THE COMPLETE IDIOT'S GUIDE® TO

WITHDRAWN

The Legacy of Lin

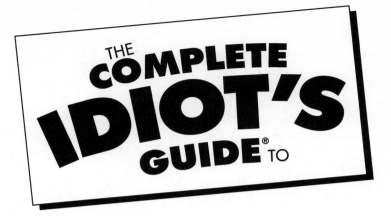

THE COMPLETE IDIOT'S GUIDE® TO

The Legacy of Lincoln

by Pamela Oldham
with Meredith Bean McMath

ALPHA

A member of Penguin Group (USA) Inc.

For Marjorie and Harold Thomas, who inspired the author's interest in history, and Lindsay Long, whose quest for understanding the past's relevance has only just begun.

ALPHA BOOKS

Published by the Penguin Group

Penguin Group (USA) Inc., 375 Hudson Street, New York, New York 10014, U.S.A.

Penguin Group (Canada), 10 Alcorn Avenue, Toronto, Ontario, Canada M4V 3B2 (a division of Pearson Penguin Canada Inc.)

Penguin Books Ltd, 80 Strand, London WC2R 0RL, England

Penguin Ireland, 25 St Stephen's Green, Dublin 2, Ireland (a division of Penguin Books Ltd)

Penguin Group (Australia), 250 Camberwell Road, Camberwell, Victoria 3124, Australia (a division of Pearson Australia Group Pty Ltd)

Penguin Books India Pvt Ltd, 11 Community Centre, Panchsheel Park, New Delhi—110 017, India

Penguin Group (NZ), cnr Airborne and Rosedale Roads, Albany, Auckland 1310, New Zealand (a division of Pearson New Zealand Ltd)

Penguin Books (South Africa) (Pty) Ltd, 24 Sturdee Avenue, Rosebank, Johannesburg 2196, South Africa

Penguin Books Ltd, Registered Offices: 80 Strand, London WC2R 0RL, England

Copyright © 2005 by Pamela Oldham

International Standard Book Number: 1-59257-405-X
Library of Congress Catalog Card Number: 2005926965

973.709
0

11/05
B & T
16.95

07 06 05   8 7 6 5 4 3 2 1

Interpretation of the printing code: The rightmost number of the first series of numbers is the year of the book's printing; the rightmost number of the second series of numbers is the number of the book's printing. For example, a printing code of 05-1 shows that the first printing occurred in 2005.

Printed in the United States of America

Note: This publication contains the opinions and ideas of its author. It is intended to provide helpful and informative material on the subject matter covered. It is sold with the understanding that the author and publisher are not engaged in rendering professional services in the book. If the reader requires personal assistance or advice, a competent professional should be consulted.

The author and publisher specifically disclaim any responsibility for any liability, loss, or risk, personal or otherwise, which is incurred as a consequence, directly or indirectly, of the use and application of any of the contents of this book.

Most Alpha books are available at special quantity discounts for bulk purchases for sales promotions, premiums, fundraising, or educational use. Special books, or book excerpts, can also be created to fit specific needs.

For details, write: Special Markets, Alpha Books, 375 Hudson Street, New York, NY 10014.

Publisher: *Marie Butler-Knight*
Senior Managing Editor: *Jennifer Bowles*
Acquisitions Editor: *Tom Stevens*
Development Editor: *Phil Kitchel*
Senior Production Editor: *Billy Fields*
Copy Editor: *Tricia Liebig*

Cartoonist: *Jody Schaeffer*
Cover/Book Designer: *Trina Wurst*
Indexer: *Brad Herriman*
Layout: *Becky Harmon*
Proofreading: *John Etchison*

Contents at a Glance

Appendixes

Contents

Appendixes

Foreword

With the thoughts you'd be thinkin'
You could be another Lincoln,
If you only had a brain

That's at least what Ray Bolger said as he sang "If I Only Had a Brain" to Judy Garland in *The Wizard of Oz*. As the Straw Man, he would have found *The Complete Idiot's Guide to the Legacy of Lincoln* to be a real treasure, because it would have made the path to thinking like Lincoln a lot easier than dealing with wizards, wicked witches, and yellow brick roads.

Thinking like Lincoln begins with understanding why Lincoln has a legacy in the first place. And that is because Abraham Lincoln, more than any other American, rescued the idea of popular government from destruction. He showed that democracies are not only worth fighting to preserve, but willing and able to do so. In Lincoln's day, the United States was the only large-scale, functioning democracy in the world. If it tore itself to pieces because the people couldn't find some way of co-operating even when they disagreed, then democracy itself would be exposed to the laughter of every king, emperor, and dictator on the planet. Democracy is about restraining the kinds of authority that can be used on people. But democratic government doesn't mean a government so unstable, so divided by opinion and interest groups, that it can't defend itself.

At the same time, Lincoln also showed that popular government—"government of the people, by the people, for the people"—was not the same thing as everybody merely doing whatever they want. Democracy is about letting the will of the people rule. But it doesn't mean that simple majorities can ignore natural law or the natural rights of others. In particular, it doesn't mean that some people can vote others into slavery.

The Complete Idiot's Guide to the Legacy of Lincoln offers many ways to think about Lincoln, as well as showing you how to think like him. The first part sketches out the plan of Lincoln's life, from 1809 to 1865, as any good biography would. But this is really a guide to Lincoln's legacy, and so it takes you step-by-step through the way Lincoln has been remembered—how he was mourned by the nation, how the mourning made him into a national Savior, and how his image has been borrowed by others as they made their own history. The other parts describe how various policies of Lincoln changed American life and still impact our lives today. Although Lincoln is best remembered for the skill and perseverance he showed in saving the Union in the Civil War, the wartime drums and bugles should not drown out the many ways—civil rights, economic policies, foreign policy—in which Lincoln's administration was a "hinge" presidency in American history. *The Complete Idiot's Guide to the Legacy of Lincoln* is a four-star reminder that, even if there had been no Civil War, Abraham Lincoln would still be remembered as one of those truly great presidents who remade the whole pattern of American public life.

In his Gettysburg Address, Lincoln referred to an "unfinished work" to which Americans needed to rededicate themselves. That "work" meant not just winning the Civil War, but winning it in such a way that opportunity for self-advancement and self-improvement could be thrown open to everyone under a single, great democratic government. That "unfinished work" remains his greatest legacy—the work of building an open and democratic society that gives to everyone the right to climb as far as talent, ambition, and natural right can take them. Thinking like that can begin right here, with *The Complete Idiot's Guide to the Legacy of Lincoln*.

—Dr. Allen C. Guelzo

Dr. Allen C. Guelzo is the Henry R. Luce Professor of the Civil War Era and Director of Civil War Era Studies at Gettysburg College. He is the only Lincoln scholar ever to win The Lincoln Prize twice, for *Abraham Lincoln: Redeemer President* (2000) and *Lincoln's Emancipation Proclamation: The End of Slavery in America* (2004). He has been featured on C-SPAN, The History Channel, and as one of The Teaching Company's "Great Professors."

Introduction

You're about to embark on a journey that will lead you to a greater understanding of Abraham Lincoln. To be sure, you'll find lots of history in the pages of this book. But more than anything else, you'll learn about—maybe for the first time—why Lincoln and his decisions still influence virtually every individual in America today. You may never look at the head side of a U.S. penny the same way again!

If you're a student who's just begun to examine Lincoln and Civil War-era history, you'll be pleased to know that this book will give you information not found in the average U.S. history text. This deeper level of detail will enrich your knowledge—and enable you to amaze and delight your teachers and professors.

For those who can barely remember learning about Lincoln in school, this book will reintroduce you to Honest Abe and his relevance to today's world. You might be surprised to see that many of the most pressing issues President Lincoln faced in his era bear a striking resemblance to those encountered by modern leaders.

If you think you already know all about our sixteenth president, stand by to have some of your beliefs confirmed and others shattered. You'll learn the factual differences between Lincoln the Saint, Lincoln the President, and Lincoln the Man.

Be forewarned: What you'll gain here is merely intended to whet your appetite. To make it easy for you to learn more about Lincoln, this book's appendixes contain a highly refined list of some of the best Lincoln resources available—including websites, books, historic sites, and annual events.

How to Use This Book

There's no right or wrong way to read this book. You will not be required to take an exam when you finish, so relax and enjoy the experience.

You can follow convention and start at the book's beginning. Unable to put the book down, you may settle into a comfortable chair and conduct yourself in the time-honored manner of many voracious readers—ignoring your family, career, and insistent knocking at your door until you've devoured every last delectable word.

Conversely, you can browse the table of contents and dive in at a spot in the book that covers a topic you find especially appealing. After satisfying your interest, you might put the book down and return to it later. (Of course, after you start reading, you may quickly find yourself unable to resist the first scenario.)

Here's what awaits you.

Part 1, **"From Humble Origins to Martyrdom,"** gives you an overview of Lincoln's life and times, from his 1809 birth in Kentucky to his untimely death in 1865. In this greatly condensed version of Lincoln's biography, we examine the challenges he faced as president, but also personal and public events that shaped him as an individual. The account provides both familiar and little-known facts, and shares the story of Lincoln's ancestors, young Abraham's early years as an adult, and his career as an attorney and fledgling politician.

Part 2, **"Lincoln's Cultural Legacy,"** describes some of the ways Lincoln changed and enriched American culture. We share the story behind Lincoln's posthumous and immediate rise to near sainthood, and why the many Lincoln myths and legends that resulted still persist today. You learn how Lincoln's death—and his young son's—created protocol for state funerals and national mourning. We explain why it took more than 30 years before Lincoln could actually rest in peace. In addition, we explore the Lincoln Memorial in Washington, D.C., and how the American people transformed this monument of post-Civil War national unity to a place where history is remembered and made.

Part 3, **"Lincoln's Political Legacies,"** explores the ways in which Lincoln impacted American politics. We begin by examining his fame as a great orator and how he changed political speechmaking. You learn how Lincoln reshaped the U.S. presidency itself—and why his decisions still influence his successors. We look at the lasting effects of his wartime actions, and find out why his contemporaries believed Lincoln the commander in chief was quite the micromanager. Lastly, we show why and how people of incredibly varied political persuasions have reinterpreted Lincoln and held him up as an example of their particular point of view.

Part 4, **"Lincoln's Personal Liberty and Legal Rights Legacies,"** discusses Lincoln's extraordinary contributions to freedom and his lifelong objections to slavery. Importantly, you learn how Lincoln's views on African Americans evolved and matured over time, and how that process of enlightenment influenced his decision-making. We provide insight into the complex issues behind states' rights versus federal rights, slavery, emancipation, and the battle for civil rights.

Part 5, **"Lincoln's Economic Development Legacy,"** shares the story of the sweeping economic changes Lincoln set in motion during his presidency—and how his efforts affect us today. You learn about how the Federal Reserve got its start, how some of our taxation practices began, and why America's western expansion was a top priority even while the country was embroiled in Civil War. We also share the stories behind little-known Lincoln legacies. We bet you didn't know, for instance, that Lincoln signed legislation that enabled the transcontinental railroad to be built or that the American dream of homeownership might have begun with our sixteenth president.

Part 6, "Lincoln's Societal Legacies," describes the legacies that established the foundation for the America we know today—many of which hearken back to Lincoln's own beginnings as a pioneer farm boy who had a passion for learning. For instance, you learn why millions of university alumni—and tens of thousands of college students enrolled in school this very moment—owe a debt of gratitude to Lincoln.

Extra Tidbits

We've also included side notes that contain information we couldn't resist sharing with you. You find these factoids scattered throughout the book, and they include Lincoln trivia, definitions, background details, intriguing stories, and more.

Notes and Orations

Quotes by or about Lincoln, both well known and obscure. All Lincoln quotes and speeches contained in this book are the genuine article. The source we used is the foremost authority: *The Collected Works of Abraham Lincoln* by Roy P. Basler, courtesy of the Abraham Lincoln Association.

Lincoln Lingo

These give definitions of terms, people, places, and events relevant to Lincoln's life and legacies. Many of these listings also include word origins and back stories that will expand your knowledge and enable you to talk like an expert from day one.

Splitting Rails

These alert you to common misconceptions and myths about Lincoln and his legacies. We clarify these issues and give you the straight scoop.

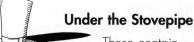

Under the Stovepipe

These contain Lincoln-related trivia, asides, and anecdotes—most of which we're betting you didn't know before you opened this book.

Acknowledgments

Although the craft of writing is conducted in solitude, no writer ever truly works alone. I'd like to take a moment to recognize the contributions of those who enabled the creation of this work.

I am most grateful for the support and encouragement of this project by numerous Lincoln scholars and organizations. Space does not allow me to thank everyone here. But a few whose contributions were especially important to this project: Dr. Matthew Pinsker, Illinois State Historian Thomas Schwartz, the Abraham Lincoln Association, Ford's Theatre, the National Association of State Universities and Land-Grant Colleges, the Abraham Lincoln Presidential Library and Museum, the Illinois State Historical Library, the Library of Congress, and the National Park Service.

The vision of Illinois native son and Lincoln enthusiast Tom Stevens, acquisitions editor at Alpha Books, wisely guided and helped shape the work. I am especially grateful for his support of and commitment to this project as well as his patient understanding of the time and research involved to see it through.

Virginia-based historian Meredith Bean McMath's expertise, knowledge, and passion for the subject proved invaluable as we set out to present Lincoln's story and its historical significance in a totally new way.

Thank you also to Rachel Dickinson, agent Marilyn Allen, and my writing "sistahs," who know why I acknowledge them here.

Lastly, I offer special thanks to my husband, Gary. In addition to helping conduct research, he gave me sustenance and emotional support while I toiled away as most writers do—in seclusion, seemingly tethered to a computer keyboard for weeks on end.

—Pamela Oldham

Thanks to the Technical Reviewer

The Complete Idiot's Guide to the Legacy of Lincoln benefited immensely from a pre-publication technical review by Dr. Matthew Pinsker. Dr. Pinsker is chair of American Civil War history at Dickinson College in Carlisle, Pennsylvania, and is the author of *Lincoln's Sanctuary: Abraham Lincoln and the Soldiers' Home* (New York: Oxford University Press, 2003) and *Abraham Lincoln*, part of the American President Reference Series. He earned his undergraduate degree from Harvard University and his doctorate in philosophy from the University of Oxford. He writes frequently about Abraham Lincoln and the Civil War era, and studied with David Herbert Donald at Harvard before completing his studies abroad.

We are truly pleased and honored that Professor Pinsker has shared his knowledge and expertise with us in this way.

Trademarks

All terms mentioned in this book that are known to be or are suspected of being trademarks or service marks have been appropriately capitalized. The author, Alpha Books, and Penguin Group (USA) Inc. cannot attest to the accuracy of this information. Use of a term in this book should not be regarded as affecting the validity of any trademark or service mark.

Part 1

From Humble Origins to Martyrdom

Welcome. You're about to embark on an exploration of one of America's most revered and influential figures. Since his death, more than 17,000 books and countless articles have examined the way Abraham Lincoln lived, pondered the decisions he made, and analyzed how he changed the course of the American experience. Yet most of us in school learn little more than a passing glimpse of what's known about Lincoln and his impact on today's world.

Let's begin by taking a look at Lincoln's life—from his simple beginnings in 1809 and the early events that shaped his complex persona to his rise to prominence, his presidency, and the final tragedy—his assassination in 1865.

Lincoln's fascinating biography—even the short version we offer in this part—is a classically American rags-to-riches saga with plenty of unexpected twists and turns.

Lincoln's Youth (1809–1831)

In This Chapter

- ◆ Lincoln's family background
- ◆ Lincoln's boyhood and insatiable appetite for learning
- ◆ Lincoln's early tragedies
- ◆ Lincoln's highly praised integrity
- ◆ Lincoln strikes out on his own

Life wasn't easy for children in the early 1800s, especially for those born to America's pioneer families. Many children of that era didn't live to see adulthood or even their first birthday, due to the lack of modern medicine and other factors.

Those who did endure were often stronger for it, emotionally and physically, having survived the harsh conditions of the time. But Abraham Lincoln was far more than a fit survivor imbued with resilience and perseverance. The challenges he faced in his youth, the obstacles he overcame, and the life lessons he learned molded his character and beliefs in ways that still reverberate throughout American society today.

Pioneer Pedigree

Abraham Lincoln never seemed particularly interested in genealogy, and he rarely talked about his ancestry. Because Lincoln was obviously intellectually gifted, his backwoods roots and the fact that his parents were ordinary may have made him a bit embarrassed about discussing his family's heritage. What's known today is largely the result of painstaking research by historians.

Lincoln's story begins in the 1780s, when his grandfather—also named Abraham—packed up his brood and moved over the mountains to the area now known as Kentucky. At the time, the region was still within the borders of the Virginia Commonwealth. Lincoln's father, Thomas, was one of five children born to Abraham and Bathsheba Lincoln, who lived in Virginia's Shenandoah Valley and had family ties to Pennsylvania Quakers. They supposedly relocated to Kentucky at the urging of family friend and distant relative Daniel Boone.

There, the elder Abraham Lincoln acquired several thousand acres of prime land, assembling one of the finest spreads in the region. He was destined to live a rich, prosperous life.

 **Splitting Rails**

Today, most parents try to give their kids first names that aren't in common use, but in the 1700 and 1800s, families would commonly re-use first names they liked, sometimes even in the same generation! It wasn't unusual for a newborn to be given the name of an older sibling who had died in infancy.

This makes things confusing for genealogists and historians; when the same names are shared so frequently, it can make reading family histories challenging. The Abraham Lincoln we know was named for his grandfather. Lincoln's father, the elder Abraham's son, was named Thomas. Got it?

But in 1786, tragedy struck when the elder Abraham was shot and killed in a surprise Indian attack as he and his sons Mordecai, Joshua, and Thomas planted corn on their new property. Just six or eight years old at the time, Thomas watched in horror as his father died instantly.

When the Indians retreated, Thomas's eldest brother, Mordecai, sent Joshua to find help and then ran to the family cabin, leaving Thomas in the field. As young Thomas sat beside Abraham's lifeless body, mourning his loss, an Indian crept out of the nearby forest and headed silently toward the little boy.

Inside the cabin, Mordecai happened to glance at the field through a crevice between the logs. To his horror, he spotted the Indian sneaking up on his little brother. Fifteen-year-old Mordecai grabbed a rifle, shoved the barrel into the narrow gap, and shot the Indian dead before he could reach the boy. Had it not been for Mordecai's quick reaction, Thomas might have been killed—and future president Abraham Lincoln would never have been born.

Shifting Fortunes

Unfortunately for Thomas, his father's death and the law of *primogeniture* also meant Mordecai, as the eldest male child, inherited his father's entire estate. That left young Thomas, his other siblings, and his widowed mother penniless. The family eventually scattered.

Lincoln Lingo

Primogeniture is the state of being firstborn. The *rule of primogeniture* comes from ancient English law, holding that the right of inheritance of a man's estate belongs solely to his eldest male child. That meant younger male siblings and females, including daughters and wives, inherited nothing. Other laws at the time reinforced primogeniture and gave a female family member's belongings, including her clothes and any income she earned, to her husband or father. Primogeniture was not uniformly followed in the American colonies, but when Thomas Jefferson, as a state legislator, abolished Virginia's statutes in the late 1700s, other colonies later followed suit.

Mordecai went on to live a well-to-do life, but Thomas never really recovered financially even though he was a very hard worker. For a time he was a drifter, working odd jobs that included carpentry work and manual labor. He eventually saved enough money to buy a small farm in Hardin County, Kentucky, where he established a home for his mother.

As an adult, Thomas was a plainspoken, uneducated man who worked hard. Others in his community described Thomas as "good natured," "respected," and above all, "honest." He loved storytelling and was known for telling funny jokes.

In 1806, when Thomas was 28, he married Nancy Hanks, whose family had also moved to Kentucky via Virginia. They'd known each other since childhood. Some who knew Nancy described her as an "intellectual" and "brilliant," but it's possible that some of these recollections may have been exaggerated after her famous son's death. She was believed to have been born out of wedlock, the child of her mother Lucy Hanks and an unknown, wealthy Virginia farmer.

Illegitimacy was a scandalous beginning for children in Lincoln's day. Children whose parents were not married were not considered "legal" offspring, and were therefore not entitled to their biological father's support, nor were they allowed to inherit money or property. Because women of that time generally could not own property in their own right and usually had no independent means of financial support, children who did not have a "legal" father to provide for them were pretty much out of luck. (Laws limiting inheritance rights and support due to illegitimacy were later abolished.) However, Abraham Lincoln later suggested his mother's parentage was the likely source of his sturdiness and many of his own mental strengths.

The couple set up married life in a small cabin Thomas built in nearby Elizabethtown. In 1807, eight months after their wedding, Nancy Hanks Lincoln gave birth to a daughter, Sarah. Now the timing of their firstborn child, coming less than nine months after the marriage, might seem scandalous. But in fact, the practice of a couple sleeping together while engaged was typical in pioneer families. Pregnancy ensured the marriage, and that was considered a positive development.

Thomas later bought another farm in Hardin County, Sinking Spring Farm, and moved his young family to a one-room, dirt-floored log cabin he built on the property. Not long after, Nancy gave birth on a cornhusk mattress bed to the couple's second child: Abraham, born on February 12, 1809.

A third child, a boy they named Thomas, died in infancy.

They eventually found the land at Sinking Spring Farm to be infertile, so Thomas bought property 10 miles away at Knob Creek, and established a smaller but more productive farm. Like the previous home, the family lived in a one-room log cabin—as did their neighbors.

Childhood Interrupted

The farm at Knob Creek was young Abraham Lincoln's home until he reached the age of seven, when a number of factors caused his father to consider relocating the family again.

Kentucky had been admitted to the Union as a slave state in 1792, and Thomas wanted nothing to do with slavery. As members of an anti-slave Baptist church,

Thomas and his wife accepted the church's strict moral doctrines, which included opposition to slavery that then thrived in Kentucky. (There were pro-slave and anti-slave Baptist churches in the South.) But he also opposed slavery because it interfered with his personal financial survival.

Thomas Lincoln had seen wealthy, slave-holding landowners set about acquiring large tracts of some of the best farming property in Kentucky, and these big operations threatened smaller farmers. Who could compete with slave labor? Males over the age of 16 also had a difficult time finding work in Hardin County, because slaves nearly outnumbered them.

Notes and Orations

"I am naturally antislavery. If slavery is not wrong, nothing is wrong. I cannot remember when I did not so think, and feel."
—Abraham Lincoln, letter to Albert Hodges, April 4, 1864

To make matters worse, it appeared that Kentucky landowners were having problems obtaining clear title to their claimed property because Kentucky hadn't been properly surveyed. Where one person's property began and ended was uncertain. Property lines were described as "to a planting of trees" or "from a large rock."

Many claimed they owned the same land tracts. The court dockets were filled with ugly property disputes. Thomas knew he couldn't afford the attorneys' fees required to straighten out such problems in court. Given the other issues, he wasn't really sure it was worth the trouble. (Interestingly, Daniel Boone gave up his property in the same way Thomas Lincoln did.)

Happily, young Abraham Lincoln's dad heard about opportunities in nearby Indiana, which had just been opened for settlement. There, slavery had been permanently prohibited and land purchasers were guaranteed clear titles by the United States government. Best of all, the place was wide open and less crowded than Kentucky. Thomas thought it sounded like a great place.

Life on the Old Frontier

During a scouting visit to southern Indiana, Thomas found what he considered to be the perfect spot to establish his new farm. He staked a claim on land abutting Pigeon Creek, a virtually uninhabited area in a heavily forested, remote wilderness. There wasn't even a footpath to the place. Talk about getting away from it all!

The Lincolns arrived in the winter of 1816, when Indiana had just been admitted to the Union. While Thomas and his boys constructed a proper log cabin, the family briefly took up residence in a lean-to—a floorless, three-sided shelter—planted smack in the middle of the wild woods.

Soon enough they moved into the log cabin, but due to its being constructed in freezing conditions, the wind whipped through the cracks and crevices all winter long, making it a cold as well as lonely place to live. Thomas, Nancy, and their two young children survived that first winter by eating deer, bear, and wild turkey meat.

Because there weren't many neighbors around to help, the Lincoln children were required to join in the backbreaking work of creating the new farm. This wasn't unusual; most pioneer kids worked just as hard as the adults. Abraham was hunting with a rifle by the age of seven and was only eight years old when his father handed him an axe and told him to help clear the land.

By the next fall, in 1817, the family began to feel more settled. Abraham's father bought additional land adjacent to their new farm and the future looked bright.

But then Abraham suffered a terrible accident. While doing his chores, he was kicked in the forehead by a horse and fell unconscious. Those who found him believed he'd been killed. For several hours, he was unable to speak. Fortunately, he recovered.

Then, Abraham's mother came down with what was called *milk sick*, a mysterious illness that commonly brought death within about seven days. Nancy Hanks Lincoln succumbed on October 5, 1818. Young Abraham Lincoln helped build a coffin for his mom. He later referred to her as his "angel mother."

Under the Stovepipe

Abraham Lincoln was seven years old when he bagged his first game, a wild turkey. He later had a change of heart and decided that killing animals wasn't something he wanted to do regularly. He might have taken smaller critters, but by his own account, in a recollection he wrote during the 1860 presidential campaign, Lincoln never again hunted anything larger than that turkey.

Lincoln Lingo

Milk sick was a disease characterized by nausea, vomiting, trembling, dizziness, and severe intestinal pain, eventually found to be caused by drinking the milk of cows who had eaten white snakeroot plants. Without medicine, symptoms worsened and ultimately led to coma and death.

A Turning Point for Young Abraham

About a year after Nancy's death, Thomas realized the family couldn't go on without a woman in the home, so he returned to Kentucky to find himself a bride!

Back in Elizabethtown, he looked up Sarah Bush Johnston, whom Thomas may have courted unsuccessfully before marrying Nancy. Sarah was recently widowed and the mother of three young children. She, too, was in desperate need of a spouse.

The two quickly married, and Sarah and her children moved into the Lincolns' Indiana cabin. The match was obviously fortunate for all, and marked a time of huge improvement in young Abraham Lincoln's life.

Sarah brought with her items that the Lincoln children viewed as luxurious—bed linens, cutlery, a Bible and other books, a spinning wheel, and more. More importantly, she introduced some class and style to the Lincoln household. She organized the entire place, and insisted that Thomas install a real floor in the cabin and build beds for the children.

What might have delighted Abraham Lincoln the most, though, was that after Sarah arrived, she and Thomas enrolled Abraham and the other children in a school that had opened about a mile from home. Classes were held in a windowless cabin owned by the teacher.

An Unconventional Education

As a youngster, Abraham Lincoln had an insatiable appetite for knowledge and Sarah encouraged him to learn, in and outside of school. People who knew him said Lincoln had a need to master every thought or idea he read about or heard. He liked to analyze every subject down to the minute details until he felt confident that he fully understood—and would remember—all the facts about whatever topic or issue he pursued.

Under the Stovepipe

Abraham Lincoln's first school was known as a "blab school," where students of all ages recited the lessons they learned aloud. But they didn't take turns, they all "blabbed" at once. The classroom must have been chaotic and the noise deafening. As the students repeated their lessons over and over, a teacher listened intently, trying to catch and correct errors made by individual students. Educators believed blabbing helped kids memorize their lessons while preventing classroom daydreaming.

On the plus side, the kids didn't have homework. Frontier schools didn't have the funds to purchase many books, and paper and writing instruments were scarce, too. If a child was lucky, he or she owned a square slate to write on and had soapstone for chalk.

School gave young Abraham the chance to interact and match wits with other children—likely nurturing a natural aptitude for what would later become his formidable debating and oratory skills. From the start, Lincoln was a natural leader among his fellow students, who admired him and believed he was clearly exceptional. They often gathered around him to hear his jokes and stories.

He also took his first forays into public speaking in the classroom. Like his father, Lincoln enjoyed storytelling, playing pranks, and sharing jokes with his classmates. Sometimes when his friends gathered to hear him tell a joke, he'd stand on a chair or tree stump, as if he was giving a speech. His early experiences must have given him tremendous self-confidence.

Unfortunately, Lincoln's first school closed after he had attended just one term. He infrequently attended other schools, most located farther away from home, which made it difficult for him to keep up with his chores and classwork. When not in school or engaged in farm work, Lincoln wrote poetry, practiced his writing skills, and read every book he could get his hands on.

Books were hard to come by on the frontier, and young Abraham treasured his reading material. His first books came from his stepmother's collection and included the Bible. Other texts were loaned or given to him by others in the community. "My best friend is the man who'll get me a book I ain't read," he said.

Because he couldn't accumulate large numbers of texts, Abraham studied each book intently, re-reading passages and committing the information to memory. Folks who knew him as a young lad said he carried a book everywhere he went, reading and studying whenever he had a spare moment. He especially enjoyed history.

Under the Stovepipe

Not everyone in the family shared Abraham's enthusiasm for learning. After marrying Sarah Bush Johnston, Lincoln's father Thomas felt enormous financial pressure as the sole breadwinner for a family of eight. He wanted his son to be able to read and write but also wanted him to take on more work around the farm.

Like most adolescents, Abraham had other ideas. His preference for reading and writing over physical labor irritated his father, and eventually their disagreement over education's value created a rift between them. Their longstanding conflict is blamed for Lincoln's absence from his father's funeral.

His sporadic formal education ended when he reached the age of 15. By then, Abraham Lincoln, the man who would eventually become president of the United States, had amassed a grand total of about a year's worth of schooling.

What he accomplished later in life is amazing when you consider how little time he actually spent in a traditional classroom. That he was able to accumulate a vast amount of knowledge on his own is inspirational and supports claims of his significant intellectual prowess.

Itchin' to Leave Home

By reading all those books about people and places outside his tiny community, Abraham began to yearn for new experiences as he entered his late teens. He had also determined that if he stayed put, his future would likely consist of nothing more than years of long, hard, physical labor.

By the time he reached the age of 16, Abraham stood six feet, two inches tall—giant-sized in that day. Weighing only about 160 pounds, he was a very skinny kid. But owing to a childhood that had included heavy chores, young Abraham was exceptionally strong. He could split rails, clear land, and skin raccoons with the best of his peers. Even so, farming and manual work didn't excite him one bit. He preferred his books and poetry.

Some of his neighbors thought Lincoln was just plain shiftless, and so did his cousin, Dennis Hanks. "Lincoln was lazy, a very lazy man," Hanks is quoted as saying. "He was always reading, scribbling, writing, ciphering, writing poetry."

However, young Abraham was actually quite enterprising. He and a friend cut and sold firewood, for instance, and Abraham hired himself out to do work for folks on the Ohio River—chopping wood, building fences, and such. Like most kids his age, Abraham probably dreamed of the day he could leave home and start fresh.

When Abraham was 17, his sister moved out and married a neighbor boy, Aaron Grigsby. The newlyweds established their home a few miles away. That might have fueled Abraham's longing to leave. Sadly, however, Sarah died while giving birth a year and a half later. The loss was a crushing blow to Abraham.

But the final straw was probably when his father decided he could make money by "renting" Abraham out to work for others. The young man's labor was worth 25 cents a day. That was a relatively large sum back then.

Under the laws in force at the time, Abraham's father actually owned him until he came of age. As you might expect, Abraham didn't like that one bit. Still, he stayed with his father and stepmother anyway, and dutifully handed over money he earned. He had integrity even back then.

The moment he had the chance, though, Abraham left the family nest. He wanted no part of farming. Instead, his first real job was as a flatboat man on the Ohio River and the mighty Mississippi. It was Lincoln's chance to be his own man, and to finally see the world.

But when a new outbreak of milk sickness emerged in southern Indiana in 1830, Abraham returned to help his parents move to Illinois, 200 miles away. He helped build yet another cabin and cleared and fenced the new farm's field.

Under the Stovepipe

Lincoln gave his first political speech in Decatur, Illinois, in 1830, responding as a citizen to addresses given by two candidates for state legislative office. The politicians had failed to serve refreshments after their talk, a fairly significant breach of etiquette at the time. Lincoln's friends coaxed him into stepping up to the podium to respond on behalf of the crowd. But instead of chastising the candidates, his brief speech consisted of an appeal for improvements to the Sangamon waterway.

But after that, he never looked back. By the age of 21, he was anxious to get on with his own life.

By 1831, his travels led him to the newly established village of New Salem, Illinois, the place where Abraham Lincoln's future greatness would truly begin.

The Least You Need to Know

- Abraham Lincoln's childhood was typical of frontier children of the era.

- Lincoln was raised on antislavery sentiment.

- Lincoln saw through land laws that legislation could create poverty or great wealth.

- As a boy, Lincoln liked reading, writing, and public speaking.

- Although raised to be a farmer, Lincoln chose a different life.

Chapter 2

Lincoln: Young Politician and Attorney (1831–1850)

In This Chapter

- ◆ Lincoln's early years in Salem, Illinois
- ◆ Lincoln's entry into politics
- ◆ Springfield's social scene
- ◆ Lincoln's courtship of Mary Todd
- ◆ Lincoln's personal and public struggles

As he entered adulthood, Abraham Lincoln really didn't have a clue about what he wanted to accomplish in life or how he'd make a living. Armed with backwoods common sense and a strong mind and body, he had many options open to him. It's apparent that he knew a good opportunity when he saw one and took advantage of all that was offered to him. Above all, Lincoln was determined to decide his own path, on his own terms.

The Likeable Giant

When Abraham Lincoln arrived in New Salem, Illinois, the tiny settlement on a hill overlooking the Sangamon River had been established for just two years. Only about 100 residents called New Salem home at that time, and they lived in a dozen or so houses all told. For a while, Lincoln boarded at a tavern owned by James Rutledge. There, he met James's daughter Ann Mayes Rutledge, whom eyewitnesses described as a beautiful and intelligent girl who was beloved by all. Lincoln and Rutledge studied together with Mentor Graham, a New Salem schoolmaster.

Splitting Rails

Rumor of a love affair between young Abraham Lincoln and Ann Rutledge has persisted—but has never been fully proven—for more than a century, fueled in large part by the recollections and accounts of New Salem residents. Soon after Lincoln arrived in New Salem, Rutledge accepted a marriage proposal from John MacNamar, a former New Yorker who was a New Salem businessman and landowner. In 1832, MacNamar left for New York to visit his parents. Some people speculate that Lincoln and Rutledge began a relationship after MacNamar failed to return to New Salem.

When Rutledge became ill (some say she had contracted typhoid fever) in the summer of 1835, she called for Lincoln. They met privately before her death on August 25, 1835, at the age of 22. Local residents reported Lincoln became severely depressed at the news of Rutledge's death. If the long-held speculation is correct, Rutledge may have been Lincoln's first serious romance. No one really knows for sure.

For Lincoln, a young man who'd spent his entire life in the wilderness, New Salem must have felt like an exciting, bustling metropolis. Here, frontiersmen bought provisions, sold goods, and enjoyed nights on the town. Farmers in the area traveled to New Salem to sell crops and have corn ground. Villagers had access to a blacksmith shop, hat maker's shop, and a tavern, among other establishments. Two mills—a gristmill and sawmill—also served the region's needs. Noticeably absent were churches.

As was the custom in that era, men of the village met each day at the general store to gossip and share stories. Lincoln fit right in. In fact, it was in New Salem that he honed his ability to tell jokes to others, and his talent for telling a good tale was appreciated and welcomed.

Lincoln worked as a laborer at first, taking odd jobs around the village to earn his keep. Later he worked in a general store, as the owner's assistant. He was paid about

$15 a month and lived in a small room, rent-free, at the back of the store. He was known as a kind, honest, and considerate man to customers. The store's proprietor was so impressed by Lincoln that he constantly bragged about him.

Strong-Man Lincoln

With its predominantly male population, New Salem was a rough-and-tumble place where physical strength and toughness were valued and revered. So naturally, when Lincoln's boss began making claims that his assistant was not just the smartest man in the village but also the strongest, other men wanted to challenge Lincoln, to see if those claims were true.

Lincoln wasn't particularly interested in physical tests, but he had no choice but to prove his mettle. The toughest roughneck in the area was Jack Armstrong—considered a champion wrestler—and who Lincoln had to take on. The entire town turned out to watch.

Under the Stovepipe

By the age of 23, Abraham Lincoln stood six feet, four inches tall and weighed more than 200 pounds. He was an imposing character with a quick mind and strong body that could intimidate just about anyone.

Time has muddled the accuracy of what happened that day. By some accounts, the outcome was a draw. Others reported that Lincoln won the contest handily, but Armstrong's supporters said Abraham won by using trickery. Lincoln offered to wrestle all Armstrong's gang and it's not known if any of them actually accepted the challenge. But ultimately, Lincoln earned the admiration and respect of Armstrong's entire group.

He also won over those village residents who were educated and more cultured and refined than Lincoln. Even college-educated villagers admired his knowledge and eagerness to learn more. Lincoln joined the New Salem Debating Society. His ability to make a reasoned argument and present his thoughts powerfully and convincingly awed all those who saw him in action.

Politics and Law Beckon

To the delight of many of the settlement's leaders, Lincoln also took a keen interest in village politics and law. In his spare time, Lincoln attended local court sessions and watched cases as they were tried. Presumably for his own entertainment, the presiding judge there, Bowling Green, sometimes asked Lincoln to address the court informally and give his opinions about cases the judge had just decided. Eventually Green recognized Lincoln as a man with an especially sharp mind.

Notes and Orations _____

"As he arose to speak, his tall form towered above the little assembly. Both hands were thrust down deep in the pockets of his pantaloons. A perceptible smile at once lit up the faces of the audience, for all anticipated the relation of some humorous story. But he opened up the discussion in splendid style, to the infinite astonishment of his friends. As he warmed with his subject his hands would forsake his pockets and would enforce his ideas by awkward gestures; but would very soon seek their easy resting place. He pursued the question with reason and argument so pithy and forcible that all were amazed... The president [of the Debating Society], at his fireside after the meeting, remarked to his wife that there was more than wit and fun in Abe's head; that he was already a fine speaker; that all he lacked was culture."

—R. B. Rutledge on Lincoln's first performance before the New Salem Debating Society, in an 1866 letter

---

As word spread of Lincoln's emerging legal ability, villagers consulted him for advice on simple matters such as deeds and wills. Residents saw that Lincoln had many talents. To them, he was a man with a future and a neighbor with a lot of friends.

Lincoln also came to the attention of New Salem's political powerbrokers. In 1832, they and Lincoln's friends convinced him to run for elected office as a candidate for the state legislature. Lincoln declared his candidacy and ran on a platform that emphasized better education and improvements to the Sangamon River, to make it more accessible to larger trade vessels.

First Steps

Lincoln's initial foray into political campaigning was interrupted by a crisis in New Salem. A 15-ton cabin steamer, the *Talisman*, had journeyed up the Mississippi and Illinois rivers and up to the Sangamon to show others how easy it was to navigate this path. Unfortunately, the Sangamon River's water level began to dangerously drop after the ship pulled into nearby Beardstown and unloaded its cargo.

As an experienced riverboat captain, Lincoln came to the ship's rescue. He took the helm and expertly piloted the *Talisman* back down the Sangamon to the Illinois River. By taking charge of the situation, Lincoln earned even greater respect from New

Salem residents. He also proved that his claim about the Sangamon River needing improvements to make New Salem a port town was correct.

Notes and Orations _____

"Every man is said to have his peculiar ambition. Whether it be true or not, I can say for one that I have no other so great as that of being truly esteemed of my fellow men, by rendering myself worthy of their esteem. How far I shall succeed in gratifying this ambition, is yet to be developed."

—Abraham Lincoln in a letter to the people of Sangamon County upon announcing his candidacy to the Illinois General Assembly; March 9, 1832

At about the same time, the owner of the store where Lincoln worked closed the place due to bankruptcy. Lincoln did his best to help the owner (and himself) save the business, including building a pen so the man could offer pigs for sale. But in the end, Lincoln was left jobless and homeless.

This diversion probably set Lincoln up for loss in the upcoming election, though he won nearly all the votes cast in his village. He wasn't well known outside his community and needed to campaign outside New Salem. But he just didn't have the time. Then, right in the midst of his first campaign, war broke out.

Lincoln the Military Man

The brief conflict known as the Black Hawk War involved land that previously belonged to the Sauk and Fox Indian tribes. Tribal leaders had been conned into giving up their ancestral homelands in northwestern Illinois, and had been forced to move westward, beyond the Mississippi River. After the Indians figured out they'd been tricked, they renounced the treaty signed with the American government and declared war.

One of the tribal leaders, an Indian named Black Hawk, returned to Illinois to reclaim tribal lands. He brought with him about 450 warriors and 1,500 women and children.

Under the Stovepipe _____

Presumably seeking refuge during the Black Hawk War, an elderly Indian carrying papers from American authorities attesting to his good character entered Lincoln's military camp one day. Militiamen believed that the Indian might be a spy and immediately threatened to kill him on the spot. Lincoln shielded the Indian with his body and told the others he'd fight anyone who tried to hurt the old man.

Federal troops tried to quell the invasion, but eventually Illinois governor John Reynolds asked for volunteers to help push the Indians back.

Lincoln joined many of his New Salem neighbors by volunteering for the militia. He was promptly elected militia captain, and his first sergeant was none other than Jack Armstrong.

Lincoln's service in the Black Hawk War was not particularly notable, as he didn't actually see much action. But he did gain some knowledge of military strategy as well as leadership experience when his company elected him captain. He was also paid handsomely—more than $100 for less than two months' service plus enlistment and land bonuses.

A Political Career Cut Short

Lincoln remained proud of his militia service, and it distinguished him as a man of courage and conviction. After the Black Hawk War had been won, Lincoln returned to New Salem. He had only a few days left to campaign before the election was held. He attended political rallies and spoke to crowds about issues of local importance. But even his stirring speeches weren't enough.

Despite all the interruptions, Lincoln made a respectable showing in the New Salem district. He received 277 votes of the possible 300. However, in his electoral region, he came in eighth out of 13 candidates. Lincoln was, of course, disappointed. But encouraged by the strong support of his home community, Lincoln knew even then that he'd run again.

On to the Next Campaign

To support himself financially, Lincoln decided to establish a new general store in New Salem with a partner named William Berry. But Berry's drinking and lack of focus on business affairs, along with New Salem's slowed growth, led to financial disaster. Lincoln and Berry's store went out of business in less than a year.

Berry died soon after and Lincoln assumed the entire debt owed by the two men, a total of about $3,000. In 1833, that might as well have been a million dollars. It was a staggering amount of money, and it took Lincoln years to recover. He called it his "national debt."

To earn extra money so he could stay in New Salem, and to help pay back his debt, Lincoln worked at odd jobs such as splitting rails, surveying land, and helping as a farm hand. Lincoln eventually repaid every cent he and Berry had borrowed for the general store. Doing so added to his ever-expanding reputation for integrity, fair dealing, and honesty. This helped him immensely in his next political campaign. As word spread of this and other deeds, Lincoln quickly became known as "Honest Abe."

His friends also helped him secure the position of New Salem's postmaster, which involved carrying and delivering the mail on horseback. Lincoln was postmaster for about three years. The job didn't pay much, but it gave him the chance to learn about current events from the newspapers he delivered.

When not hard at work, Lincoln joined in conversations with other male villagers, discussing issues of the day, gossiping, and speculating about the Bible's accuracy. In New Salem, various religious groups sparred over philosophical and doctrinal differences—even though the town still didn't have any churches.

Under the Stovepipe

Abraham Lincoln never claimed membership in any church, Christian or otherwise. When pressed about his lack of affiliation, he said he had never denied scriptural truth and had never spoken with disrespect about any religion or Christian denomination. He went on to describe a spiritual doctrine he had learned in early childhood, the Doctrine of Necessity, which held that a power outside human experience compelled the mind to move a person to take action.

Much of Lincoln's personal morality came from studying the Bible, one of the first books he read. "But for [the Bible] we could not know right from wrong," he said. As Lincoln's spiritual views matured, he expressed a poetic, almost romantic, understanding of faith and belief in God. According to author William Lee Miller in *Lincoln's Virtues*, Mary Lincoln said her husband was not a "technical Christian," but "was a religious man always."

When the notes came due on the Lincoln and Berry store, Abraham thought it was time to run for office. He needed the money. In 1834, he declared his candidacy for a seat in the Illinois state legislature.

This time he campaigned from a position of political strength. More people knew him than when he had previously run for office, and he was widely trusted. He attended barbecues, spoke at races, and used his positions as postmaster and surveyor to reach voters. Already a savvy politician, Lincoln also reportedly struck a deal with local Democrats. It all paid off and Lincoln was elected.

At the age of 25, Abraham Lincoln left New Salem for Vandalia, the Illinois capitol at that time, to take his seat among other legislators. The young man had finally "arrived."

Lincoln was reelected in 1836 and moved to Springfield after helping make that city the new state capitol of Illinois. An extremely popular state legislator, Lincoln was re-elected again in 1838 and 1840.

After his reelection in 1836, Lincoln never returned to New Salem to live. The village never did conquer its river transportation problems; the settlement declined economically and its residents scattered. By 1840, New Salem no longer existed.

Splitting Rails

The proliferation of Lincoln legends is rather remarkable. Lincoln's time as a shopkeeper in New Salem, for instance, inspired a number of stories that have been erroneously passed down as truths for many decades. Two of these longstanding legends found their way into history books.

One story tells of Lincoln traveling three miles from his store to return a few pennies to a customer he'd inadvertently shortchanged. The other legend describes Lincoln buying a barrel of unknown contents from a mysterious man who passed through New Salem while moving west in a covered wagon. According to the legend, Lincoln discovered that the barrel contained a treasure trove of law books, enabling him to launch his law career.

Neither story has ever been verified as fact.

When he wasn't at the statehouse, Lincoln was studying law. A man he'd met during the Black Hawk War, Major John Todd Stuart, had also been elected to the Illinois state legislature. Stuart encouraged Lincoln to become a lawyer and even loaned him his law books. In characteristic fashion, Lincoln studied the texts and statutes intently, eventually reading everything required by a law school.

Back in 1837, lawyers didn't take an exam before being admitted to the bar. Those for whom they apprenticed vouched for their knowledge of the law and also for the other requirement to obtain a law license back then: good moral character. Lincoln easily met the requirements—especially that last one—and on March 1, 1837, he was granted a license to practice law.

Lincoln in Love

Springfield in 1837 was a rustic place with no paved roads, railroads, or even street-lights. Its most memorable features were mud and pigs, which were allowed to roam free and often rolled in the mud.

However, as Illinois' capitol city, Springfield was a place of power—and a bachelor's paradise. Lincoln met his best friend, Joshua Speed, in Springfield and the two became part of the town's young social set.

Under the Stovepipe

As Lincoln headed to Springfield's statehouse in 1836, he considered marrying a woman named Mary Owens. He'd met her three years earlier in New Salem, and Abraham thought she'd do just fine as a wife. That is, until she showed up in Springfield. Seems she'd gained a significant amount of weight, and Lincoln viewed her new appearance as an impediment to romance. In a letter he wrote to Mrs. Orville H. Browning in April 1838, Lincoln wrote of Mary Owens, "When I beheld her I could not for my life avoid thinking of my mother."

Lincoln did everything possible to dissuade Mary's affections, even acting rudely toward her at times. But he finally had to break it off. In a carefully worded letter to Mary Owens, sent ironically on April Fool's Day in 1838, Lincoln cancelled the engagement. (Seven months later, he had a change of heart, reversing his earlier decision—and half-heartedly offered his hand in marriage. Mary Owens turned him down flat.

Mary Todd Catches Lincoln's Eye

Among the many young women being courted by Springfield bachelors was 21-year-old Mary Todd, a pretty, blue-eyed Kentucky belle who'd enjoyed a privileged upbringing. Todd had attended private schools and had an engaging quick wit. Among the most persistent of her many suitors was future congressman Stephen Douglas.

But then Mary met Abraham in December 1839 at a cotillion ball.

Lincoln immediately began pursuit. Some members of Todd's family thought Abraham was too uncouth and lacked the level of education and family background needed to be a suitable husband for young Mary. She didn't see it that way, though, and did her best to get Lincoln to fall in love with her.

They shared a love of poetry and spent their time together discussing politics as well as their individual aspirations and beliefs. By the end of 1840, Lincoln decided to make Mary his wife. He proposed and she accepted.

Uncertainty, Then Sadness

Then things suddenly fell apart on New Year's Day in 1841. Lincoln's roommate and best friend in the world, Joshua Speed, decided to pack up and move away from Illinois. On the same day, Lincoln broke off his engagement to Mary Todd.

He'd previously caught her flirting with Stephen Douglas and viewed Mary's act as a betrayal. But it's also believed that it was more than mere jealousy: Lincoln might have gotten nervous about giving up his freedom, or felt a bit overwhelmed about the responsibilities of marriage. No matter what his reasons, the events that day proved to be too much for the introspective Lincoln to handle. He descended into a deep depression.

Splitting Rails

Some contemporary writers suggest Lincoln's sadness in early 1841 was triggered by Joshua Speed's departure rather than his breakup with Mary, and that Lincoln and Speed were involved in a homosexual relationship. Those assertions have been soundly rejected by the vast majority of historians and Lincoln scholars for lack of evidence.

Lincoln's sexuality has been questioned in modern times because he and Speed shared a bed as roommates in 1837. However, bed sharing was a common practice in nineteenth-century America that arose from economic necessity, not sexual orientation. In fact, American frontiersmen often slept two and three to a bed.

After breaking off his engagement with Mary, Lincoln reportedly stayed in bed for several months, forsaking his law practice and his duties as a legislator. He stopped eating and started losing weight. Finally, a doctor advised him to quit moping and take a little vacation to visit his friend Joshua Speed, who'd moved to his family's Kentucky plantation.

The change of scenery was exactly what Abraham needed. Not long after Lincoln arrived, Speed proposed marriage to a young Kentucky woman who had captured his heart. Ironically, Speed later began to doubt himself and his relationship with Fanny Henning, his fiancée. Like Lincoln, Speed broke off the engagement and he, too, fell into a serious depression. (Talk about fear of commitment!)

Making His Own Home

Lincoln's faith in himself returned and he overcame what little sadness remained by helping Speed pull out of his depression. Abraham eventually refocused on obtaining Mary Todd's hand in marriage.

Abraham Lincoln and Mary Todd were finally married in an impromptu evening ceremony on November 4, 1842. Earlier that day, Lincoln had engaged the services of an Episcopal minister by telling him, "I want to get hitched tonight." Todd's well-to-do family was a bit irritated by the short notice.

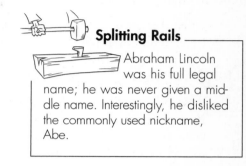

Splitting Rails

Abraham Lincoln was his full legal name; he was never given a middle name. Interestingly, he disliked the commonly used nickname, Abe.

Within nine months, Mary and Abraham welcomed their firstborn, a son named Robert Todd, named for Mary's father.

Mr. Lincoln Goes to Washington

To support his young family, Lincoln worked as a *circuit lawyer*. Lincoln's cases typically involved criminal as well as civil matters, including bad debts, fights, land disputes, divorces, murders, and public drunkenness.

Lincoln became well known in the circuit and gained many friends, including people who would later become influential and prominent. Illinoisan William H. Herndon was one of these individuals. In 1844, Herndon joined Lincoln's law practice.

Lincoln Lingo

As a **circuit lawyer,** Abraham Lincoln traveled every fall and spring by horse from one county courthouse to the next, completing a circuit of about 15 courthouses in about 10 weeks' time.

Because each courthouse in the circuit was in session for only a few days, the pace was frenzied. Court Days, as they were called in many locales, took on a festive atmosphere and drew residents from miles around. Residents took the opportunity to visit with one another and gossiped about the latest court happenings.

Today's county circuit courts are vestiges from the old circuit court system, which originated under British rule in colonial times.

Not long after Robert was born, Abraham's law practice began to produce a comfortable income. In 1844, Lincoln purchased his first home, a small frame cottage that cost him about $1,500 in cash and land. His young family settled in. (Real prosperity for the Lincolns didn't come until the mid-1850s.)

Life was good, but Lincoln also thought again about running for office—this time setting his sights on a congressional seat. It would be a couple of years before the timing would be exactly right for him to win the Whig nomination.

Congressman Abraham Lincoln

In March of 1846, a second Lincoln child was born: a son, Edward Baker, named after a close friend. That fall, 37-year-old Lincoln ran on the Whig ticket for the U.S. House of Representatives seat from Illinois' Seventh Congressional District.

Lincoln was elected in August 1846. His visibility as a circuit attorney had paid off. But incredibly, Lincoln served just one two-year term. Why? There were several reasons, but the most obvious one was that by nonbinding prearrangement, up-and-coming young Whigs agreed to rotate their service. While in Congress, Lincoln showed that he wasn't afraid to take a stand against what he perceived as abuse of power.

When Lincoln arrived in Washington for his first session in December 1846, the country was involved in war against Mexico. Like all Whigs, Lincoln strongly opposed the war and U.S. policy toward Mexico. (Interestingly, Congressman Lincoln cast votes in favor of supplying soldiers while vigorously objecting to the Union's decision to go to war with Mexico.)

The Union's War Against Mexico

As you might remember from history class, the Mexican War arose from a conflict between Texas and Mexico. After gaining independence from Spain in 1821, Mexican rulers invited white pioneers from the United States to settle Texas. In 1836, American Texans revolted against Mexican rule, and successfully battled Mexico in a war of independence. For about a decade after that, Texas was an independent country, known as the Republic of Texas. Mexico stubbornly refused to recognize Texas as a sovereign nation.

In 1845, the Republic of Texas applied for U.S. statehood. That step renewed tensions between Texas and Mexico. But what shocked Mexico even more was that the U.S. president, a Democrat named James K. Polk, made it clear that he not only wanted to annex Texas, he also intended to snatch up two other Mexican territories—New Mexico and California—and bring them into the Union.

Mexico refused to give up its land, so war broke between the Union and Mexico in 1846. Consistent with the concept of *Manifest Destiny*, many people believed the United States should expand across the continent.

Lincoln Lingo

Manifest Destiny was a nineteenth-century doctrine that viewed U.S. territorial expansion as its obvious fate. Many Americans in the 1840s believed the destiny of the United States of America was to expand across the entire continent, holding all land from the Atlantic to the Pacific oceans. What's more, they believed it was God's will that this expansion take place.

Interestingly, no U.S. president or secretary of state ever outlined this doctrine. According to author and historian Matthew Pinsker, the term was coined by a journalist, and the concept provoked a great deal of controversy at the time.

In the Mexican War, Union forces pushed Mexican nationals from their homes and farms in territories that had been held by Mexico. By the time Lincoln arrived in Washington in 1847, the United States had won the war and its spoils—more than 500,000 square miles. Texas became part of the United States, plus the Union gained what would later become California, Nevada, New Mexico, Utah, Arizona, and parts of Colorado and Wyoming.

To some, it was a huge land grab that displaced a lot of Mexicans, most of whom were peaceful farmers with no means of defending themselves against the mighty U.S. invasion. Lincoln believed the entire affair was unwise and outrageously unjust. The acquisition of this new land also reopened the debate over slavery and its impact on the U.S. economy.

An Unjust War, Says Lincoln

Practically the entire northern Whig Party in Congress opposed the war. But owing to the widespread belief in Manifest Destiny as well as issues involving national patriotism, the folks who spoke out against the Mexican War were considered traitors.

However, within his first weeks as a freshman congressman, Lincoln openly challenged the war's instigator, President Polk, and asked that Polk prove the Mexican

War was justified. Whigs saw the issue—the president's role in instigating the Mexican War—as the only one on which Democrats were vulnerable.

Polk claimed that Mexico had invaded the State of Texas, triggering a response from the United States to protect American citizens on American soil. In a series of resolutions, Lincoln demanded to know the exact spot where that had occurred. Was that spot ever part of Texas? Had the people who lived on that spot pledged allegiance to the United States or to Texas? Had they voted in elections? Had they served on juries?

Lincoln and other Whigs also argued that Congress, not the president, had the constitutional authority to start a war. Professing that no one man should hold such power, Lincoln charged that Polk had acted in violation of the Constitution when he ordered American troops into Mexico. Lincoln and more than 80 Whig representatives supported a resolution introduced by Massachusetts Representative George Ashmun that declared Polk had acted unnecessarily and unconstitutionally.

However, Lincoln's position on the Mexican War wasn't popular and was viewed as politically motivated; a Whig's personal attack against a popular Democrat. His "Spot" resolutions were never debated or acted upon, and Polk ignored Lincoln's demands for explanation.

Under the Stovepipe

Abraham Lincoln's name will always be associated with the Thirteenth Amendment, which ended slavery. But during his term in Congress, Lincoln actually argued against making changes to the United States Constitution. He said the document should be viewed as "unalterable."

In the midst of a renewed debate over slavery as it related to the newly acquired land, Lincoln also took a tentative first step toward freeing slaves during his term in Congress. He composed and read a proposed amendment to a congressional resolution. The amendment called for the abolition of slavery in the District of Columbia and, among other provisions, required compensation for D.C.'s emancipated slaves.

Perhaps recalling the backlash from Lincoln's stand on the Mexican War, his backers quickly abandoned him after hearing the piece of legislation he planned to propose. Absent the support of his colleagues, Lincoln never formally introduced the amendment.

Lincoln's time in office was far too short for the young congressman to make his mark. Still, he supported and voted in favor of the Wilmot Proviso to ban slavery in the territory acquired from Mexico. (The proposed legislation was passed by the U.S. House of Representatives in 1846 and 1847, but the Senate never passed the measure.) He had the opportunity to be among some of the most famous lawmakers in history, including John Quincy Adams. Lincoln also distinguished himself as an orator and a man who stood up for what he believed, even when it was politically risky.

Public Pride, Private Tears

Despite these setbacks, Lincoln continued to make progress as an attorney after returning to private life. In 1849, he was admitted to practice law before the United States Supreme Court. By 1850, the Lincoln–Herndon law practice was one of the most successful in Springfield, handling more than a third of all cases heard in Sangamon County, Illinois. But it was on the court circuit that Lincoln felt most comfortable. He didn't have to put on airs of sophistication and city refinement; Lincoln could just be himself.

On the homefront, Lincoln learned that his father, Thomas Lincoln, was near death in May 1849. When Lincoln arrived at his father's home, he discovered that the man was out of danger and had recovered quite nicely. The next winter, Lincoln's stepbrother sent another series of urgent letters to Abraham about Thomas's failing health. Believing his stepbrother was unnecessarily alarming him again, Abraham ignored the correspondence.

Lincoln had what he considered far more serious worries. His son, Edward, had always been a fragile, sickly child. In December 1849, the boy became deathly ill.

After several long weeks of battling a mysterious illness (today believed to have been *pulmonary tuberculosis*), little Edward Baker Lincoln died on February 1, 1850. The child hadn't yet reached the age of four. The loss of their son absolutely devastated Abraham and Mary.

On December 21, 1849, Lincoln's third son, William Wallace, was born.

Under the Stovepipe

Toward the end of Lincoln's term as a congressman, he sent his wife and two children to live at Mary's family home in Lexington, Kentucky. Although they had tried to live in Washington, he decided they were distracting him from his congressional duties. Letters that were passed between Lincoln and his wife during this separation illustrate how much they missed each other.

Lincoln Lingo

Pulmonary tuberculosis is a contagious bacterial infection caused by Mycobacterium tuberculosis (TB). The infection primarily involves the lungs but can spread to other organs. In Lincoln's time, there was no known cure for the infection and it was usually fatal.

Then on January 27, the following year, Lincoln's father finally succumbed. Abraham had written Thomas before his death, but decided not to attend his father's funeral. He and Thomas weren't close. Abraham, whose world was so vastly different from that of his father, didn't see the point in returning to bury the man.

The Least You Need to Know

♦ Lincoln had a long-established reputation for integrity.

♦ Lincoln gained his law license and built a successful law practice using formidable self-study skills.

♦ Lincoln was a romantic who eventually found and married the love of his life.

♦ Although at first defeated, Lincoln went on to serve four terms as a state legislator.

♦ Lincoln wasn't afraid to speak out against injustice.

3

Lincoln's Emerging Public Presence (1851–1861)

In This Chapter

- ◆ Lincoln's law practice grows and changes
- ◆ Lincoln's wealth and reputation as an orator
- ◆ Lincoln's surprising racist views
- ◆ The 1860 presidential nomination and Lincoln's election
- ◆ Lincoln's inelegant Washington arrival

His term as a U.S. representative over, Lincoln settled into a more private but still prominent life in Springfield. While Mary tended to the children, Abe ambitiously continued building his law practice. But he never totally abandoned politics. He continued to form opinions and speak out about the major issues and conflicts of his time. Lincoln's views continued to evolve and mature. And just as the country was about to fracture from internal strife, the allure of elective office beckoned him once again. This time, Abraham Lincoln found himself aiming for the White House.

"Lawyering" with Integrity

Lincoln turned 40 in 1849. Although he was engaged in ambitious business pursuits, the early 1850s marked a time of personal peace and introspection for the former congressman. The change of focus must have seemed like blessed relief, especially after the previous few years in which Lincoln endured great personal losses.

Lincoln was a very busy attorney and was also heavily involved in partisan activities, even though he wasn't a candidate for office. But during this time, he was able to return to his beloved books and continued to develop his mind. He reconnected with his family and finally enjoyed time at home with his wife and kids, after having been away—or otherwise distracted—for a very long time.

The balance in his life helped to fuel his business success, and his continued personal development led to changes at his law practice. Over time, Lincoln's clientele changed. In addition to its smaller mainstay cases, the firm began taking on big corporate clients. Railroad cases especially appealed to Lincoln because of his interest in transportation and its ties to economic growth.

Under the Stovepipe

Lincoln was at his best as a lawyer when he was convinced he represented the side of justice. Knowing that his cause was right gave Abraham confidence. He also needed lots of time to prepare his legal argument. Lincoln typically conducted painstakingly tedious legal research to ensure he possessed all the legal ammunition he could possibly gather before he ever set foot in the courtroom. Lincoln didn't like to lose a legal battle.

Workin' on the Railroad

As America's railroad system expanded, legal problems arose on issues such as right-of-way, taxation, and passenger rights. The work was important and often complex, and represented a major new source of income for lawyers of the era. From a business perspective, Abe was in the right place at the right time!

Lincoln's first major railroad case was litigated in 1851. His client, the Alton and Sangamon Railroad, sued a *subscriber* (an investor) who refused to pay the balance of his pledge money to the company. The subscriber didn't want to pay because the railroad company changed the route it previously advertised, when it solicited funding. The original path would have run by the subscriber's property, significantly increasing the land's value. Instead, the railroad shifted the route to save money.

Lincoln Lingo

To offset construction costs, railroads in the 1850s often solicited financial pledges, or "subscriptions," from investors, who were typically folks who stood to benefit from the railroad's route—individuals, businesses, and even entire towns. People who purchased these subscriptions were commonly known as **subscribers.**

In those days, economic boom or bust was largely dependent on the location of railroad routes and stations—a requirement for the transport of goods and people. If a railroad company did not receive the pledges it needed in a given area, the company took its business elsewhere, rerouting the railroad through or along the lands of those who had provided financial support.

Lincoln successfully argued that the subscriber was actually a stockholder in the company and that made him liable for the debt. The case was an important one because if Lincoln had lost, other subscribers might have had the right to withhold pledge payments if they didn't agree with railroad decisions. That would have played havoc with the entire railroad industry and hampered its expansion.

The case law that was established as a result of Lincoln's effort helped establish the principle that corporate charters could be amended when in the public interest. Lincoln immediately became a much sought-after expert in railroad law.

The advent of the railroad system in Illinois also brought Lincoln a personal benefit. Previously, he'd traveled the circuit on horseback and had been away for weeks at a time. With the establishment of a nearby station, Lincoln could hop a train, work the court circuit, and return home that weekend. That meant more time with his family.

Appeasing the Wife

By now, Mary was having a hard time. She'd suffered the loss of little Eddie in 1850 and, in the course of the next three years, had given birth to two more sons. Throughout that time, her husband was frequently away, leaving the burden of managing the Lincoln household on her shoulders. It was about this time that neighbors noticed her mood changing. Mary was irritable and sullen, often getting downright nasty with Abe—and other folks, too.

Many history books carry accounts of Mary's moodiness and rants sometimes characterized as craziness, according to her neighbors. However, it's likely that she simply became resentful of her husband and his freewheeling, esoteric ways. How would you like to spend your youth at lovely parties, the center of everyone's attention, and then find yourself stuck in the house for days on end with three kids, including a newborn and a toddler going through his "terrible twos"?

Under the Stovepipe

As an infant, Abraham's youngest son, Thomas, had an unusually large head and a long, skinny body. The child's physique reminded Abe of a tadpole, so he decided to call the kid Tad. The nickname stuck.

Mary's propensity toward excitability is notorious. Lincoln's response was said to be that he simply lived through it, never raising his voice to his wife or taking any other punitive action. He helped out with babysitting chores when he was around, a rarity for men of that era. The fact is, he enjoyed doting on his children and liked being a father. However, neighbors gossiped that Abe was henpecked. Mary and Abraham paid no mind to their detractors. Still, Lincoln was frequently away from home and his son, Robert, would later complain that while growing up he barely knew his father.

Keeping Tabs on Current Events

Even though Lincoln was busy with (and growing wealthy from) his prosperous law practice, he kept up with issues facing the nation. Now considered an elder statesman in Illinois politics, Lincoln lent his support to various Whig candidates and worked on their campaigns. Among other issues of the day, the economic and political battles over slavery continued to divide the nation.

In the years following the Mexican War, the *Compromise of 1850* settled the question about whether the newly acquired lands would allow slavery or not. But then land west of Iowa and Missouri, part of the Louisiana Purchase, became the subject of debate again in the U.S. Congress. Southern congressmen soundly defeated several bills that would have established the territories as free soil.

Then in 1854, Democratic Senator Stephen Douglas of Illinois (the same man who some whispered had been Lincoln's rival for Mary Todd's affections years before) proposed the Kansas–Nebraska Act. Douglas's proposal was to divide the land into two territories, Nebraska (north) and Kansas (south), and to allow each of these two jurisdictions to decide the slavery question on their own.

Because Douglas's proposed act violated another law concerning slavery north of the boundaries of the western territories, the Missouri Compromise of 1820, he added language to his proposed law that repealed (or cancelled) the previous compromise. The law passed. Lincoln was appalled by this turn of events.

Lincoln Lingo

The Missouri Compromise (1820) and the **Compromise of 1850** settled slavery issues related to lands acquired from France in the Louisiana Purchase—an 828,000-square-mile tract of land that would later become 13 states. They were designed to appease congressmen who represented northern abolitionists and southern slaveholders. The Missouri Compromise allowed Missouri to enter as a slave state, while prohibiting slavery in western territories north of Missouri's southern border.

Among other provisions, the Compromise of 1850 settled the slavery issue for lands acquired in the Mexican War. This law admitted California to the Union as a free state, and permitted the territories of Utah and New Mexico (which included land that would later become Arizona and Nevada) to decide the slavery question on their own.

It's important to understand that in the 1850s, Lincoln was not a true abolitionist in that he did not actively work to ban slavery where it already existed. Lincoln figured that if the number of slave states could be strictly contained, slavery would eventually disappear on its own. Unlike most Americans of his era, Lincoln believed blacks were entitled to human and economic rights equal to those of whites. He was skeptical about possible social and political equality, but it's not clear whether that was because he believed in white superiority (a commonly held belief in Lincoln's day) or if Lincoln simply didn't believe whites would ever accept full equality of the races.

Lincoln vigorously objected to the practice of keeping humans captive, as slavery violated his moral principles. But he also strongly opposed slavery on the basis of its economic and societal impacts.

Taking a Stand

When the Kansas–Nebraska Act was passed and the Missouri Compromise was repealed, Lincoln was "aroused" (his word) to seek national office again. Fearing slavery's spread would ultimately lead to the downfall of the Union and the end of democracy, Lincoln believed that allowing slavery in new territories was a huge mistake. As an American patriot, he had no choice but to act. But following the Kansas–Nebraska Act's passage, the political climate was volatile. Those who opposed the new law were not organized.

Lincoln took time to carefully evaluate the situation and decided to take part in the 1854 fall elections by campaigning for the reelection of Whig congressman Richard

Yates of Illinois. While he stumped for Yates and advised him as his campaign manager, Lincoln also worked on behalf of the anti-Nebraska cause. He also had his sights on running for U.S. Senate. But during the campaign, political party leaders urged Lincoln to run for state legislature, even promising to sway support for Yates if Lincoln would accept nomination. Lincoln eventually agreed.

Yates lost the congressional election, but Lincoln was elected to serve in the Illinois state legislature. Almost immediately after the state legislative elections had concluded, Lincoln began campaigning for the Senate position. But there were legal and political problems. According to Illinois law, Lincoln couldn't be elected to the Senate seat as long as he held the state office. But if he didn't run for the Senate seat, he might end up having to cast a vote for a political foe.

Lincoln considered his options, and decided not to accept election to the Illinois House of Representatives. He felt he'd have the opportunity to make a far bigger impact as a U.S. senator.

When the Illinois legislature assembled for the election, Lincoln had about half the votes he needed. But as the election played out, Lincoln had to make a difficult but savvy political decision. When it appeared that a proponent of the Kansas–Nebraska Act might win, Lincoln directed his supporters to cast their votes for Lyman Trumbull, a Democrat who shared Lincoln's anti-Nebraska beliefs. Trumbull won, and by rallying members from several political parties, Lincoln helped establish the foundation of the Republican Party in Illinois.

A New Political Party Emerges

Although Whig and Democratic candidates often prevailed in the era's elections, voters had many other choices, and that's the way it had been since the beginning of democracy. New political parties regularly formed, usually to rally support for an issue of importance.

In the 1840s, for example, antislavery sympathizers founded a political party known as the *Free-Soilers*, and nativists who opposed immigrants, especially Catholics, established the *Know-Nothing Party*. Candidates from each of these parties gained seats in local and state or territorial elections.

But after the Kansas–Nebraska Act was passed, individuals within several political parties decided to join together to fight slavery. Free-Soilers joined with Democratic and Whig hard-line abolitionists to form the Republican Party in 1854. Lincoln didn't join the new party right away, partly because of their extremist reputation but also because he felt a strong loyalty to the Whig Party and thought the more moderate approach advocated by that party would eventually work. However, the Whig Party quickly weakened and Lincoln changed his position. By the end of 1855, Lincoln concluded that a new party was needed, one that could effectively consolidate all the groups who opposed the expansion of slavery. Lincoln took the lead in creating the new party, known as an "Anti-Nebraska" party.

Lincoln Lingo

Free-Soilers were against slavery but they were not abolitionists. They believed that white men should receive property in the western territories free of charge. Some Free-Soilers sought to ban all blacks from these newly acquired lands.

Organizers of the **Know-Nothing Party** opposed foreign immigration and were widely believed to be anti-Catholic.

A Moment to Remember

Not long after, the old party collapsed—undoubtedly nudged by an eloquent speech Lincoln made on May 29, 1856 at the new party's state convention in Bloomington, Illinois.

His appearance at the podium marked Lincoln's first public appearance as a Republican—even though it would be two years before Illinois party loyalists would use the term "Republican" to describe the newly formed political organization. In his impassioned address, he argued that antislavery factions of the Whig and Democratic parties should join with Free-Soilers and Know-Nothings to win that year's election.

Following the 1856 presidential election, won by Democrat James Buchanan, the Whig, Free-Soilers, and Know-Nothing parties dissolved. That left just the two major political parties, Republican and Democrat—the same two we know today.

Lincoln vigorously campaigned for the Republican nominee, John C. Frémont. He regrouped by turning his attention back to his law practice and family again. But the period of relative calm didn't last long.

Just two days after Buchanan's inauguration in 1857, the U.S. Supreme Court handed down a terrible legal decision. The ruling further agitated the conflict between the North and the South.

Under the Stovepipe

Throughout the years, Lincoln's address at the Illinois State Republican Convention has been widely praised as his most stirring oratory achievement. It's said that Lincoln was so incredibly compelling that the newspaper reporters covering the event actually stopped taking notes. Like others present that day, the journalists were supposedly spellbound, and they wanted to hear—and experience—every moment.

Sadly, we have no record of Lincoln's inspirational speech, calling for unity among anti-slavery factions of four political parties, because he delivered it extemporaneously. Unlike his many other addresses, Lincoln hadn't prepared a written copy of the speech before he gave it. The awed reporters who stopped to listen to him speak didn't record Lincoln's words, either. Today, this historic address is remembered only through eyewitness accounts and is known as The Lost Speech.

On the Verge of Greatness

A decade before, a Missouri slave named Dred Scott sued for his freedom when his master died. Scott's master, an army surgeon, had taken him to live for several years in Illinois and later to the Minnesota territory, both of which outlawed slavery. Scott argued that even though his master eventually brought him back to Missouri, where slavery was allowed, Scott's time in these northern lands made him a free man. (It took 10 long years for this case to wind its way through the legal system, leaving Dred Scott legally captive all that time.)

Dred Scott, they ruled, had no right to sue his master. He was a Negro, and therefore not a citizen of the United States. The justices declared that when the nation was created, blacks were considered inferior to whites, and therefore America's founding fathers had not included Negroes in either the Declaration of Independence or the U.S. Constitution. As owned property on par with cattle and mules, blacks had absolutely no rights at all.

But they didn't stop there. According to the Supreme Court's 7-to-2 decision, Congress also had no constitutional right to bar slavery. So the Missouri Compromise and all other laws limiting or governing slavery anywhere in the United States were immediately declared null and void.

At first, Lincoln believed other legislative decisions being weighed in other courts might correct the damage done by the Dred Scott Decision. But as Lincoln further contemplated the decision and its impact, his initial ambivalence was replaced by righteous indignation. What riled Lincoln was the audacity of Supreme Court Chief

Justice Roger B. Taney. How could that man interpret the language of the Declaration of Independence as exclusionary?

Under the Stovepipe

Chief Justice Roger B. Taney of the U.S. Supreme Court, a Maryland slaveholder, was the architect of the 1857 Dred Scott Decision, which stripped African Americans of all rights and eliminated laws limiting or governing slavery. Four years after handing down that decision, southern sympathizer Taney drew a most distasteful task. As Chief Justice, Taney was required to administer the oath of office to a man whose policies he detested: the newly elected President Abraham Lincoln. Now that's sweet justice!

Referring to the Dred Scott Decision, Lincoln wrote, "In those [America's founding] days, our Declaration of Independence was held sacred by all and thought to include all, but now, to aid in making the bondage of the Negro universal and eternal, it is assailed, and sneered at, and construed, and hawked at, and torn, till if its framers could rise from their graves, they could not at all recognize it."

Lincoln realized there were two chilling possibilities: If blacks had no rights, then nothing prevented whites from owning them anywhere in the country. And if one group of people could be excluded from constitutional protection, others could, too.

Under the Stovepipe

Because he feared African Americans might never be permitted full rights, Lincoln toyed with the idea of establishing a federal government program to solve the problem. His ideal solution involved providing financial support and other logistical assistance that would enable freed slaves to leave the United States and resettle in Africa or the Caribbean. Once back in their African homeland, he believed, blacks could finally regain their civil liberties, including the right to self-govern.

Upon later reflection, however, Lincoln realized that his idea was impractical. Aside from logical difficulties that couldn't be overcome, blacks had been in the United States for so long that they no longer recognized Africa as "home." Organizations were formed to help send blacks back to Africa (which is how Liberia, meaning "freedom," was founded), but the attempt failed. Most settlers wanted to return to America.

During the next year, Illinois Republicans nominated Abraham Lincoln as their candidate for U.S. Senate, to run against the incumbent, Democrat Stephen Douglas.

(It's important to note that state legislatures, not voters, selected U.S. senators at the time.) In accepting his party's nomination on June 16, 1858, Lincoln drew on a well-known biblical verse as he uttered these immortal words:

Notes and Orations

"I shall have my hands full. He is the strong man of the party—full of wit, facts, and dates—and the best stump speaker, with his droll ways and dry jokes, in the West. He is as honest as he is shrewd."

—Incumbent U.S. Senator Stephen Douglas of Illinois, 1858, upon learning that his opponent for re-election was Abraham Lincoln

"A house divided against itself cannot stand. I believe the government cannot endure, permanently half slave and half free. I do not expect the Union to be dissolved—I do not expect the house to fall—but I do expect it will cease to be divided. It will become all one thing, or all the other."

Lincoln's message was like a rallying cry for abolitionists, who had for decades professed that it was impossible for freedom and slavery to co-exist in society. Of course, Abe's opponent didn't see it that way.

Let the debates begin!

The Road to the White House

Lincoln's national prominence and path to the presidency actually began in 1858, with the now famous Lincoln–Douglas debates. By that time, the two men had known each other for many years. (They'd first met when Lincoln was a shopkeeper in New Salem.)

Both Lincoln and Douglas were highly regarded as orators, and some of the debates between them drew crowds of more than 10,000 people at a time. Full-length photos of the two men standing side-by-side would have instigated a few laughs. Stephen Douglas was a stout little guy—only five feet, four inches in height. Tall, lanky Lincoln towered over him. The subject of their intense verbal contests was of vital interest to all: slavery.

In the debates, Lincoln argued that slavery was morally abhorrent, and that the Union could not go on as a nation divided on the issue. Douglas attacked Lincoln, suggesting that Abe was in favor of dissolving the Union to eliminate slavery.

The Lincoln–Douglas debates were reasoned, heated, and entertaining, but that's not what made them famous or historically important. These two oratorical powerhouses synthesized and more clearly defined both sides of the slavery issue for the entire American public. They allowed stenographers to take down their speeches so they could be reprinted statewide and, later, nationwide.

Each debate produced no clear champion, although after each contest, supporters from both sides insisted their candidate absolutely crushed the other. After the election results were tallied, though, Stephen Douglas learned he had retained his Senate seat. Lincoln had suffered yet another bitter defeat.

Splitting Rails

Lincoln has been widely hailed as an unwavering abolitionist and a steady voice for racial equality. That perception is not exactly accurate. Lincoln's views on slavery and African Americans evolved over time and were intertwined with economic as well as social issues.

During his fourth debate with Stephen Douglas in 1858, for instance, Lincoln said he was not in favor of blacks voting, serving on juries, holding office, or intermarrying with white people. He went on to say that he believed the differences between blacks and whites would forever prevent the two races from living together in social and political equality. But it's important to note that Lincoln didn't rule these out forever. He made these statements in response to vicious race-baiting by Douglas and the Democrats.

During the debates, Lincoln's goal was not to express ideas of white superiority. (In fact, he claimed blacks had equal human and economic rights with whites.) Instead, Lincoln sought to avoid distractions in an argument about slavery extension.

Honest Abe for President!

Even though he lost his bid for U.S. Senate, Lincoln benefited tremendously from the national media attention that the debates had attracted. He became widely known and respected among Republicans in the North.

In 1859, Lincoln believed Douglas would try to run for president, so he made himself available to lecture wherever Douglas spoke. Lincoln considered Douglas "a dangerous enemy of liberty." Lincoln continued to express the concepts he'd expressed in his debates with Douglas but he also elaborated on other issues that he hadn't thoroughly explored the previous year. Economic freedom was a recurring subject.

As Lincoln traveled throughout the country, his name began coming up as a possible candidate for president. Some newspaper editors actually wrote editorials suggesting they were endorsing Lincoln's candidacy before he'd even declared!

It may surprise you to learn that Lincoln was more than pleased by the reaction. Behind the scenes, Lincoln courted the media and sought endorsements. He provided biographical materials and worked to arrange for the national Republican convention to come to Chicago in 1860. Among his many invitations, Lincoln was asked to speak before a sophisticated New York crowd in February 1860. He somehow knew this event would be an important one, and he took great pains to prepare. He even bought a brand-new suit. On February 27, 1860, Lincoln appeared before a near-capacity crowd—including many skeptics—at New York's Cooper Union. Folks who heard the speech said the experience was positively spine tingling. Those city slickers saw that Abe Lincoln was no backwoods hick. Instead, they recognized him for who he was: a great American leader. When Lincoln finished, the audience went wild.

The next day, Lincoln's speech was reprinted in its entirety in four New York newspapers. Among many superlatives, he was hailed as "the greatest man since Saint Paul." Newspapers throughout the North also reprinted his speech. Not surprisingly, the reaction to Lincoln's Cooper Union speech provided the momentum he needed to gain the Republican Party's presidential nomination. In the election held later that year, Lincoln faced his old nemesis, Stephen Douglas, and two other rivals.

You already know how the contest ended. Despite having suffered previous back-to-back defeats, Abraham Lincoln won the election handily. Some Lincoln scholars believe that his Cooper Union speech made all the difference in the election's outcome.

But it's also important to understand that the 1860 election was a pivotal point in American history and a harbinger of events to come.

Divided Parties

In April 1860, southern and northern Democrats couldn't agree on a platform—or a candidate—at the Democratic Party's national convention in Charleston, South Carolina. Southern Democrats walked out in protest and Stephen Douglas failed to gain the two-thirds majority required to secure his party's nomination. Leaders decided to adjourn the convention and meet at a later date.

While Democrats struggled against deep devisions within their party, Lincoln was nominated on the third ballet as the Republican Party's candidate the following month. Because of the turmoil in the Democratic Party, Republicans believed they had nominated the next president of the United States.

But meanwhile, the Constitutional Union Party formed, consisting primarily of conservative Whigs who had refused to join the new Republican Party and like-minded "Know Nothings." In May 1860, the group met in Baltimore, Maryland, to nominate its candidate, John Bell.

In June, Democrats met again—this time in Baltimore. Douglas won the presidential nomination on the second ballot, but southern Democrats who had walked out of the Charleston convention hadn't been allowed to be seated. Members of the group that had previously bolted decided to meet on their own in Baltimore. They nominated John C. Breckinridge as their presidential candidate, a decision that was later ratified at yet another southern Democratic convention held that year in Richmond.

Southern Democrats had expected Douglas to withdraw, but he didn't. The Democratic Party, which had been the dominant political force, was split in two—North and South. Lincoln won the election handily.

But with all the emphasis on Lincoln and Douglas and their famous debates, you may be surprised to learn that Douglas didn't place second in the 1860 presidential election. Lincoln won with 180 electoral votes and 40 percent of the popular vote. Breckinridge finished second with 72 electoral votes. Bell received 39 electoral votes. Although Douglas finished second to Lincoln in the popular vote (he was the choice of 29 percent of the voters), he placed last in the election, having won only 12 electoral votes. As you might imagine, Lincoln won with northern voters and Breckinridge's voter support came from the South.

Mr. President

On February 11, 1861, Lincoln packed up his family and said a tearful goodbye to their friends in Springfield. Together, he and Mary and their children boarded a train to begin the long journey to Washington, stopping at numerous towns and cities along the way to acknowledge and address well-wishers who turned out to greet him.

By the time Lincoln's train reached Pennsylvania, Lincoln and his supporters had learned of a plot to kill the new president. Southern sympathizers wanted Lincoln dead.

Allan Pinkerton, head of the Pinkerton Agency, the first detective agency in the country, protected Lincoln from Baltimore to Washington. While under contract to the Philadelphia, Wilmington and Baltimore Railroad, Pinkerton and his operatives infiltrated *secessionist* organizations in Baltimore to investigate a possible threat to the railroad company's property.

Lincoln Lingo

A **secessionist** advocates withdrawing from an association, organization, or other alliance. In Lincoln's time, the term related to advocates of southern states withdrawing from the Union. From 1860 to 1861, 11 states seceded, triggering the Civil War.

During that investigation, they reportedly uncovered the plot to kill Lincoln when he passed through Baltimore. Pinkerton immediately notified his client and arranged to meet with Lincoln in his hotel room in Philadelphia. It's said Pinkerton's quick thinking probably saved Lincoln's life. However, some Lincoln contemporaries and a number of historians think Pinkerton may have made up the plot.

Under the Stovepipe

Imagine Mary Todd Lincoln's quandary when her husband was elected president of the United States—and she realized her wardrobe was all wrong. Now that she, too, was about to become an important person, Mary wanted her clothing to reflect high style and refinement, but she had to consider her family's budget. When she learned that Abe's salary as president would increase their already hefty household income by at least five times, Mary did what any red-blooded American woman would do in her situation. She left the kids with her husband and headed for New York City's fashion houses. My, she looked fine when she arrived at the White House.

Unfortunately for Abraham, Mary didn't limit herself to the cash in her pockets during her shopping spree. Instead, she took advantage of the credit lines New York merchants gleefully offered her, and she rang up a huge debt. (By the way, the presidential salary in 1860 was $25,000. That may not sound like much money, but in today's dollars, it's roughly equivalent to the current presidential salary.)

To ensure his safety, Lincoln exchanged his easily identifiable top hat for a wool hat and switched trains, sneaking into Washington unnoticed. (In 1861, after safely escorting the president-elect to Washington, Pinkerton served as head of intelligence for the Army of the Potomac. The newspapers had a field day when they learned about Lincoln's inelegant arrival.

The Least You Need to Know

- Before being elected president, Lincoln was a successful and wealthy Illinois lawyer.

- The passage of the Kansas–Nebraska Act reignited Lincoln's political ambitions.

- The 1858 Lincoln–Douglas debates brought Abe national fame and defined both sides of the slavery issue.

- Lincoln's compelling 1860 speech at New York's Cooper Union led to his party's presidential nomination.

Chapter 4

President Lincoln (1861–1865)

In This Chapter

- ◆ Little-known challenges Lincoln faced as president
- ◆ Lincoln's controversial domestic policies
- ◆ Lincoln's role in Civil War military strategy
- ◆ Lincoln's assassination led to chaos and mourning
- ◆ Lincoln's path to American sainthood, myth, and legend

Lincoln reportedly once said that his first months in office went so badly that he wanted to hang himself. The comment was undoubtedly delivered half-jokingly—Abraham was known for his self-deprecating humor as well as his bouts with depression—but after you know the magnitude of the troubles he faced, such a remark isn't really so startling. If you had been in Lincoln's shoes, chances are you would have uttered similar words.

The Lincoln presidency was riddled with tragedy as well as triumph, laced with a series of seemingly endless personal losses and national crises. Thankfully, the man from Kentucky never gave up.

A Grim but Hopeful Beginning

On March 4, 1861, his inauguration day, Abraham Lincoln awoke in his suite at the Willard Hotel in Washington, anxious and exhausted. It was no secret that his life was in danger. Secessionists had openly placed a bounty on his head—offering a hefty reward for Lincoln's immediate assassination.

Not long after putting on his new suit, tall stovepipe hat, and leather boots, Lincoln picked up his gold-headed cane and walked to the hotel lobby. There, he greeted outgoing Democratic president James Buchanan, who had arrived at the Willard a few minutes before noon to accompany the president-elect on his short journey to the inauguration ceremony. The two men exchanged pleasantries, and then headed down Pennsylvania Avenue in an open carriage bound for the Capitol building.

The new leader of the United States of America must have felt as though he had entered a hostile, foreign land. The city was unadorned, eerily quiet, and tense. Most Washingtonians didn't support the new president; the majority had already sided with the South and the secessionists. The atmosphere that day starkly contrasted with his big send-off in Springfield and the huge celebrations he had experienced during his 12-day, 1,904 mile journey from his hometown to Baltimore.

Although it might have offered Lincoln some measure of comfort and safety, the scene surely had to be troubling and even a little depressing to him. Instead of the customary festive banners and other celebratory decorations along the route, Lincoln saw armed guards lining the avenue leading to the Capitol steps. Soldiers had blocked off some of the cross-streets.

Under the Stovepipe

Some historians say that by the time he arrived in Washington for his inaugural ceremony, Lincoln's right hand was swollen and nearly paralyzed from shaking the hands of thousands of well-wishers during his 12-day trip from Springfield, Illinois, to Washington, D.C.

Riflemen on rooftops scanned the streets along Lincoln's route and the areas immediately surrounding the yet-to-be-finished Capitol Rotunda. Along nearby hills stood two batteries of light artillery—great guns—that had been positioned and manned to respond to any major threat. All were ready to defend the United States Capitol and the new president.

Although taking such precautions to protect America's leaders isn't unusual today, it was in Lincoln's era. Never before had any United States presidential inauguration called for such extreme security. Still, it's mind-boggling that no one thought of transporting Lincoln in a covered carriage to avoid making him such an easy target.

Because of Washington's aversion to Lincoln, the crowd that assembled that day for his inauguration was largely imported, comprised of Lincoln supporters from the North. Even so, some of Lincoln's former rivals showed up that day to wish him well. His old nemesis, Stephen Douglas, sat alongside other dignitaries on the Capitol's east portico and reportedly held Lincoln's hat while he addressed the country.

Under the Stovepipe

During the trip to Washington from Springfield, Lincoln asked his eldest son, Robert, to guard a satchel that contained the one and only handwritten copy of his inaugural address. The 17-year-old, who was normally pretty straightlaced, got caught up in all the excitement. He flirted with girls, took a turn at operating the locomotive, drank too much wine—and totally forgot about the importance of that satchel.

Robert gave the bag to a porter, who casually tossed it on a stack of unguarded luggage! Well, you can just imagine what Lincoln had to say when, during the trip, he discovered his satchel was missing. After an uncharacteristically heated discussion with the boy (Lincoln rarely showed anger toward his children), Abraham rummaged through a pile of baggage to find his case. Luckily (for us and young Robert), no harm had come to the papers.

Once at the podium, the great orator placed his notes on the stand and finally relaxed. He pulled out his steel-rimmed spectacles from his pocket, put them on, and began to speak just as the sun broke through the clouds, warming the otherwise cold and somber winter day. Some historians suggest that for his first inaugural address, Lincoln had originally planned a stern address, but acting on the advice of trusted associates, he softened his message to avoid provoking his detractors.

Lincoln delivered an impassioned plea for peace among American countrymen, urging citizens in the North and South to be friends, not enemies, and to resist revolution. By the time he reached the conclusion of his address, however, Lincoln had left no doubt about his determination to preserve—and protect—the Union. After completing the speech, he took the oath of office and became the sixteenth president of the United States.

Notes and Orations

"In your hands, my dissatisfied fellow countrymen, and not in mine, is the momentous issue of civil war. The government will not assail you. You can have no conflict, without being yourselves the aggressors. You have no oath registered in Heaven to destroy the government, while I shall have the most solemn one to 'preserve, protect, and defend' it."

—Abraham Lincoln, First Inaugural Address, March 4, 1861

The Confederacy Rises

Ironically, two weeks earlier, citizens of the newly formed Confederate States of America had gathered in Montgomery, Alabama, to hear President Jefferson Davis's inaugural address. The Confederate States of America represented only a few southern states at first, but more were soon to follow—eventually numbering 11.

Georgian Alexander H. Stephens, an old Whig congressional colleague of Lincoln's and someone Lincoln hoped might support him and the Union, was installed as Davis's vice president. Military outposts in Texas had been surrendered to the secessionists that day, too.

Even as Lincoln spoke at his own presidential inauguration, serious trouble brewed just outside Fort Sumter in South Carolina. The new president didn't hear about it until he arrived at the White House after midnight, having enjoyed the evening at his inaugural ball—an event which, by the way, was boycotted by Washington's southern-sympathizing social elite.

On that first night as president, Lincoln received word that Confederate forces had surrounded the fortress, located on a tiny island in the middle of Charleston's harbor. Supplies couldn't get in or out. Without help from Washington, federal troops inside the fort would run out of supplies in less than two months. The unexpected communiqué would set the tone for Lincoln's 50 months in office and began the first of many sleepless nights for the new president.

Splitting Rails

Lincoln wasn't universally beloved during his time in office, particularly during his first term, and many critics were downright nasty. His reputation as a backwoods prairie lawyer, his homely and often bedraggled appearance, and his down-home sense of humor rubbed a lot of people the wrong way. Democratic newspapers (the media was partisan in those days) often published cartoons depicting Lincoln as a buffoon, and they harshly criticized his decisions and ridiculed the jokes he told. Republican newspapers supported the president almost uniformly. In the process, neither side worried too much about accuracy. For "Honest Abe," life was truly lonely at the top.

Over the next few weeks, as Fort Sumter's rations dwindled, members of Lincoln's Cabinet disagreed on the best course of action and gave the president conflicting advice. Some advisors favored pulling the troops out of the fort and giving it up.

Others wanted to send reinforcements, to fight the Confederates. Others wanted simply to send food and supplies.

In the end, Lincoln was left to make the decision on his own. He chose to send an expeditionary team armed with provisions to Fort Sumter, under strict orders not to engage the rebels unless they were fired upon. Although he believed civil war might be inevitable, Lincoln didn't want the Union to fire the first shot.

What Abraham didn't know when the team and provisions left for Charleston from New York on April 1, 1861, was that the Confederacy had already decided to start the war. On April 10, rebel forces surrounding the fort demanded that the Union garrison at Fort Sumter surrender. The Union commander declined. On April 12, the Confederates opened fire and attacked the fort. Unable to mount an effective response (supplies were low and the men were exhausted), Sumter surrendered about 33 hours later, on April 13.

In response, Lincoln immediately put out a call for 75,000 volunteers to protect Washington and battle the insurgent Southern army. Lincoln offered command of the Union army to one of the most respected military men in the nation: Colonel Robert E. Lee of Virginia.

Lee was Lincoln's first choice for good reason. The son of a Revolutionary War hero, a distinguished graduate of West Point (second in his graduating class), and himself a veteran of the Mexican War, Lee loved his country. However, when Virginia voted to secede from the United States on April 18—two days after he received Lincoln's offer—the colonel saw no choice but to refuse the appointment. "I cannot raise my hand against my relatives, my children, my home," Lee explained in a letter to his sister.

Rather than support what he viewed as the Union's suppression of Virginia, Lee resigned from the Union army and accepted the position of major general of Virginia forces. On May 23, when Virginia officially joined the Confederacy and they combined military forces, Lee was named brigadier general. He later held other commands, including his appointment as General-in-Chief of the Confederacy, an appointment made in February 1865. For Lincoln, losing Lee *and* Virginia to the South were crushing blows.

Opening Skirmishes

Almost immediately after Virginia seceded, Lincoln ordered Union troops based in Washington to cross the Potomac River into northern Virginia and secure the neighboring towns of Alexandria and Arlington. Not surprisingly, one of the first buildings seized and occupied by Union forces was Robert E. Lee's family mansion in Arlington.

Although the raid was a success for the Union, Lincoln was devastated to learn of the loss of Colonel Elmer Ellsworth, who led one of the Union regiments in the foray. Ellsworth, a former law student of Lincoln's and a close family friend, was shot and killed in Alexandria after he impulsively climbed to the roof of a local hotel and took down a Confederate flag. He was the first officer to die in the conflict. Lincoln wept when he heard the news, and gave Ellsworth a White House funeral.

Under the Stovepipe

After Union troops captured Robert E. Lee's mansion in Virginia, the Union came up with an innovative way to prevent Lee from ever returning to his home. Union soldiers buried their dead in his front yard. Lee never lived in the house again, and in June 1864, the Union secretary of war officially appropriated Lee's home and the nearly 200 acres of land surrounding it for a military cemetery. Today, Lee's mansion is a National Park Service Museum, perched on a hill overlooking the hallowed ground now known as Arlington National Cemetery.

Even though the Union army had achieved its objective in the Virginia raid, there weren't enough soldiers in Washington to defend against an attack. The volunteers Lincoln requested hadn't arrived yet from the North. In fact, some never made it. About the same time Lee resigned from the Union army, violence broke out in Maryland as a regiment of Massachusetts soldiers bound for Washington was attacked. Several of them were killed by a rioting mob of southern sympathizers in Baltimore.

Things got so bad that for a time it looked like the capital might fall into Confederate hands within the first month of Lincoln's presidency. But when reinforcements from New York, Rhode Island, and Massachusetts finally arrived on April 25, Washington's pro-Union residents went wild. They knew their city was safe. Many were so relieved and optimistic that they thought the Union army would easily quell the rebellion and win the war within 90 days. They were only off by about four years.

A Hands-On Commander in Chief

Tennessee, North Carolina, and Arkansas were the next states to withdraw from the Union. The rapid secession of three more states, the escalating violence in neighboring Maryland, and the presence of spies and traitors throughout the area caused Lincoln to stun some people by suspending the *writ of habeas corpus*, thus allowing Union military personnel to arrest individuals at will. He also increased the size of the regular army without first gaining congressional approval. These moves understandably alarmed some citizens, but Lincoln had overwhelming public support for his actions in the North.

Supreme Court Chief Justice Taney decided against Lincoln. But Lincoln believed his actions were justified to quell the rebellion and preserve the Union. In sharp contrast to his background as an officer of the court and his reputation as a defender of personal freedom and the United States Constitution, Lincoln did something unimaginable— he ignored the ruling. But he didn't ignore the issue Taney raised. Lincoln decided to explain his actions to Congress on July 4, 1861. Members ratified his authority to act in time of rebellion.

Lincoln Lingo

Its Medieval Latin translation is "you shall have the body." Also known as the Great Writ, the **writ of habeas corpus** is an order that may be issued to release a person from unlawful restraint; the protection against imprisonment without cause, one of the personal liberties guaranteed by the United States Constitution. When Lincoln suspended the writ of habeas corpus in selected geographic areas in the spring of 1861, some citizens no longer had this constitutional right. Congress later formally approved Lincoln's initiatives. The civil liberties of most northern citizens were kept intact during the Civil War.

The president didn't stop there. Although Lincoln respected Union General Winfield Scott, he wasn't confident in the elderly (and overweight) commander's stamina. So Lincoln studied military books and maps and determined that the best place to attack and stop the Confederates was at Manassas (Bull Run) in Northern Virginia.

Scott and another leader, General Irvin McDowell, protested unsuccessfully that their men were green and not ready for battle. But like so many others, Lincoln wanted a quick and decisive end to the war, so he ordered the troops into battle. The confrontation at Manassas resulted in a massive, humiliating defeat for the Union for which Lincoln was widely criticized.

A Long, Long War

The loss at Manassas, or Bull Run, convinced Lincoln that the Union needed to be resolute, and that it was crucial for him to take an even more active role in military affairs. When the Army of the Potomac embarked on a campaign in the Virginia peninsula in March 1862, Lincoln turned control over to General George B. McClellan, a cocky, diminutive man, known as "Little Napoleon," who drilled the raw Union volunteers into a real army. McClellan was beloved by the troops for how well he supplied and looked after them, but—despite his arrogance—he was notoriously cautious when it came to actually engaging the enemy. In July 1862, Lincoln appointed General Henry W. Halleck, a distinguished military strategist, as general in chief. After McClellan failed to act decisively, Lincoln fired him as commander of the Army of the Potomac in November 1862, and replaced him with Ambrose Burnside. Those would not be the last changes Lincoln made to Union command.

Splitting Rails

During the Civil War, the North always named battles after the most prominent topographical feature near the battlefield. The South named battles after the closest town. The North called the first battle of the Civil War the Battle of Bull Run, after the stream that flowed near the battlefield, and the subsequent confrontation on the same site the Second Battle of Bull Run. The South, which was victorious in both battles, named them after the closest town, Manassas Junction. The Battle of Antietam was named by the North after Antietam Creek. The South referred to confrontation as the Battle of Sharpsburg, for the town of Sharpsburg, Maryland.

The National Park Service, which manages battlefield parks, uses the name chosen by each battle's victor. If you visit the battlefield Lincoln called "Bull Run," located in Virginia's Prince William County near the city of Manassas, you'll see signs that read Manassas Battlefield. To avoid confusion, we've adhered to the park service's practice in this book.

As time went on, Lincoln became increasingly frustrated by those who were to lead the Union Army. No matter how strongly he pressed his generals, none seemed capable of overcoming the rebels. He seemed to be constantly searching for a man with the "right stuff," a general with unflinching courage and commitment. The lack of military progress not only prolonged the war and the reestablishment of the Union, it undermined Lincoln's later goals for eliminating slavery. He knew nobody would even consider his proposals if the Union kept losing battles.

McClellan, in command again after Lincoln became frustrated with McDowell, overcame Confederate forces under the command of Robert E. Lee at Antietam Creek near Sharpsburg, Maryland. The victory gave Lincoln renewed hope. The September 1862 battle provided the military win Lincoln needed to unveil his Emancipation

Proclamation, which he had written several months before. (More about this and other momentous occasions appear in the next sections of this book, beginning with Part 2.)

Throughout the Civil War, Lincoln remained intimately involved in military strategy and execution. He frequently left the relative safety of the White House and boldly traveled to the war front to see firsthand the status of the war effort. He took his role as commander in chief of the armed forces quite literally. He routinely made personnel changes when he saw that the effort wasn't going the way he'd planned, and he also made troop deployment, movement, and battle decisions. He even personally led an attack on Norfolk, the first president ever to command a military assault while in office.

Some of Lincoln's strategies didn't work, such as the decision to order unready troops into battle at Manassas. But other ideas worked well. Lincoln's greatest overall military contribution to the Union's eventual victory was his early decision, proposed by old General Scott, to order a naval blockade of southern ports.

Lincoln's hands-on style irritated many of his generals, who viewed him as a micromanager. From Abraham's perspective, though, he was doing what was needed to win the war.

Under the Stovepipe

Lincoln's forays into the field of battle once put him directly in harm's way and provide insight into his own personal courage. He came under fire in July 1864 while visiting Fort Stevens, located on the outskirts of Washington near the Maryland border. He'd hoped to gain a firsthand look at the enemy, to determine the strength of the Confederate forces. While Lincoln engaged in conversation with a Union general, enemy soldiers shot directly at Lincoln's party.

Another Campaign

By 1863, Civil War death tolls had escalated on both sides and partisan political battles were heating up. Although Lincoln faced his worst criticism in 1862, the tides had turned and his popularity grew. As election time drew near, Lincoln was alternately praised by Republicans and criticized by Democrats. His political adversaries accused him of cold indifference to the losses and attacked him in intensely personally ways—calling attention, for example, to his gangly frame and lack of military experience. His opponent in the 1864 election was General George McClellan, who was popular in the army and among Democrats but was not a universally loved hero.

Republicans ran on a platform calling for the preservation of the Union and the abolition of slavery everywhere. Democrats who opposed the policies of Lincoln's administration chose McClellan as the presidential candidate in 1864, on a platform that denounced the war as a failure and called for negotiating peace with the South. In accepting his party's candidacy, McClellan rejected the platform, presumably because of his loyalty as a soldier to the troops he once commanded.

Under the Stovepipe

The Democratic Party broke apart in 1860 when divisions over sectional issues and platforms resulted in two presidential candidates being nominated by two separate factions—northern and southern Democrats. During the Civil War, northern Democrats were generally more conciliatory toward the South than Republicans, but internal bickering and divisions within the Northern Democratic Party grew. During the Civil War, the party further splintered into two groups, the War Democrats and the Peace Democrats.

War Democrats, representing the majority of Democrats in the North, supported the Union's military efforts but were critical of Lincoln's conduct of the war. Peace Democrats (also called "Copperheads" by their opponents), were primarily Midwesterners who wanted to preserve the Union but charged that Republicans had provoked the South into war and secession for their own personal aims. Many in this group maintained economic and social ties to the South and favored negotiated peace.

It was clear to everyone that the 1864 presidential election would decide the future of America. Would the war end in unconditional surrender or a negotiated peace? Would slavery be maintained in the United States or be outlawed?

Republicans and War Democrats joined forces to form the National Union Party and renominate Lincoln for a second term. The party selected former Democratic Senator Andrew Johnson of Tennessee as its vice presidential candidate, replacing Vice President Hannibal Hamlin of Maine.

Lincoln risked everything in the election. The vote of the people would be nothing less than a referendum on Lincoln's conduct of the war and his support for emancipation. Lincoln could have cancelled the elections because the country was embroiled in civil war. However, Lincoln didn't think canceling was the right thing to do. So he stood for reelection in 1864—and won, by more than 500,000 votes. His largest margin of support (4-1) came from Union soldiers.

Notes and Orations

Lincoln's spiritually powerful Second Inaugural Address, delivered on March 4, 1865, was brief but inspiring, and is widely considered to be one of the most remarkable political documents in American history. He closed his brief but powerful speech:

With malice toward none; with charity for all; with firmness in the right, as God gives us to see the right, let us strive on to finish the work we are in; to bind up the nation's wounds; to care for him who shall have borne the battle, and for his widow, and his orphan—to do all which may achieve and cherish a just and lasting peace, among ourselves, and with all nations.

In the weeks that followed, Union forces racked up victory after victory in Confederate strongholds throughout the South. Richmond, Virginia, the capitol of the Confederacy, fell to the Union on April 3, 1865. A week later, Lee surrendered and the Union was saved. Although April 9, 1865, is commonly cited as the end of the Civil War, other Confederate forces continued to fight and battles were waged through most of the next month.

The Final Tragedy

On the morning of April 14, Lincoln told everybody how happy he was. The war was ending at last. The years of extreme stress had finally lifted, and he had every reason to feel cheerful and optimistic. He and his wife Mary talked of their personal future, too. For Lincoln, the day was glorious in all respects. The future of America, he said, was limitless.

But on the other side of Washington at the National Hotel, actor John Wilkes Booth finalized his plot to murder Lincoln that night and to reignite a revolution.

That evening, Abraham and Mary boarded a carriage bound for Ford's Theatre, to conclude their wonderful day with a grand finale: seeing the play *Our American Cousin*. As they entered the second-floor box reserved for Lincoln and his party, the band struck up "Hail to the Chief." The audience rose and cheered. After acknowledging the greeting, Lincoln sat down in a large cushioned rocking chair, his wife seated beside him.

Around 10 P.M., as Mary and Abraham tenderly held hands, Booth crept into the theatre box, pointed a small derringer pistol at Lincoln's head, and fired. The president never regained consciousness. He died the next morning.

The nation was plunged into a long period of mourning. Abraham Lincoln was the first United States president to be assassinated in office. The timing—he was shot on Good Friday—also triggered his swift elevation to near saintly status. The day after Lincoln died, ministers stood in their pulpits on Easter Sunday, comparing his humble beginnings with those of Christ.

Like Jesus, they said, the man from Kentucky rose up to prominence to free an enslaved people, and was sacrificed on their behalf. In a very short time, people forgot the real man and remembered him only as a pure and great martyr.

The Least You Need to Know

- Lincoln's storied presidency got off to a terrible start, with months of personal and national calamity.

- As commander in chief of the Union, Lincoln was intimately involved in determining military strategy.

- Lincoln was cut down at the height of his popularity, after years of struggle and criticism.

- Lincoln's greatest contributions to American life sprang from decisions made during the Civil War, to protect the Union and its future.

- Many of Lincoln's longstanding legacies were obscured by his saintly martyrdom following his assassination in 1865.

Part 2

Lincoln's Cultural Legacy

Perhaps the most visible legacies Abraham Lincoln left behind are the contributions he made to American culture.

In this part, we discuss the ways Lincoln's death and funeral affected how we as individuals and as a nation mourn fallen leaders. We also explore the factors that helped create Lincoln myths and legends. What took place after Lincoln's death illustrates how American heroes are often raised up to near-godlike stature, sometimes muddling their true greatness.

Finally, we visit a hallowed place—the Lincoln Memorial in Washington, D.C. A permanent reminder of our sixteenth president, the memorial is a sacred spot where voices still rise, demanding to be heard.

Chapter 5

National Mourning

In This Chapter

- ◆ How young Willie Lincoln died and the state funeral

- ◆ How doctors tried to save President Lincoln

- ◆ Why it took nearly a month and a 1,700 mile-long journey to bury Lincoln

- ◆ How Lincoln's death started what has become an honored American tradition

When he planned to kill Abraham Lincoln, John Wilkes Booth hoped that his act would undo the fragile truce between the North and South. Lincoln's murder actually had the opposite effect. As the first United States president to be assassinated, Lincoln's tragic death triggered extreme sorrow nationwide, drawing the country together in a common resolve to keep the peace.

And how our nation reacted and mourned his loss established a precedent that became both a national tradition and a cultural legacy. But before we grieved for Lincoln, the country mourned when he and his wife buried one of their young sons.

The First Family

When Abraham Lincoln and his wife, Mary, took up residence in the White House in 1861, they also established a new home for their three sons: Robert Todd, age 17; William Wallace, age 10; and Thomas, age 7. (Their second-born, Edward Baker Lincoln, died at the age of three on February 1, 1850, after contracting an illness believed to be tuberculosis.) The Lincoln boys were among the first of many young children who have lived at 1600 Pennsylvania Avenue.

Born in a rooming house on August 1, 1843, Robert was a bright child who challenged Abe and Mary's parenting skills and authority from the start.

Presumably to instill some scholarly discipline, Lincoln sent Robert to a private school in Springfield. In his late teens, Robert initially failed Harvard's entrance exams—a common occurrence at the time. After attending Phillips Exeter Academy in New Hampshire to improve his chances, Robert passed the exams and started at Harvard in the fall of 1860. He attended his father's inauguration while on winter break.

Under the Stovepipe

Abraham Lincoln's eldest son, Robert, was his only child to survive to adulthood. (Robert's youngest brother, Thomas, died on July 15, 1871, at the age of 18.) After completing his undergraduate studies at Harvard College in 1864, Robert entered Harvard Law School. Four months later, he became a captain under General Grant's command and had the honor of being present at Appomattox when Robert E. Lee surrendered.

Robert went on to become a successful Chicago lawyer and businessman who further distinguished himself in government service as secretary of war under presidents Garfield and Arthur and as U.S. ambassador to Great Britain under President Harrison. Robert Lincoln died in 1926 at the age of 82. Abraham Lincoln's bloodline ended with the death of Robert's great-grandson, Robert Todd Lincoln Beckwith, who was born in 1904 and died in 1985.

William was born on December 21, 1850, just 10 months after young Edward died. Known as Willie among members of his family, he carried the mixed blessing of serving as the "replacement" child for his deceased brother. Abraham recognized in Willie many of his own characteristics, including charisma, intelligence, and a questioning and thoughtful mind, so it's no surprise that Willie became the favorite child.

Thomas Lincoln, the fourth of Abraham and Mary's sons, was named for Abe's father and was born on April 4, 1853. His parents had supposedly hoped for a girl. Thomas was inquisitive, but a little spoiled. He was born with a cleft palate and an unusually large head and slim body that prompted his father to nickname him "Tadpole," which he shortened to "Tad." Along with his older brother Willie, Thomas was doted on by his father.

Beloved Willie, Gone

On February 5, 1862, the Lincolns threw an unusually large and extravagant party for more than 500 invited guests. The White House had just been refurbished, and Mary wanted to show the place off to Washington society.

That night, young Willie was so sick with a mysterious illness that Mary considered canceling the gala. But acting on the advice of a physician, she and Abe held the party as scheduled rather than disappoint the expected crowd. Still worried, they both sneaked away from the party several times that night to check on the feverish boy.

Later, Tad also came down with the same illness. Known only as "bilious fever" at the time, it's believed today that the two children contracted typhoid fever from drinking tainted water, the source of which was either the White House's own water system or an outdoor stream the children had found. Although Tad began to recover, Willie's symptoms worsened.

Under the Stovepipe

Lincoln's son Willie had a strong aptitude for mathematics, and liked reading, writing poetry, and memorizing railroad schedules. When he was eight years old, Willie accompanied his father on a business trip to Chicago and enjoyed a wonderful father-son adventure.

Abraham and Mary spent nearly every waking moment caring for their beloved, favored son. But on February 20, 1862, Willie lost the battle and died, just two months after his eleventh birthday.

The death completely devastated the Lincolns. When he announced the child's passing to White House staffers, Abraham reportedly burst into tears. Tad was still in bed and quite ill, but undoubtedly the loss of his brother frightened him and broke his heart, too. Mary was inconsolable, and never truly recovered from the loss.

Willie's White House state funeral was the first ever held for a child of a United States president. His body was placed in a small coffin and taken to the Green Room to lie in repose. Dressed in his favorite clothes, Willie's hands reportedly held a delicate bouquet of flowers at his chest. Dignitaries came by and offered condolences to the

Lincoln family, but Mary was so aggrieved that she could not bear to leave her bed. Mary's decision to remain away from visitors and even the funeral may sound odd, but it was actually customary at the time. Abraham tended to young Tad, and at the height of his grief, attempted to carry on his wartime responsibilities as president.

> ### Splitting Rails
>
> Throughout the ages, American schoolchildren were commonly taught that Confederate president Jefferson Davis was so moved that he sent a message of condolence to Lincoln upon the death of his son, William. The legend's accuracy has never been verified.
>
> Davis and Lincoln shared the sorrow of losing young children. Six children were born to Davis and his second wife, Varina Howell, and most died early in life. In fact, Davis lost a son two years after Willie Lincoln died. Joseph Evan Davis was just five years old when he was tragically killed in 1864 after accidentally falling from a banister outside the Confederate White House.

On February 24, 1862, Willie's funeral was held in the adjoining East Room of the White House, a place where the boy had liked to frolic and play. The somber ceremony was conducted out of the general public's sight. Willie's school classmates attended, and Abraham was surrounded by family, friends, and his closest allies that day. Senators, ambassadors, and Union generals prayed with Lincoln and dabbed at their eyes, struggling to maintain composure.

The young boy was buried temporarily in Georgetown. After Abraham Lincoln's assassination, Willie's body was exhumed and placed on Lincoln's funeral train. Today the two are interred near one another at Oak Ridge Cemetery in Springfield, Illinois.

Abraham Lincoln was a man who not only led a nation and a great military force, but was also a loving father who struggled to balance work and parental responsibilities long before such personal conflicts became commonplace. Lincoln showed others that he was as honest in his grief as in the other aspects of his life, a lesson for all to emulate.

Then We Mourned Abraham

After Abraham Lincoln was shot at Ford's Theatre on April 14, 1865, doctors in the audience that night made their way through the melee and rushed to his side. The assassin's bullet entered Lincoln's brain just behind his left ear. He had no pulse.

A young physician resuscitated Lincoln and restarted his heart. Then, accompanied by soldiers, a group of men carried a still breathing but unconscious Lincoln out of the theatre and across the street to a boarding house. He was placed diagonally on a bed too short for his long frame. Even as doctors monitored the fallen president, an investigation into the shooting began.

In addition to seeing to Lincoln's comfort, doctors used a long metal probe to explore his head wound while attempting—unsuccessfully—to dislodge the bullet from his brain. The invasive probing probably didn't help Lincoln's condition. Some people later claimed the doctors' actions might have hastened or even caused the president's death, but given the nature of Lincoln's wound, that's unlikely.

Lincoln lingered through the night, but never regained consciousness. He was pronounced dead at 7:22 the next morning. Robert Lincoln sobbed openly as he stood by his father's side.

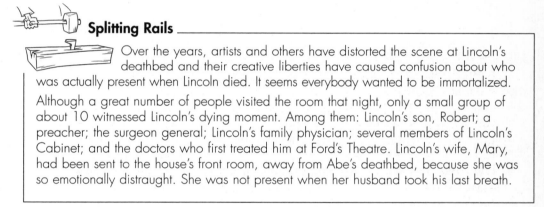

Splitting Rails

Over the years, artists and others have distorted the scene at Lincoln's deathbed and their creative liberties have caused confusion about who was actually present when Lincoln died. It seems everybody wanted to be immortalized.

Although a great number of people visited the room that night, only a small group of about 10 witnessed Lincoln's dying moment. Among them: Lincoln's son, Robert; a preacher; the surgeon general; Lincoln's family physician; several members of Lincoln's Cabinet; and the doctors who first treated him at Ford's Theatre. Lincoln's wife, Mary, had been sent to the house's front room, away from Abe's deathbed, because she was so emotionally distraught. She was not present when her husband took his last breath.

An Event to Remember

When Washingtonians awoke that morning, most didn't have a clue about the tragedy that had occurred overnight. However, it didn't take long for them—and the rest of the country—to learn that Lincoln had been murdered. Operators quickly tapped out the sad news and sent their messages along telegraph lines, which had been strung throughout the nation to aid in Civil War communications.

America's editors then carried the story on the front pages of the nation's newspapers. Unlike any other previous time in history, the entire populace mourned together because they received news reports of Lincoln's death quickly and virtually simultaneously.

Back in Washington, members of Lincoln's administration made funeral arrangements. Their goal was to create the most exquisite event ever seen in the history of the world. Some of their arrangements were a bit unusual, such as the Temple of Death, a gigantic *catafalque* that stood 11 feet high and was actually built inside the East Room of the White House.

Lincoln's coffin was placed atop the catafalque and his body was ready for viewing by Tuesday, April 19, the day before his Washington funeral. Flags were ordered lowered to half-staff throughout the country. Soldiers wore black armbands, signifying mourning. Schools and businesses closed. In cities and towns throughout the nation, churches held memorial services at the exact same time Lincoln's funeral took place.

Lincoln Lingo

A **catafalque** (pronounced *cat-a-folk*) is a decorated platform used to hold a coffin while in state or repose during a funeral and for public exhibition of the body. Decorative additions might include an overhead canopy, extensive corner draping, and other such things. Fabric used to drape the structure's framework is almost always black. Sometimes the catafalque is used to transport the body to its final resting place.

Lincoln Lingo

To **lie in state** is used exclusively to describe the formal honor of placing a person's remains in the Rotunda of the United States Capitol. When placed anywhere else for public or private viewing, the body is said to be lying *in repose*.

In the East Room of the White House, about 600 invited mourners gathered to hear the funeral service and pay their last respects. Too consumed by grief and trauma to attend, Mary Todd Lincoln remained upstairs in the family quarters.

When the White House service ended early that afternoon, a military escort transferred Lincoln's casket to a horse-drawn funeral hearse that waited outside. Thousands of mourners stood along the route of the long procession, which carried Lincoln's body down Pennsylvania Avenue to the Capitol Building. There, the casket was carried up the steps of the East Portico and placed atop a second catafalque inside the Rotunda, where Lincoln's body was to *lie in state*.

After a second service, crowds lined up to view Lincoln's body as the casket's lid was kept open. Lincoln had delivered his second inaugural address near the very same spot just six weeks earlier.

Lincoln's body remained in the Rotunda until Friday, April 21, when his coffin was ceremoniously moved and taken to the train station in Washington and placed on a nine-car funeral train. Alongside Lincoln's body was the coffin carrying the exhumed remains of his son William. About 300 dignitaries, Robert Lincoln among them, were onboard when the train left Washington to take Lincoln home to Springfield, Illinois.

The Long Journey Home

By today's standards, the route to Springfield was anything but direct. From Washington, it headed north to Baltimore, then northwest to Harrisburg, Pennsylvania. From there, the train headed east to Philadelphia, then north again to New York City and Albany. Then it proceeded east, toward Rome and Buffalo, and south to Cleveland and Columbus. Eventually, the train headed west to Indianapolis. It then turned north to Michigan City and took a quick jog west to Chicago, before heading back south to Springfield.

Lincoln's funeral train made 12 extended stops during its journey to allow for public viewing and local funeral services. Each city had hastily planned and hosted complex memorial events that were uniquely their own.

Under the Stovepipe

Abraham Lincoln's son Robert has the dubious distinction of being "invited" to the assassinations of three U.S. presidents. He was invited to accompany his parents to the theatre the night Abraham Lincoln was shot but went to bed instead. In 1881, Robert was present when President Garfield was shot. The young man had accepted Garfield's invitation to meet him at Union Station. And Robert also accepted an invitation to meet with President McKinley in Buffalo when he was shot, too.

After McKinley's assassination in 1901, Robert decided he'd had enough. He never accepted another invitation to meet with any U.S. president again.

Millions of people turned out to say a last goodbye to Lincoln, and the procession instigated frenzied reaction among mourners wherever the train passed, paused, or stopped. In Philadelphia, for instance, the train's arrival triggered riots among those fighting to catch a glimpse of Lincoln's flag-draped casket. Later, about 300,000 people viewed the body at Independence Hall after an elaborately decorated, canopied hearse moved his remains there from the Philadelphia station.

In New York City, hoards of people waited for hours at City Hall, where Lincoln's body was taken for public viewing. On the day the train departed, about 100,000 people marched in an hours-long funeral procession from City Hall to the New York train depot.

In Cleveland, viewing was conducted outdoors and more than 10,000 citizens each hour passed by in a steady line in front of Lincoln's open casket. In Indianapolis, rain prevented the procession that had been planned. The day after the train's departure, the city held its funeral and procession, in-absentia, which allowed the city's citizens to properly mourn their fallen leader.

The train finally reached its final destination on May 3, weeks after the journey from Washington had begun. A public viewing was held at Springfield's State House, and then a final funeral procession transported Lincoln's remains to the Oak Ridge Cemetery on May 4, 1865. Muffled drums played in the distance and *rifle volleys* rang out as thousands of mourners watched.

Following behind the funeral hearse was a riderless horse who was led by the Reverend Henry Brown, a black minister. The steed was Lincoln's favorite, a horse he called Old Bob.

After a final service and prayers at the cemetery, the public was ushered out. A lone bugler played "*Taps*." Then, at last, the gates to Lincoln's tomb were closed and locked.

Lincoln Lingo

Full military honors at the interment (or burial) of a president of the United States typically include the firing of three **rifle volleys** over the fallen leader's grave. This longstanding tradition arose from the practice of halting battlefield fighting to allow for the removal of dead soldiers on both sides of a conflict. After the field had been cleared, three volleys were fired to signal that the battle could be resumed. In modern times, seven service members usually fire the three volleys. But don't confuse this high honor with the 21-gun salute. That's something completely different.

"**Taps**" is the military call signaling soldiers to "extinguish lights." First penned in 1862 by Brigadier General Daniel Butterfield of the Army of the Potomac, the melodious bugle call was adopted in 1863. Lincoln's funeral marked the first time "Taps" was played at a presidential funeral.

How America Grieves

One of the legacies from that terrible time in 1865 is the acknowledgement that Americans share a common need to publicly mourn the loss of great leaders. When a president dies, we grieve together, as a nation united, regardless of our political views. From Lincoln's meticulously planned funeral, we also gained strong traditions for exactly how our leaders are to be mourned. The description of Lincoln's Washington, D.C., funeral may remind you of the state funerals held for President John F. Kennedy in 1963 and President Ronald Reagan in 2004. Both Kennedy's and Reagan's ceremonies were modeled after Lincoln's funeral.

All U.S. presidents—whether in office at the time of their death or not—are entitled to a state funeral, an occasion of general mourning that's steeped in tradition and strict protocol. The U.S. secretary of state, as a representative of the sitting president, is responsible for planning state funerals.

Funeral duties are performed by the secretary of state's designates. These representatives include the secretary of the army and the commanding general of the Military District of Washington, whose mission—among other homeland security and defense duties—is to provide presidential escort and to carry out all ceremonial arrangements.

Some of the customs observed in today's state funerals originated in the military, while others evolved from ancient practices dating back to the Roman Empire. But regardless of origin, the funerals of our presidents are based on traditions that were more firmly established with Lincoln's death.

The families of our presidents ultimately decide if a state funeral will be held and, if so, what takes place. Following John F. Kennedy's assassination, for instance, his widow specifically asked that her husband be given a state funeral like the one held in Washington for Abraham Lincoln.

Under the Stovepipe

Although she may have been consulted, Mary Todd Lincoln probably wasn't too involved in making plans for her husband's Washington funeral. Mary was so emotionally distraught by the loss—and so traumatized by the violent assassination itself—that she was unable to attend the ceremonies.

As a woman who valued history and tradition, Kennedy's widow likely recognized the parallels between John F. Kennedy's fight for civil rights and Abraham Lincoln's battle to end slavery, among other similarities. So it seems natural that she chose a funeral event that would closely mirror the traditions established by Lincoln's death. Other presidents who have died since Lincoln's assassination were given state funerals that were based on the 1865 funeral, but they did not compare to the pomp and circumstance afforded Lincoln. Nobody had ever actually tried to duplicate Lincoln's funeral before.

Jacqueline Kennedy's seemingly simple request immediately sent historians and protocol experts scrambling to presidential archives to search through old records in an attempt to gather every last detail about Lincoln's funeral. Like its 1865 predecessor, the result was an occasion that every American living at the time would remember forever.

Like Lincoln's funeral events, Kennedy's body first lay in repose in the East Room of the White House. Following a private service, his body was later moved with great ceremony to the Capitol Rotunda, to lie in state as members of the public paid their last respects. An Armed Forces honor guard kept watch throughout the day and night.

The elaborate catafalque constructed for Lincoln's funeral was replaced by a tastefully simple and elegant stand. Unlike Lincoln's, Kennedy's body was not exposed for viewing. However, both presidents' caskets were draped in the stars and stripes.

Kennedy's casket was transported down Pennsylvania Avenue by a horse-drawn *caisson*, which was followed by a caparisoned (or riderless) horse, named Black Jack. Led by a lone soldier, the horse wore an empty saddle with riding boots reversed in the stirrups, symbolizing the commander's final ride and his last, parting glimpse at his troops behind him.

Lincoln Lingo

Originating in the 1800s, the **caisson** is a flat-decked, wheeled cart that was first used to transport military artillery and was often pressed into service to carry dead soldiers from the battlefield. As it was in Lincoln's day, the use of a caisson and riderless horse are traditional elements of a funeral procession for a military leader. U.S. presidents are accorded this honor in recognition of their former role as commander in chief.

The caisson that was used in President Reagan's funeral procession was built in 1918, and was attended by the Caisson Platoon of the 3rd U.S. Infantry Regiment, known as The Old Guard. The roots of this military regiment date back to 1784.

In 1865, the arrival of Lincoln's funeral train halted all business and other activity to allow citizens to pay their respects and attend local services. People in other parts of the country went on with their business. But in 1963, no funeral train was necessary to enable individuals a time and place to share their grief.

Television and radio had connected people from coast to coast, and for the first time, a presidential funeral was broadcast live. For several hours, the entire nation stopped. Virtually every person in America listened to live radio reports or sat glued to their television screens to witness—as it happened—the procession, funeral, and graveside ceremony of John F. Kennedy.

Just as in Lincoln's era, a great leader was eulogized and his contributions to America were honored and remembered. Muffled drums played a droning, sorrowful cadence as millions of mourners across the country wept.

After a brief ceremony and prayers at Arlington National Cemetery, rifle volleys rang out. "Taps" was played. And then the live reports ended as the individuals present were ushered out.

Thanks to Lincoln's legacy, Americans were given the chance to publicly mourn Kennedy together. And as Lincoln's assassination did in 1865, Kennedy's murder and the period of national mourning that followed his death pulled a divided nation together.

Other notable state funerals that followed Lincoln traditions include presidents Herbert Hoover, Harry Truman, Dwight D. Eisenhower, Lyndon Johnson, and Richard Nixon. President John F. Kennedy's brother, senator and presidential candidate Robert F. Kennedy, was also given a state funeral after being assassinated in 1968.

The Least You Need to Know

- ◆ Willie Lincoln was the first child to be given a funeral at the White House.

- ◆ When Abraham Lincoln died, members of his administration planned an elaborate funeral that set the bar for subsequent state funerals.

- ◆ U.S. state funerals today commonly consist of elements drawn from Lincoln's funeral, which include military customs.

- ◆ President John F. Kennedy's funeral was based on Lincoln's funeral as requested by his widow, Jacqueline.

Chapter 6

The Stuff of Myth and Legend

In This Chapter

- ◆ How clergymen helped shape today's view of Lincoln
- ◆ Why so many Lincoln artifacts and relics exist today
- ◆ What happened to Mary Todd Lincoln after her husband's assassination
- ◆ How and why early biographers rewrote Lincoln history
- ◆ Why Lincoln mythology is so much a part of American culture

The desire to immortalize Abraham Lincoln began the moment he died. As is the case with many fallen heroes, Lincoln's biography was almost immediately sanitized and his "pure" life held up for others to idolize. And so, great Lincoln myths and legends were born.

But what we gained culturally from this saint-making activity are innumerable Lincoln "shrines," such as his boyhood home, his home in Springfield, Ford's Theatre, and a vast collection of memorabilia—from locks of hair and photographs to apparel and writings.

The Making of Saint Abe

For Christians, one of the most sacred religious holidays is Good Friday, an occasion that commemorates the crucifixion of Jesus Christ. In 1865, Good Friday fell on April 14—the day Lincoln was shot. He died less than 24 hours later, on Saturday.

On Easter Sunday, when Christians filled churches throughout the United States to celebrate the risen Christ, the sermons they heard eulogized their assassinated president. How bereaved clergymen described Lincoln that day helped reframe perceptions about Lincoln, the man.

In pulpits throughout the country, preachers compared Lincoln to the risen Messiah, as a humble yet remarkable man who rose from poverty to lead the greatest nation on Earth. Like Jesus, they said, Abraham was the only son of a poor, illiterate carpenter and his saintly wife. Why, Lincoln was even born in a ramshackle structure similar to the Bethlehem stable! What's more, he spent his first night in this world on a bed of straw and corncobs. Talk about public relations spin doctoring!

Under the Stovepipe

Mary Todd Lincoln remained secluded in her White House room for nearly five weeks after her husband's assassination. In late May of 1865, she and her sons returned to Illinois. While Robert continued his legal studies, she and Tad escaped to Europe for a time, mostly to avoid the bad press that followed her every move. But when they came back to the United States in 1871, Tad contracted an illness believed to be tuberculosis. He died at the age of 18. After that, some say Mary's emotional health dramatically declined.

In 1875, Robert Lincoln, then a prominent lawyer, had his mother declared legally insane and committed to a hospital. Mary was released three months later, after vigorously battling her son in court. She died at the age of 63, on July 16, 1882, at her sister's home in Springfield.

From these Christlike beginnings, the clergymen said, the savior Abraham Lincoln was sent into the world by God Himself to free the slaves and save the Union. Ex-slaves referred to him as "Father Abraham," a name Union soldiers gave him while he was alive.

Further drawing on Jesus' story, the preachers explained that the pure, unstained human being known as Abraham Lincoln was struck down on Good Friday, the very same day that Christ had been killed. This was all tangible evidence, they implied, that Lincoln had died to atone for the sins of the American people.

However, Christians were not alone. Lincoln's death also came during Passover. Jewish rabbis lauded Lincoln, calling him a second Moses.

From that day forward, Lincoln—an extraordinary man in his own right, a true hero whose life needed no embellishment—was no longer a common mortal. Almost instantaneously, he had become the first American martyred saint.

 Splitting Rails _____

When writers sanitized Lincoln facts, that effort was often overt but not always as noticeable as you might think. For example, when *Harper's Magazine* reported on Lincoln's death in April 1865, reporters wrote that Lincoln was taken to a "private residence" across the street from Ford's Theatre. However, in fact, Petersen's was a privately owned *boarding house*.

In the nineteenth century, boarding houses were common but sometimes considered unseemly. To report that President Lincoln had been delivered to—and later died—in what some might arguably consider a distasteful, undignified place would have been unthinkable at the time, given Lincoln's newly acquired saintly status.

Had he actually been able to gaze down from Heaven's gate, Lincoln probably would have been surprised to see such unrestrained adoration. In their grief, folks obviously got a bit carried away.

Relic Frenzy

In life, Lincoln never received this level of praise, as he was adored and hated. You might recall that the media, in particular, had not been particularly kind to him. But Abraham's death and the public's reaction to the loss changed all that.

Anything connected with Lincoln suddenly became sacred—the items he'd touched, the places he'd lived or visited, and, of course, the words he spoke. What's more, everybody wanted to be connected to Lincoln and his legacy.

The entire state of Illinois quickly became known as the "Land of Lincoln." Tens of thousands of visitors were immediately drawn to Lincoln's hometown of Springfield. There, folks reverently gazed upon his former home, touched the walls of buildings he'd frequented, and followed the same streets and pathways that Lincoln once walked.

Kentucky and Indiana each proudly claimed him as a native son, and both states set about preserving the homes in which Lincoln had lived as a child. Sites where Lincoln spoke soon became hallowed ground, too.

The Petersen Boarding House to which Lincoln was taken after being shot and where he died at 7:22 A.M. on April 15, 1865, became known as "The House Where Lincoln Died." Visitors flocked to the site. However, in later years they weren't as interested in the building across the street from the Petersen House. Ford's Theatre was considered a place where evil still lurked.

Places Lincoln never actually saw while he lived also joined the frenzy. Small communities along the path of Lincoln's funeral train claimed connections to Abraham by virtue of his coffin passing through their area.

Under the Stovepipe

While still clinging to her mourning bed, Mary Todd Lincoln attempted to contact and communicate with her dead husband with the help of spiritualists. Trance mediums and other psychics conducted bedside séances—in the White House. There are no verifiable reports that she was successful. She had done the same following Willie's death. But so did many middle-class Americans. Spiritualism was a very popular fad of the era.

Hundreds of statues and monuments immortalizing Lincoln, sometimes including members of his family, were erected throughout America. Today, thousands of American streets are named for Lincoln, as are hundreds of schools and dozens of cities and towns.

Under the Stovepipe

Among the largest monuments that include Lincoln's image is Mount Rushmore in South Dakota. Work on the project began in 1927, and was intended as a way to pay homage to America's heroes while drawing visitors to the Black Hills region. Along with three other U.S. presidents, a colossal face of Lincoln—roughly the equivalent of a six-story building—was carved into solid granite on the face of the tallest mountain in the vicinity. The monument cost nearly $1 million to create and 14 years to finish.

Mount Rushmore sculptor Gutzon Borglum died in 1941, before completing the project. His son, Lincoln Borglum, finished the carvings seven months later—just as funding ran out.

Most of the photographic images taken of Abraham Lincoln throughout his life were kept and preserved. As a result, Lincoln's face is one of the most recognized images of all time. But Americans don't need to visit a gallery to see a portrait of Lincoln. Chances are you're carrying a picture of Lincoln in your pocket, purse, or wallet at this very moment. His face is on our penny and five-dollar bill.

A Lock of Hair, a Piece of Cloth

Up until now, we've only talked about the preservation of Lincoln places and the establishment of monuments. But some of the most treasured Lincoln artifacts are relics, particularly those from his assassination.

Reminiscent of what occurs when a candidate for religious sainthood dies, the gathering of Lincoln relics began at the very moment of his death.

According to various Lincoln relic inventories, it appears that the U.S. surgeon general who attended to Lincoln at death took a few strands of Abraham's hair and placed them in a gold locket. He wasn't the only one. Several collectors and museums possess locks of hair believed to be Lincoln's. At least one of these relics bears a note testifying that the hair was snipped near Lincoln's bullet wound.

Lincoln Lingo

Generally, a **relic** is a memento that is kept because of its association with the past. The term is more commonly used to describe an object of religious veneration, including a saint's personal items or a piece of the saint's body.

Thousands of items belonging to or associated with Lincoln have been kept and preserved for future generations. The objects—some of them decidedly creepy—are found in hundreds of public and private collections throughout the world. There are, in fact, so many relics that it's unlikely a single museum could hold them all.

Upon the death of its owner, the walnut bed and mattress on which Lincoln died was sold at auction to a collector. The same collector also acquired the bed's sheet, one sleeve of a man's undershirt reported to be Lincoln's, and a piece of wood molding said to have been taken from Ford's Theatre. The Chicago Historical Society now owns these items. The bloodied pillow upon which Lincoln's head rested while dying is at Ford's Theatre.

The bullet that was removed from Lincoln's brain as well as bone fragments from the president's skull are at the National Museum of Health and Medicine, on the grounds of the Walter Reed Army Medical Center. The derringer used by John Wilkes Booth is part of the collection on display at Ford's Theatre National Historic Site. Bone fragments from Booth's spine, removed during his autopsy on the ironclad ship *Montauk* docked at the U.S. Naval Yard, are at the Navy Museum in Washington, D.C.

Under the Stovepipe

Because of the care taken to preserve Lincoln artifacts, it's almost unthinkable that a group of people once wanted to destroy Ford's Theatre. Right after Lincoln's assassination, residents of Washington, D.C., threatened to burn the place to the ground because of the evil that had taken place there. Secretary of War Edwin Stanton saved the theatre by ordering that soldiers surround the brick building and guard it 24 hours a day.

The angry mob eventually dispersed. But it wasn't until 1968 that Ford's Theatre reopened—as a living memorial to Abraham Lincoln.

Today, Ford's Theatre National Historic Site is owned by the U.S. Park Service and includes Ford's Theatre, the Petersen House (called "The House Where Lincoln Died"), and the Ford's Theatre Museum. In addition to other events, three to five theatrical productions are presented at Ford's Theatre each year.

Bloodied Flags, Furniture, and Something More

The massive, black-shrouded catafalque that supported Lincoln's coffin is stored at the U.S. Capitol, two floors beneath the Rotunda in a special chamber. Mary Todd Lincoln's blood-stained cape as well as many other assassination relics are owned by the Chicago Historical Society.

One of two Treasury Guard flags that adorned Lincoln's theatre box, and which he clutched upon being shot, is at the Connecticut Historical Society in Hartford; the other remains at Ford's Theatre. Another U.S. flag, bloodied when used to cushion Lincoln's head before his transport from Ford's Theatre to the Petersen Boarding House, is in The Columns, a museum of the Pike County Historical Society located at Milford, Pennsylvania.

The last painted portrait for which Lincoln sat is at The Lincoln Museum in Fort Wayne, Indiana. The top hat Lincoln wore to the theatre on the night of his assassination is a treasure in the National Museum of American History, a part of the Smithsonian Institution. The Henry Ford Museum in Dearborn, Michigan, owns the bloodstained rocking chair in which Lincoln sat when he was shot. (Replicas of the chair are on display elsewhere.)

What's in Your Pocket?

Some of this relic business may seem to serve more macabre than historic interests. But consider what you might learn about Lincoln right now if I told you about the contents of his pockets on April 14, 1865. Well, you can see these items at the Library of Congress in Washington, D.C., because someone thought to keep them.

When Abraham Lincoln was shot at Ford's Theatre, he was carrying two pairs of reading spectacles, a lens polisher, a pocketknife, a watch fob, and a linen handkerchief. Lincoln also carried a brown leather wallet that contained a Confederate five-dollar note (imagine that!), and nine newspaper clippings, including several favorable to Lincoln and his policies.

These personal effects were given to Robert Lincoln when his father died. They remained in the Lincoln family until 1937, when Abraham's granddaughter, Mary Lincoln Isham, donated them to the Library.

Those few intimate items from Abraham's pockets reveal an incredible amount of information about Abraham Lincoln the man. Sharing that insight with future generations is one of the reasons folks kept all that stuff. For instance, take a moment now to ponder all the reasons why Lincoln might have carried that Confederate note in his wallet. (He probably collected the note a few weeks earlier when he visited conquered Richmond.)

Under the Stovepipe

Although he'd studied the Bible from an early age, Lincoln never formally joined a church or affiliated himself with an organized religion. He sought spiritual comfort upon the death of his son, Edward, from a Presbyterian minister in Springfield, and attended that pastor's church for a short while.

Rewriting History

Our sixteenth president's life may be the most documented in all of history. Thousands of books and articles have been published about Lincoln. And they're not all strictly birth-to-death biographies. Some of these volumes explore a single event in Lincoln's life or contain page upon page of commentary and analysis about just one of the many speeches he delivered during his lifetime.

However, that doesn't mean that all we think we know about Lincoln is true. Even today, historians continue to sift through new and old artifacts to try to make sense of Lincoln and to separate fact from fiction. The confusion that has endured for nearly two centuries began on that Easter Sunday in 1865.

Taking their cue from the pulpit sermons that took place the day after Lincoln's death, early biographers were inspired to write cleansed versions of their subject's life. One of the first posthumous Lincoln biographies was published about a year after his death, and was written by Josiah G. Holland, a New York author who'd reportedly never met Lincoln. That book, like many others that came after it, cast Lincoln as something of an untouchable deity who always possessed unquestioned purity of thought and deed.

Under the Stovepipe

Lincoln is often referred to as the "Great Emancipator," a label believed to be first coined by biographer Isaac N. Arnold. Published in 1866, Arnold's book was the second Lincoln biography released that year and contained the author's remembrances based on first-hand accounts.

However, the eventual publication of personal journals and notes written by those who knew Lincoln well helped historians gain a more balanced view of Abraham. Lincoln's law partner, William H. Herndon, wrote and published his own version of Lincoln's life called *Herndon's Lincoln* in 1888. His goal was to set the record straight.

Although it contains some legend-style material, too, Herndon's book is considered by many experts to be one of the most vivid personal accounts of the pre-presidential Abraham Lincoln. It's also the most candid of the early biographies.

Under the Stovepipe

So what happened to John Wilkes Booth? Well, after he fled from Ford's Theatre on April 14, Booth rode to Maryland and met up with a co-conspirator, David Herold. They arrived the next morning at the home of Dr. Samuel Mudd. The doctor hadn't heard about the assassination yet. He set Booth's broken leg and then Booth and Herold left, spending the next several days hiding from federal troops.

The cavalry finally cornered the pair in a tobacco barn in Port Royal, Virginia, on April 26. The two men had crossed the Potomac River from Maryland a few days earlier, expecting (but not receiving) a hero's welcome. Herold gave himself up. But Booth refused to come out—and one of the soldiers shot and killed him.

Twelve weeks after Lincoln's assassination, David Herold, Mary Surratt, Lewis Paine, and George Atzerodt were hanged for their involvement. Some historians characterize the conditions of their incarceration, trial, and hangings as unjust.

Other close Lincoln associates also wrote historically important biographical works. In 1890, his onetime White House aides John Nicolay and John Hay wrote *Abraham Lincoln: A History*, a 10-volume biography that is considered the most comprehensive of all. The volumes included a massive amount of detail. Given the work's size, it's hard to imagine that Nicolay and Hay left out a single fact. However, unlike Herndon, they did weed out material that might have been construed as being in conflict with the Lincoln legend. (Still, it's a great read—if you can find the set and you have lots of time.)

Sandburg's Take on Lincoln

Another writer who helped accelerate Lincoln's rise to iconic status was none other than renowned American poet Carl Sandburg. Virtually unknown until a group of his poems was published in 1914 in *Poetry* magazine, Sandburg later achieved international acclaim for his children's fairy tales as well as his volumes of poems. Based on the success of a book Sandburg wrote in 1922 for young readers, his publisher suggested that he write a biography about Abraham Lincoln for children.

But after three years of research, Sandburg decided to write a book about Lincoln for adults. His two-volume biography, *Abraham Lincoln: The Prairie Years*, was published in 1926. In Sandburg's skillful hands, Lincoln's story was powerfully conveyed in a lyrically eloquent and mostly factual way. It also brought Sandburg his first taste of financial success.

Over the next several years, he wrote four additional volumes, collectively published as *Abraham Lincoln: The War Years*. That second set earned him a Pulitzer Prize in 1940.

Problems Faced by Biographers

To be fair to Lincoln's early biographers, it's important to know that more than a few obstacles stood in the way of their getting at the truth. One of the problems they faced, for example, was that Robert Lincoln reportedly censored a lot of biographical material. That made many important facts and details inaccessible to writers.

Plus, as guardian of his father's papers, Robert alone possessed the treasure trove of Lincoln's personal journals, correspondence, and other writings. While he lived, he chose not to share them publicly and they were closed to the public until after World War II. Today's historians now have access to these documents, many of which are available online.

So in the absence of what we'd call cold facts, anecdotal information gathered from a variety of sources had to suffice. Colored by grief and the passage of time, many of these stories got bigger and better each time they were told. Pretty soon, some folks started to believe that Abraham Lincoln actually was a real giant, for instance. (In fact, schoolchildren were—and perhaps still are—taught songs that perpetuate that very idea.)

Splitting Rails

Between Lincoln's assassination in 1865 and John F. Kennedy's in 1963, two other presidents were murdered while in office: James Garfield in 1881 and William McKinley in 1901.

(By the way, other U.S. presidents who died while in office—but from natural causes—include William Henry Harrison, Zachary Taylor, Warren Harding, and Franklin D. Roosevelt.)

Another difficulty for biographers was that the Lincoln legend became part of American culture. History textbooks unwittingly conveyed mythical information alongside the factual. When a writer tried to correct the errors by publishing details not previously known, the article or book immediately became controversial. Imagine trying to report on Lincoln in a balanced, reasoned way when all your readers viewed him as godlike. Why, you'd be accused of blasphemy, labeled a liar—or worse, called a traitor!

Lincoln's larger-than-life persona hasn't diminished much since that Easter Sunday in 1865. Interest in him has also remained high. New books about Lincoln are published every year. Millions of people each year visit historic sites dedicated to Lincoln's memory—places such as the Lincoln Memorial in Washington, D.C., for instance. And schoolchildren continue to memorize his words.

In fact, he's such a huge part of our culture that debates about Lincoln take place on Internet blogs. Who would have imagined back in 1865 that so many people would still be talking about Lincoln today, more than a hundred years after his death?

Rest in Peace?

Had Lincoln been just an ordinary man, his story would have ended when they closed the gates at Oak Ridge Cemetery on May 3, 1865. But even in death, this man wasn't allowed to rest.

The vault into which Lincoln's body was placed was merely a temporary way station. A few days after Lincoln's death, a group of Springfield citizens formed the National Lincoln Monument Association and raised funds for a magnificent tomb to be located nearby. In 1869, construction of the $171,000 tomb began.

In 1871, Lincoln's body and the remains of his three sons were moved to the unfinished tomb and placed in crypts. The memorial was dedicated in 1874, and Lincoln's remains were interred in a marble sarcophagus in the center burial room.

Just two years later, in 1876, members of one of the largest counterfeiting rings in the nation hatched a plot to steal Lincoln's body and hold it for ransom. Their Chicago-based engraver had been imprisoned and the gang's supply of counterfeit money was nearly gone. The plan was to trade Lincoln's body for $200,000 in gold and the engraver's freedom.

On Election Day in 1876, the graverobbing ringleader, "Big Jim" Kinealy, led the gang to Oak Ridge Cemetery, where the men broke into Lincoln's tomb and opened the sarcophagus that held his coffin. The wooden casket had already been partially removed from the sarcophagus when authorities arrived.

> **Under the Stovepipe**
>
> To thwart grave-robbing attempts, Lincoln's coffin was actually moved 17 times before it was permanently sealed in its present location. What's more, the coffin was opened five times after the remains were first interred in May 1865—December 21, 1865; September 19, 1871; October 9, 1874; April 14, 1887; and September 26, 1901. (Folks wanted to make sure Lincoln's body was still inside.)

The gang's plan was foiled only because they had unwittingly allowed a Secret Service agent to infiltrate the ring and join in the crime. As the team worked to remove the coffin, the undercover agent was asked to bring the wagon to the tomb, to ready it for Lincoln's body and the getaway. Instead, the agent alerted detectives hiding nearby.

> **Under the Stovepipe**
>
> Among many other responsibilities, Secret Service agents protect U.S. presidents as well as presidential candidates and other officials. But those duties weren't in the job description right away.
>
> The United States Secret Service was formed in July 1865 as part of the Treasury Department, to suppress the manufacture and distribution of counterfeit currency. Allan Pinkerton, the very man who kept Lincoln safe on his way to his first inaugural, headed the service. It wasn't until 1902, the year after President McKinley was assassinated, that Secret Service agents assumed full-time responsibility for protecting the president of the United States.
>
> From 1862 to 1865, the War Department assigned an infantry company to guard the White House and Soldiers' Home as well as a cavalry unit to accompany President Lincoln when he rode around town. Washington police detectives were added to the protection force in the fall of 1864, but those officers didn't stay with Lincoln at all times. Consistent with that policy, the detective who accompanied Lincoln from the White House to Ford's Theatre then left.

The graverobbers were tried and convicted in 1877, and were sentenced to a year in prison. But the attempt to steal Lincoln's body shook everybody. Members of the National Lincoln Monument Association moved Lincoln's remains to another part of the memorial.

When Mary Todd Lincoln died in 1882, her body was placed beside her husband, as she had requested. However, the remains of Lincoln and his family continued to be relocated, to stave off the possibility of theft.

After the monument was rebuilt and restored in 1901, Robert Lincoln asked that Lincoln's body be exhumed and moved one last time. After a group of people verified that the body inside the casket was indeed Abraham Lincoln, the coffin's lid was welded back into place.

Then, the casket was lowered into a steel cage located 10 feet beneath the original burial room. To ensure that no one could ever disturb Lincoln again, workers then permanently encased the casket and steel cage in 4,000 pounds of cement.

The extreme measures taken to protect his father's remains must have given Robert Lincoln tremendous peace of mind.

The Least You Need to Know

- Easter Sunday sermons the day after Lincoln's death led to his immediate saintly status.
- After Lincoln's assassination, all that he had touched in life suddenly became sacred.
- After his death, Lincoln's biography was sometimes embellished and that helped perpetuate myths and legends about him.
- Lincoln relics are found in public and private collections throughout the world.
- Lincoln's final interment didn't take place until 1901—more than 35 years after his death.

Chapter 7

The Lincoln Memorial

In This Chapter

- ◆ Learning the Lincoln Memorial's history, facts, and figures
- ◆ Discovering why the site selected for the Lincoln Memorial caused controversy
- ◆ Knowing how and why the memorial's dedication ceremony was racially segregated
- ◆ Learning about the historic moments that have taken place at the memorial
- ◆ Disagreeing over the memorial today

Although Lincoln's body is entombed in Springfield, Illinois, his indomitable spirit lives on—and still guides us—in the majestic memorial on the National Mall in Washington, D.C.

When it was dedicated in 1922, the Lincoln Memorial was touted as a mighty symbol of unity between the North and South, a national monument to America's Civil War. Its construction took place in the wake of World War I, so the memorial's architects created a victorious symbol of American democracy and a tribute to Abraham Lincoln's role as its savior.

But from the very beginning, the people of the United States had other ideas for this special place. The symbolism of the Lincoln Memorial, unlike any other memorial, has continued to evolve since its dedication. Future generations restored the dual themes of unity and social justice, which the memorial's designers had originally intended to convey.

Unlike any other site in the nation's capitol, the Lincoln Memorial is a temple of hope and promise, hallowed ground upon which history is not merely contemplated but made.

The People's Monument

On busy weekday mornings, thousands of harried, twenty-first-century workers travel to offices in Washington, D.C., by way of the Memorial Bridge, which spans the Potomac River to link northern Virginia with the capital city. Historic sites abound, but their familiarity often blinds commuters to their presence as they make their way to "the District."

To the rear are Confederate General Robert E. Lee's former home and Arlington National Cemetery in Virginia, where dozens of solemn military funerals take place each day. Across the river, the Washington Monument peeks out above the tree line. Toward the right are the Thomas Jefferson Memorial and the Tidal Basin encircled by blossoming trees. But dead ahead, at the end of Memorial Bridge and usually surrounded on all sides by tourists, stands an edifice that demands attention: the Lincoln Memorial.

Under the Stovepipe

The Lincoln Memorial, including construction of its adjacent reflecting pool, cost a total of $2,957,000 to build. Today, the memorial's grounds span 6.3 acres of prime Washington, D.C., land.

The memorial's exterior height is 99 feet above grade; measuring from the top of its foundation, it stands 80 feet. The reflecting pool outside was built to hold nearly seven million gallons of water. The pool's deepest point, 30 inches, is at its center.

Built in a style reminiscent of an ancient Greek temple, the memorial's design features 36 exterior columns, symbolizing the number of states in the Union at the time of Lincoln's death. Each column is 44 feet high, and is seven feet, five inches in diameter. The exterior colonnade measures 188 feet high by 118 feet wide.

What makes the Lincoln Memorial so different from all other monuments in the nation's capital? Visitors stand inside the Jefferson Memorial to marvel at its beautifully crafted dome and consider Jefferson's revolutionary words, which are carved into the shadowy granite walls. At the Vietnam Veterans Memorial, visitors weep as they realize the magnitude of our country's loss. The glorious World War II Memorial engenders pride—and gratitude to a generation of Americans who saved the entire world. And the Washington Monument? To be blunt, there's not much to see up close. Locals fly kites while tourists climb stairs to gain a better view of the area.

But with all due respect for differing viewpoints, we believe the Lincoln Memorial is in a category all its own.

The Lincoln Memorial Experience

The sight of the Lincoln Memorial at the end of that bridge is simply breathtaking at any time. But at night, just viewing the orange, sunlike glow that emanates from the structure's core where Lincoln's statue sits warms even the coldest soul.

Visiting the Lincoln Memorial is almost indescribable. Merely ascending the marble staircase of this hallowed place is emotionally moving, knowing that so many prominent Americans once walked the same path and made history on this very location. One of its most distinguishing hallmarks is that the Lincoln Memorial has become a place where citizens feel free to publicly express opinions. The Lincoln Memorial is the people's monument.

Under the Stovepipe

The Lincoln Memorial is maintained by the United States National Park Service, which staffs the site from 8 A.M. until midnight each day. The memorial is open to visitors 24 hours a day, 365 days a year.

Stepping inside the memorial is a profoundly spiritual experience, akin to entering a sanctuary where an endless hymn of freedom plays. Inscribed on the walls of its three interior chambers are words that still resonate today—the Gettysburg Address, Lincoln's second inaugural address, and excerpts from other speeches and writings on equality, freedom, emancipation, and more. Painted murals depicting Lincoln's principles, values, and deeds adorn spaces above his speeches, and these illustrations further heighten the memorial's impact.

Of course, in the central chamber is the memorial's most prominent interior feature: a massive, seated statue of Lincoln—his face set in a determined expression, his strong hands resting on the arms of a simple concrete throne. Inscribed on the wall directly behind the Lincoln statue are these words:

IN THIS TEMPLE
AS IN THE HEARTS OF THE PEOPLE
FOR WHOM HE SAVED THE UNION
THE MEMORY OF ABRAHAM LINCOLN
IS ENSHRINED FOREVER

Under the Stovepipe

The statue of Abraham Lincoln is 19 feet high by 19 feet wide, and was inspired by the statue of Zeus crafted by ancient Greek sculptor Phidias for the Temple of Zeus in Olympia. The bundled rods carved into Lincoln's armrests are classic Roman symbols of authority, representing justice and republican government.

Visitors to the memorial can often be seen wiping tears from their eyes, for many recognize that this place is far more than a repository for historical rhetoric. Within the walls of the Lincoln Memorial, it feels as though the past, present, and future of the American people converge in one sacred spot. Perhaps that's why millions of people are drawn to the memorial every year.

Back in 1922, who would ever have imagined that a simple structure would today arouse such reverence, inspire so many of us, or cause such controversy?

Building a Unique Symbol of Democracy

After Lincoln's death in 1865, folks in Washington, D.C., immediately talked of building a suitable memorial. In 1867, in fact, Congress established the Lincoln Monument Association to do just that. However, years of disagreement followed. No one could decide on the type of monument, where it should be located, or how it could be funded.

Real progress wasn't made until 1911, when members of Congress finally succeeded in moving the project again. That year, a federal bill was passed to establish the Lincoln Memorial Commission and provide $2 million in funding for a memorial to be located in Washington, D.C. At last, the project could proceed.

The commission selected a site on land known as the Potomac Flats, located west of the Capitol near the banks of the Potomac River. That decision immediately triggered fierce controversy. Back in 1911, that property was reclaimed marshland, and many folks were displeased by the selection of such a site for a memorial to a man of such great stature. The Speaker of the House of Representatives that year, Congressman Joseph Cannon of Illinois, was especially furious. Cannon reportedly said, "I'll never let a memorial to Abraham Lincoln be erected in that g--damned swamp."

Splitting Rails _____

Like virtually all U.S. cities established in the seventeenth and eighteenth centuries, much of Washington, D.C., was established on low lands adjacent to tidewater. America's European colonists called it "swampy," which at the time meant land too wet to be farmed. Today's definition of a swamp is wooded land that floods seasonally. Potomac Flats in the nineteenth century wasn't forested, and flooding likely only resulted from the Potomac River's high tides. So, by a twenty-first-century definition, it's more accurate to say that the Potomac Flats was a tidal marsh.

Nevertheless, after a few more years of haggling and a lot of site preparation, ground-breaking for the Lincoln Memorial took place on February 12, 1914, the 105th anniversary of Lincoln's birth. Architect Henry Bacon, sculptor Daniel Chester French, and artist Jules Guerin were selected to design the memorial. The memorial's cornerstone was laid a year later, on February 12, 1915.

Given that it took so many years to actually start construction, considering all the decisions that had to be made, it's a wonder the project was ever finished. Out of all the addresses Lincoln made in his lifetime, which two speeches would you have chosen to immortalize in Indiana limestone?

You might think the Gettysburg Address was selected solely because it was so famous. (Or maybe because it's short and would fit nicely on a wall!) But in considering which speeches (and excerpts) to carve into the memorial's interior walls, the designers and the commission sought addresses that were indicative of Lincoln's character and beliefs.

Under the Stovepipe _____

Consisting of 28 pieces of white Georgia marble, the Lincoln statue was constructed on-site atop a 10-foot-high pedestal of Tennessee marble. Its total weight is about 120 tons. The central chamber in which the statue is located measures 60 by 74 feet. (The two side chambers are 63 by 38 feet.) Each interior column stands 50 feet tall and measures five feet six inches in diameter.

The memorial's interior walls and columns are made from Indiana limestone, and the ceiling is Alabama marble saturated with paraffin to create a lustrous translucent effect. Floor and wall base material are pink Tennessee marble.

The Gettysburg Address was selected because it displays Lincoln's strength and determination to see a successful conclusion to the American Civil War. What's more, the address vividly illustrates that Lincoln's goal was not only to reunite the nation but also to finish what the Founding Fathers began—creating a nation in which all citizens are considered equal.

Commission designers also chose to engrave the words of Lincoln's second inaugural address, which he delivered one month before the end of the Civil War. It was selected because it shows Lincoln's compassion. Even as northerners pressed for retribution for hundreds of thousands of Union dead, President Lincoln urged forgiveness. His speech also created the policy for reunification.

These speeches also suited the memorial's original theme of national unity and social justice. But something rather shocking occurred at the memorial's dedication that altered, albeit temporarily, the memorial's ideals.

A Divided Celebration of National Unity

On May 22, 1922, the Lincoln Memorial was finally dedicated in a ceremony witnessed by a crowd of more than 50,000 people. Lincoln's only surviving son, Robert Todd Lincoln, then 78, was in attendance. President Warren G. Harding and former president and chief justice of the U.S. Supreme Court William Howard Taft both delivered addresses.

However, given Lincoln's role as the Great Emancipator, it was fitting that an African American was selected to serve as the featured speaker. Tapped for this honor was Virginia-born Dr. Robert Russa Moton, who was then president of the Tuskegee Institute (formerly known as Tuskegee Normal School). It was established by the state of Alabama in 1881 to educate freed African Americans and their children.

When former President Taft asked Moton to deliver the featured address at the Lincoln Memorial dedication, many considered Moton to be the most powerful African American in the country. But certainly nothing could have prepared Moton or other African Americans for the indignity that took place on May 30, 1922.

The only African American to address the crowd that day, and one of the nation's most prominent individuals, was not permitted to sit on the speaker's platform. The dedication of the Lincoln Memorial was a racially segregated event.

Several years of progress, marked by the repeal of old ordinances that had treated blacks—slave or free—unfairly, had occurred since Lincoln's death. But all those reforms had gradually fallen by the wayside. By 1922, segregation had settled into Washington, D.C. Like all other African Americans who attended the dedication,

Moton was required to sit in the *colored section*—a separate, roped-off area away from white attendees, located at the side of the main seating. Reserved exclusively for African Americans, this separation was meant to diminish rather than celebrate their presence.

Under the Stovepipe

Dr. Robert Russa Moton, the only African American speaker at the 1922 dedication of the Lincoln Memorial, was born in 1867 in Amelia County, Virginia. Among Morton's ancestors was a powerful African chief who, after successfully battling a rival tribe and selling survivors to an American slave trader, was reportedly hoodwinked into boarding the vessel that held his former captives. Undoubtedly to his great horror, the African chief soon found himself chained with the others and bound for America's slave market.

An 1890 graduate of the Hampton Institute, Moton was the protégé of Booker T. Washington, the famed African American educator and founder of Alabama's Tuskegee Institute (now Tuskegee University). Moton became president of Tuskegee following Washington's death in 1915. Armed with considerable influence and status among America's white political and financial elite, Moton is responsible for significantly advancing the cause of African Americans in his lifetime.

Editorials published in African American newspapers after the ceremony at the Lincoln Memorial urged readers to find a way to rededicate the memorial to the unfinished cause of equality and civil rights. Over the years, that's exactly what's happened there.

The next year, Moton was in the papers again. He worked with the federal government to establish the Tuskegee Veterans Hospital on land donated by the Tuskegee Institute. His decision against hiring an all-white professional staff at the hospital drew national attention and criticism.

Moton refused to back down—even after angry Ku Klux Klan members staged statewide protest marches and threatened violence. When the hospital opened in 1923 (the year after the Lincoln Memorial was dedicated), the Tuskegee Veteran's Hospital became the first facility to have an all-black medical staff. Moton continued at Tuskegee, receiving honors for his work in race relations before retiring in 1935. He passed away in 1940.

In Lincoln's Name

Since its segregated dedication in 1922, the Lincoln Memorial has been the site of many history-making gatherings, including major civil rights demonstrations—even one that featured an opera concert.

Opera on the steps of the Lincoln Memorial as a means of protest? It happened in 1939, and what took place forever changed how Americans viewed the memorial. Famed contralto Marian Anderson had come to Washington to perform at Constitution Hall, which was owned by the Daughters of the American Revolution. When the DAR realized that the internationally renowned opera singer was African American (a fact that had apparently eluded DAR officials earlier), the organization immediately barred the 37-year-old Anderson from using the hall—solely based on her skin color.

The uproar that resulted from the DAR's decision was quick and significant. First Lady Eleanor Roosevelt resigned from the DAR in protest, and then supported NAACP officials who sought the federal government's approval to hold Anderson's concert on the grounds of the Lincoln Memorial.

On Easter Sunday, April 9, 1939, an integrated crowd of more than 75,000 people turned out to hear Anderson sing. At 5 P.M. that evening, before a huge array of radio microphones and loudspeakers, and with the statue of the Great Emancipator as a backdrop, Anderson opened her concert by singing "America."

In that single moment in 1939, the Lincoln Memorial was transformed. Its original theme of national unity and social justice was restored, and the memorial instantly became a powerful public forum—a treasured place where Americans could go to bring attention to and discuss the national citizenry's most pressing issues.

March on Washington

Anderson's concert cleared the way for another famous Lincoln Memorial gathering that took place in 1963. That year, issues involving racial segregation and equality had become a national crisis.

In the years that immediately preceded what became known as the March on Washington for Jobs and Freedom, hundreds of demonstrations had been held throughout the country. Many political figures and even law enforcement of the era often minimized the issues being raised.

Regardless of their size or nature, protests were commonly known as *civil disturbances*, a minimalist term that further hindered the American public's awareness. Media coverage of "disturbances" was often spotty, and civil rights leaders saw that no real progress was being made to improve race relations.

In early 1963, civil rights leaders decided that a massive march in Washington, D.C., might raise the public's awareness of the issues and more rapidly bring about changes in America's laws. They asked Martin Luther King Jr. to deliver the event's keynote address from the steps of the Lincoln Memorial. King was an Alabama preacher who had gained national attention for organizing a boycott of Montgomery's segregated bus system in 1955.

On August 28, 1963, more than 200,000 people participated in the historic March on Washington in what was at the time the largest American civil rights demonstration ever assembled. All three major television networks carried live coverage of the event; CBS broadcasted the entire event as it unfolded. Plus, later that evening, network newscasts replayed portions of King's speech as part of their news reports.

The year after the March on Washington, Congress passed and President Lyndon Johnson signed into law the Civil Rights Act of 1964, which worked to offer equal protection in public accommodations, public schools, voting, and the workplace.

Sadly, King was assassinated four years later in Memphis, Tennessee.

A Memorial—and Platform for All

Since 1963's March on Washington, the Lincoln Memorial has hosted demonstrations and rallies that reflect the diversity of America. People have gathered in the shadow of Lincoln's statue to speak out in support of abortion rights as well as fetal rights. Evangelical ministers, Nazi sympathizers, Mothers Against Drunk Driving, Vietnam War veterans, the National Organization for the Reform of Marijuana Laws, and newly elected U.S. presidents have all used the memorial as a platform to address and inspire crowds.

Unlike any other monument in America, the Lincoln Memorial's significance has been defined by the public. The people have given substance to the memorial's themes of national unity and social justice. What's more, America established how its sixteenth president's ideals should be remembered. Wouldn't Abe be proud?

The Least You Need to Know

- The Lincoln Memorial was dedicated in 1922.
- The dedication ceremony was racially segregated.
- People from all walks of life are drawn to the Lincoln Memorial, and many share a powerful experience.
- The Lincoln Memorial is a site where history is not only remembered, but made.

Part **3**

Lincoln's Political Legacies

Most people know that Abraham Lincoln was one of the greatest orators of all time, but he was also a consummate politician and strategist. This is often overlooked in favor of the more popular image of Lincoln as a humble backwoods lawyer.

In this part, we observe Lincoln's long-standing influence on American politics, the marks Lincoln left on the United States presidency, and another long-standing Lincoln phenomenon: how individuals and groups have sought to interpret Lincoln's life and words to promote their own political causes.

Known for taking controversial and often unpopular political stands, Lincoln is still a part of the American political scene, 150 years after his death.

Chapter 8

Political Oratory

In This Chapter

- ◆ Discovering the origins of Lincoln's public speaking skills
- ◆ Remembering Lincoln's most famous addresses
- ◆ Learning why Lincoln's words are still relevant today
- ◆ Learning from Lincoln's public speaking success
- ◆ Emulating Lincoln, the orator

When Abraham Lincoln stood before an audience and began to speak, it was as if all the elements of his greatness converged. At the podium, Lincoln embodied wisdom, compassion, courage, and a command of the facts. To hear him—especially in his later years—must have been a powerful, moving experience. More than a century later, we remember his words because they still stir the hearts of Americans.

But behind Lincoln's exquisite speechmaking is a compelling human story about how a man with less than a year of formal education grew to become the greatest public orator in American history. That triumph is a precious inheritance for all of us.

The Great Orator

No one is born with public speaking talent, and Lincoln was no different in this regard. He had to practice speaking before a group to gain confidence and he worked hard to build his *oratory* skills. Keep in mind also that at no time in his career did Lincoln have speechwriters at his beck and call. He gained renown as an orator the old fashioned way—on his own merits.

Lincoln, like all good writers, didn't always work alone. Lincoln frequently relied on his aides and cabinet officers to help write some or part of his public papers. William Seward, for example, provided lines in the First Inaugural. John Hay wrote many of Lincoln's letters, possibly including the famous Bixby letter. But Lincoln researched and crafted virtually every single address he ever delivered.

Lincoln Lingo

Oratory is the art and science of delivering an eloquently crafted speech designed to sway an audience. Oratory's origins arise from ancient Greece and Rome, when such skills were highly valued and taught as part of a classical curriculum. The word oratory is derived from the Latin term *orare,* "to pray." Political oratory emerged as a major force in the American colonies and in Europe in the eighteenth century. Today, the term oratory is erroneously used for all public speaking and is sometimes defined as a "pompous" speech. Oratory techniques and skills are most commonly employed in law, politics, and religion.

The Importance of Oratory

Early in America's history, only property owners (typically wealthy, well-educated, white males) were eligible to vote in elections. Candidates and those they courted for votes were of the same societal class. Campaigns, especially in southern states, were more reflections of social standing and a gentleman's character than his learning. Early American political campaigns often excluded speeches altogether. (Congressional speeches, however, were different from political campaign speeches and were complex and high-minded, and often referenced classical literature and symbolism.)

But as voting rights were slowly extended to all white males on a state-by-state basis during the nineteenth century, the ability to convey complex concepts to a vastly more diverse, sometimes less educated audience became absolutely crucial. In

Lincoln's time, politicians who could communicate effectively and persuasively with this growing electorate naturally gained wider voter support. It's not hard to see why many of the most prominent political leaders of the nineteenth century were the most highly skilled orators.

It's interesting to consider that although Lincoln was widely heralded as a writer and debater, his own peers had mixed opinions about his oratorical skills. Even most Republicans thought there were better orators than Lincoln in the middle of the nineteenth century.

Challenges for Orators

In the 1800s, successfully pulling all the elements of great oratory together in a single moment was no small feat. Highly regarded orators possessed far more than just strong personal presence and good delivery skills. They also had to have complete command of the subjects about which they spoke, including critical analysis and an in-depth knowledge of all sides of the topic.

The most successful orators of the time researched and prepared their arguments carefully and thoughtfully. It took time to do that properly. Sometimes an orator's preparatory work in crafting even a short speech was equal to the effort required to produce a high-quality research paper today.

 **Splitting Rails**

Contrary to what many people believe, Abraham Lincoln did not hastily pen the Gettysburg Address on the back of an envelope while on the train from Washington to Pennsylvania.

Lincoln was known for taking great care in preparing his speeches, and his public address at the dedication of the cemetery at Gettysburg was no exception. He composed his first drafts in Washington on White House stationery, and later revised and finished the manuscript in the guestroom of David Wills's home in Gettysburg.

Lastly, the best orators in Lincoln's time were also expert wordsmiths who possessed especially strong persuasive writing skills. What set Lincoln apart is that for him, every word counted. Rhythm and pace of delivery also mattered. (Lincoln's study of poetry probably added to the power of his speeches.)

Most nineteenth-century oratory was long-winded and full of wasted, empty words. Lincoln's efficiency of expression was respected in his day, but is absolutely revered in our more fast-paced age today.

The goal of an orator then—as it continues to be today—was to communicate a well-crafted, well-reasoned message or argument to inform, persuade, entertain, and move an audience emotionally. So considering all that's involved, oratory is a much bigger deal than what we normally think of when we say "public speaking."

Oratory craft wasn't the only challenge Lincoln faced when he set out to prepare a public address. Because the first modern typewriter wasn't invented until 1868 (three years after Lincoln's death), he had to write out all his speeches—including draft versions and extra copies—in longhand!

Under the Stovepipe

Reading Lincoln's speeches in his own hand adds a significant dimension to even his most familiar addresses. In addition to the opportunity to see his penmanship, viewing the manuscripts offers fascinating personal insights about Lincoln. You can easily spot points at which he appears to search for just the right word or phrase.

In his second inaugural address, for instance, the words "Fellow countrymen" appear at the top edge of his reading manuscript in a lighter hand than the rest of the speech and with great flourish. It looks like he added those words at the very last minute. Guess he wanted to make absolutely sure he didn't forget to properly address his audience!

Images of many of Abraham Lincoln's speeches written in his own hand can be found online at the Library of Congress's electronic American Memory archives at http://memory.loc.gov/ammem/alhtml/malhome.html.

Origins of Lincoln's Oratory Skills

Lincoln's oratory prowess began to take shape in his youth. His sharp, questioning mind; the massive amount of knowledge he acquired; and his fondness for storytelling laid the foundation.

Lincoln's father most likely introduced him to the art of storytelling, which Lincoln later honed and incorporated into his speechwriting and delivery style. In his youth, Lincoln's first forays into public speaking came when his classmates and friends assembled to hear him tell jokes and witty stories.

As you'll recall from earlier chapters, Lincoln read and reread books as a young boy (and continued the practice into adulthood) for one primary purpose: to educate himself. But he sought and gleaned more than just facts from each volume, and that helped build his oratory skills, too.

Lincoln's mind worked to analyze and understand all the knowledge contained in books, not just the factual details. In fact, according to his stepmother, Lincoln sought to master and truly understand every concept an author presented. By studying Aesop's *Fables*, for example, young Abraham likely learned how to craft a story with a universal message—and how to argue a point by using parables. Later, his study of Shakespeare's works added significantly to his depth of understanding.

Undoubtedly, reading the Bible taught Lincoln the importance of drawing on historical references, demonstrated the emotional power of lyrical prose, and gave him further food for thought on the subject of parables. But Lincoln's study and understanding of the Bible also greatly influenced the content of his speeches and main themes—far beyond mere storytelling. Scripture study and critical analysis of the Bible helped frame Lincoln's personal morality and the spiritual concepts he gleaned, refined, and embraced as truths were reflected in his speeches.

After reading the words of others, young Abraham Lincoln soon felt compelled to write, too. His essays and poems were often about issues that troubled him and members of his local community—temperance, human cruelty, and other issues. These writing exercises tested Lincoln's ability to artfully convey his thoughts while he learned the principles of debate and persuasive writing.

Later, as a lawyer, Lincoln learned how to develop and deliver a sound argument based on legal principles. When Lincoln combined that expertise with his other talents and accumulated knowledge, he was virtually unstoppable in the courtroom. Lincoln's compelling stories about his clients added power to his closing arguments. His folksy, down-home manner of delivery disarmed his opponents and endeared jurists. His reputation for honesty heightened his credibility.

By the time he first sought national office, Lincoln had learned to leverage his skills and knowledge to expertly craft persuasive public speeches with widespread appeal. What's more, as the son of an illiterate pioneer, Lincoln the orator understood first-hand the most pressing issues facing the largest number of voters—and he knew how to reach that audience.

In the span of a few short decades, Lincoln had replaced the axe of his youth with oratory, a far more refined yet even more powerful weapon. To use an oratory device, Lincoln proved "the pen is mightier than the sword." What's more, he offered audiences more than mere technique. Lincoln's speeches illustrated that this was a man who had spent significant time examining moral concepts and their applicability to solving the problems of his era.

The Orator at Work

Examples of the principles of oratory can be identified everywhere in Abraham Lincoln's speeches (as well as those delivered by modern-day orators):

- **Rhetorical devices.** Includes rhetorical questions, exaggeration, understatement, contrast and juxtaposition, and quotations from well-known sources.

  "A house divided against itself cannot stand." A derivative of a Bible verse (Matthew 12:25) Lincoln used in his "A House Divided" speech in Springfield, Illinois, on June 16, 1858.

- **Planned use of pronouns.** Used to address the audience (for example, "Fellow Americans")—inclusionary pronouns such as "we" and "us," to pull audience members to the orator's side; and exclusionary pronouns such as "they" to distance audience members from opponents.

  "I stand here surrounded by friends—some political, all personal friends, I trust." From Lincoln's last speech of the 1858 campaign in Springfield, Illinois, on October 30, 1858.

- **Emotionally evocative, vivid language.** Triggers visual recall and influences audience members to choose a side, preferably that of the orator.

  "The world will little note nor long remember what we say here, but it can never forget what they did here." From Lincoln's Gettysburg Address on November 19, 1863.

- **Sound.** Repetitious use of consonants, words, or phrases; use of rhyming words or other techniques that improve listeners' recall.

  "Let us have faith that right makes might …" From Lincoln's Cooper Union speech in New York on February 27, 1860.

- **Figurative language.** Grabs the listener's attention and retains his interest (for example, metaphors, similes, and giving human qualities to inanimate objects).

  "A husband and wife may be divorced and go … beyond the reach of each other; but the different parts of our country cannot do this." From Lincoln's first inaugural address on March 4, 1861.

◆ **Other devices.** Includes such things as repetition of points; repetition of phrases and groups of words; use of lists of statistics, quotes, and other items for emphasis.

"Here I have lived a quarter of a century, and have passed from a young to an old man. Here my children have been born, and one is buried." From Lincoln's farewell address in Springfield, Illinois, on February 11, 1861.

Ten Simple but Immortal Sentences

Incredible as it may seem today, Abraham Lincoln was not the featured speaker that day at Gettysburg. That honor went to another orator, Edward Everett. In fact, organizers of the event at which Lincoln spoke—the dedication of the cemetery at Gettysburg—didn't even ask Lincoln to speak until almost the last minute. But Lincoln's role—to dedicate the cemetery—was exactly appropriate for a president. He perceived no slight.

After the Battle of Gettysburg had been fought, the people of Gettysburg had no choice but to find a place to bury the thousands of dead soldiers whose bodies were strewn throughout the town and its countryside. Within days of the battle's end, Pennsylvania Governor Andrew Curtain asked prominent Gettysburg attorney David Wills to secure property for a new military cemetery and to plan its solemn dedication.

Wills quickly bought up a 17-acre tract of land for the new Soldiers' National Cemetery, and engaged an architect to draw up plot plans. Burials began soon after.

Under the Stovepipe

From July 1 through July 3, 1863, more than 160,000 Confederate and Union soldiers fought in the Battle of Gettysburg. Of these, a total of about 33,200 troops were wounded or captured; nearly 11,000 reported missing in action by both sides; and another 7,058 soldiers killed in battle. Combined Union and Confederate casualties exceeded 50,000.

In late September, Wills invited the man considered to be the nation's foremost orator at the time, Everett, to serve as the featured speaker at the event. Everett immediately accepted—but with one caveat: he needed more time to prepare his oration. In response to Everett's requirement, the event's date was moved out a month, to November 19, 1863.

Historical records suggest that Lincoln was added to the speaker list as an afterthought. At some point, though, it must have occurred to someone on the planning team that it might be a nice idea to ask the president of the United States to speak at the affair.

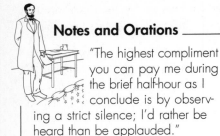

Notes and Orations

"The highest compliment you can pay me during the brief half-hour as I conclude is by observing a strict silence; I'd rather be heard than be applauded."

—Abraham Lincoln, Lincoln–Douglas debates, 1858

Not until November 2 did Wills finally extend a formal written invitation to Lincoln, asking that he make "a few appropriate remarks." Given that Lincoln was a busy president, it's more likely that organizers hoped but didn't necessarily expect he would attend the event. They certainly wouldn't have demeaned Lincoln by asking for a long historical lecture of the sort Everett delivered that day.

Wills's invitation included a warm welcome to the president and the offer of a place to stay—Wills's own home in the town of Gettysburg.

Everett and Lincoln at Gettysburg

On November 19, Lincoln had breakfast at the Wills house and then returned to the guestroom to polish his speech. He and his colleagues then left for the dedication and arrived around 10 A.M. After mounting a chestnut horse, Lincoln rode in a procession that began at about 11 A.M.

Fifteen minutes later, Lincoln and other dignitaries arrived at the dedication site. Before taking his seat, President Lincoln, as commander in chief of the Union forces, received a military salute from soldiers assembled for the event. All was ready, except that Everett had not yet arrived. (Cue the musical interlude …)

At 11:40 A.M., Everett arrived and was introduced. He spoke—eloquently, of course—for more than two hours. After Everett finished and received the crowd's applause, Abraham Lincoln was introduced at 2 P.M. Lincoln rose from his seat and, two-page manuscript in hand, strode purposefully to the center of the platform to begin his address. (Cue the paparazzi …)

As Lincoln spoke his first few sentences, photographers calmly moved their equipment about and made adjustments to their cameras. They obviously wanted to set up for what they hoped would be that perfect photo, the shot that would run in newspapers and magazines throughout the Union. Little did they know that Lincoln's speech consisted of just 10 sentences. (Okay, the last sentence was really, really long.)

So before any of the photographers was able to snap a single camera shutter, Lincoln completed his speech and headed back to his chair. The stunned disappointment of the photographers must have been palpable. The audience was so surprised it was over, they delayed their applause and when it finally came, it was scattered.

Four score and seven years ago our fathers brought forth on this continent, a new nation, conceived in Liberty, and dedicated to the proposition that all men are created equal.

Now we are engaged in a great civil war, testing whether that nation, or any nation so conceived and so dedicated, can long endure. We are met on a great battle-field of that war. We have come to dedicate a portion of that field, as a final resting place for those who here gave their lives that that nation might live. It is altogether fitting and proper that we should do this.

But, in a larger sense, we can not dedicate—we can not consecrate—we can not hallow—this ground. The brave men, living and dead, who struggled here, have consecrated it, far above our poor power to add or detract. The world will little note, nor long remember what we say here, but it can never forget what they did here. It is for us the living, rather, to be dedicated here to the unfinished work which they who fought here have thus far so nobly advanced. It is rather for us to be here dedicated to the great task remaining before us—that from these honored dead we take increased devotion to that cause for which they gave the last full measure of devotion—that we here highly resolve that these dead shall not have died in vain—that this nation, under God, shall have a new birth of freedom—and that government of the people, by the people, for the people, shall not perish from the earth.

—Abraham Lincoln's address delivered at the dedication of the cemetery at Gettysburg, November 19, 1863

Lincoln's Oratory Influence

Modern-day presidents and candidates for public office have routinely invoked Lincoln's name and employed Lincolnesque oratory techniques—regardless of their party affiliation.

President John F. Kennedy

Democratic President-elect John F. Kennedy, for example, reportedly asked the speechwriter who crafted his inaugural address to study Lincoln's Gettysburg Address—to uncover its "secrets."

Given that instruction, it's not surprising that Kennedy's inaugural address was short, emotion-packed, and set the stage for a new era. Poetically phrased one-syllable words made up nearly three-quarters of the speech. After he delivered the address, Kennedy's inaugural was hailed as one of the best public speeches of all time, capable of moving even the dead. (Kennedy's "Ask not" line was his idea, by the way.)

Don't miss these two great Lincoln speeches, which are reprinted in Appendix G of this book:

◆ Last Public Address (April 11, 1865)

◆ Cooper Union Address (February 27, 1860)

Notes and Orations _____

Let every American, every lover of liberty, every well wisher to his posterity, swear by the blood of the Revolution, never to violate in the least particular, the laws of the country; and never to tolerate their violation by others. As the patriots of seventy-six did to the support of the Declaration of Independence, so to the support of the Constitution and Laws, let every American pledge his life, his property, and his sacred honor;—let every man remember that to violate the law, is to trample on the blood of his father, and to tear the character of his own, and his children's liberty. Let reverence for the laws, be breathed by every American mother, to the lisping babe, that prattles on her lap—let it be taught in schools, in seminaries, and in colleges; let it be written in Primers, spelling books, and in Almanacs;—let it be preached from the pulpit, proclaimed in legislative halls, and enforced in courts of justice. And, in short, let it become the political religion of the nation; and let the old and the young, the rich and the poor, the grave and the gay, of all sexes and tongues, and colors and conditions, sacrifice unceasingly upon its altars.

—Abraham Lincoln's address before the Young Men's Lyceum of Springfield, Illinois, January 27, 1838

See if you can find the Lincoln influence in these excerpts from Kennedy's inaugural, delivered on January 20, 1961 in Washington, D.C.:

In your hands, my fellow citizens, more than mine, will rest the final success or failure of our course.

Let every nation know, whether it wishes us well or ill, that we shall pay any price, bear any burden, meet any hardship, support any friend, oppose any foe, to assure the survival and the success of liberty. This much we pledge—and more.

United, there is little we cannot do in a host of cooperative ventures. Divided, there is little we can do, for we dare not to meet a powerful challenge at odds and split asunder. We dare not forget today that we are the heirs of that first revolution. Let the word go forth from this time and place, to friend and foe alike, that the torch has been passed to a new generation of Americans, born in this century, tempered by war, disciplined by a hard and bitter peace, proud of our ancient heritage, and unwilling to witness or permit the slow undoing of these human rights to which this nation has always been committed, and to which we are committed today at home and around the world.

Martin Luther King Jr.

In the months leading up to Kennedy's assassination, another great orator emerged: Martin Luther King Jr., an Alabama preacher and highly influential leader of the civil rights movement. On August 28, 1963, more than 200,000 people turned out for the March on Washington, a peaceful demonstration that brought unity among African Americans and raised awareness of the need for a new civil rights bill.

At the conclusion of the march, a day-long rally was held on the steps of the Lincoln Memorial, and it was there that King delivered his "I Have a Dream" speech. Here's the second paragraph of King's address:

> *Five score years ago, a great American, in whose symbolic shadow we stand today, signed the Emancipation Proclamation. This momentous decree came as a great beacon light of hope to millions of Negro slaves, who had been seared in the flames of withering injustice. It came as a joyous daybreak to end the long night of their captivity.*

Using many of the same oratory devices Lincoln employed and invoking Lincoln's memory, King successfully argued his case to the American people and garnered widespread support. Congress passed the new Civil Rights Act a few months later.

President Ronald Reagan

Republican President Ronald Reagan, known as the Great Communicator for his formidable oratory skills, also admired and studied Lincoln's speeches. A former professional actor, Reagan had a soothing baritone voice and more than three decades of experience delivering lines on stage and before cameras. As an orator, Reagan was completely at ease and extremely effective.

President Reagan's first inaugural address was particularly unique. Its form and delivery were specifically created for the millions of television viewers who would witness the speech in their own homes. Because of the camera angles made available by Reagan's choice of the Capitol's West Wing, viewers also caught glimpses of a background containing America's most recognizable memorials and national monuments, further heightening the patriotic experience of the historic moment. Reagan's inaugural was but the first of many oratory triumphs for the two-term president.

But even great orators are not infallible. Reagan's most notable error as a speaker came when he erroneously attributed to Lincoln a quote he used in one of his speeches. The unfortunate gaffe occurred during his rousing 1992 speech at the Republican National Convention, at which President George H. W. Bush was about to be renominated to run for his second term. (Bush's Democratic opponent, Bill Clinton, had already been nominated at the Democratic Convention.) Reagan obtained the quotations from a widely used source that erroneously attributed them as Abraham Lincoln's words.

Splitting Rails

Some of the most famous quotes attributed to Lincoln have more in common with urban legend than with our sixteenth president. Here's an example:

"We may congratulate ourselves that this cruel war, which has cost a vast treasure of blood and money, is almost over. But I see in the future a crisis approaching which fills me with anxiety. As a result of the war, corporations have become enthroned, and an era of corruption in high places will follow."

This widely diseminated "Lincoln quote" appeared in a 1931 book by Emanuel Hertz, *Abraham Lincoln: A New Portrait*, citing a purported 1864 letter from Lincoln to a Colonel William F. Elkins. The letter was a forgery. Archer H. Shaw "authenticated" the fraudulent quote by including it in his 1950 *Lincoln Encyclopedia*. (Other fact checkers have attributed the source of this false quote to a séance in Iowa, but that's not right.)

How can you determine if a Lincoln quote is genuine? For starters, refer to the *Collected Works of Abraham Lincoln*, compiled by the Abraham Lincoln Association and available online at www.alincolnassoc.com. Recollected quotes are less reliable, but the best single source is Carl Sandburg's six-volume biography of Lincoln.

Reagan's address was a huge success that night. He told conventioneers (and millions of television viewers):

> But we knew then what the liberal Democrat leaders just couldn't figure out: the sky would not fall if America restored her strength and resolve. The sky would not fall if an American president spoke the truth. The only thing that would fall was the Berlin Wall.

> I heard those speakers at that other convention saying, 'We won the Cold War'—and I couldn't help wondering just who exactly do they mean by 'we'? And to top it off, they even tried to portray themselves as sharing the same fundamental values of our party! What they truly don't understand is the principle so eloquently stated by Abraham Lincoln: 'You cannot strengthen the weak by weakening the strong. You cannot help the

wage-earner by pulling down the wage-payer. You cannot help the poor by destroying the rich. You cannot help men permanently by doing for them what they could and should do for themselves.

Afterward, Lincoln scholars recognized that, although stirring, the statements Reagan credited to Lincoln were not in Abraham's voice or style. Upon further investigation, it was determined that the words were indeed not Lincoln's.

In fact, Reagan had quoted from 10 statements of moral principle written by Reverend William John Henry Boetcker, a Pennsylvania-reared Presbyterian minister who lived from 1773 to 1862. Boetcker's "Ten Cannots" was first published in a 1916 leaflet entitled "Lincoln on Private Property," which also contained Abraham Lincoln's words.

And in Conclusion ...

Not only are the words of many of Lincoln's speeches remembered today, but excerpts from his addresses have become part of the common lexicon. His unique personal style and way with words are emulated by public speakers in all walks of life—and of all skill levels.

The Least You Need to Know

- ◆ Abraham Lincoln's oratory skills were built, not born.

- ◆ Among many reasons, oratory was important during Lincoln's era because many voters were illiterate.

- ◆ Politicians who possessed strong oratory skills usually gained widespread voter support.

- ◆ Lincoln was not the featured speaker at Gettysburg, but his speech is the one we remember.

- ◆ Modern-day orators employ many of the same oratory devices used by Lincoln; they also quote (and sometimes misquote) him while invoking the Lincoln name!

Lincoln's Impact on the United States Presidency

In This Chapter

- ◆ How Lincoln's personal integrity and honor influenced future political leaders—and voter expectations

- ◆ How Lincoln redefined the presidential role of commander in chief

- ◆ Why Lincoln's reputation for promoting personal liberties must be balanced against his wartime orders

- ◆ How Lincoln influenced public opinion through the media—and how modern-day presidents emulate him

As president, Lincoln broke new ground in a variety of areas, from involvement in military strategy to rallying or calming citizens. He established precedents that his successors considered and frequently adopted, even decades after his death. Above all, Lincoln was a man of high integrity, a fact that's sometimes needlessly minimized.

As a wartime president, Lincoln was also called upon to make tough, highly unpopular decisions that seemed to contradict his lifelong commitment to personal freedom. He tested the limits of executive branch powers in ways that still draw criticism—and praise—today.

Politics, Personal Honor, and Morality

In the quest to put down myths and saintly legends about Abraham Lincoln, the true facts about his personal integrity are frequently overlooked. It's no myth that Lincoln rarely acted in ways that contradicted his high values.

And in today's world of corporate scandals, legal trickery, and exposure of political misdeeds, it's often difficult for many people to truly grasp what it meant to be a man of honor in Lincoln's time. As you might expect, during Lincoln's career, rivals and various political opponents accused him of dishonesty, deception, and other unseemly behavior. As a mere mortal, Lincoln occasionally didn't live up to his high ideals. But "Honest Abe" wasn't an empty label. Abraham Lincoln earned that nickname—coined during his lifetime—because of his longstanding and well-known practice of honest dealings with others. Like Lincoln's nickname, honor and duty weren't mere words in nineteenth-century America. To be sure, not all men and women behaved honorably in Lincoln's time. However, a person's standing in society was largely measured by his or her personal integrity. Honesty was but one factor that comprised a more expansive set of desirable values found in true "ladies" and "gentlemen."

To examine Lincoln's virtues and their impact on the U.S. presidency, we need to view him in the context of his own era. The world was a vastly different place in the nineteenth century.

In Lincoln's time, a man's *word of honor* meant more than just about anything. Folks relied on the integrity of others. The concept of a handshake agreement as a valid, binding contract between two parties was derived from this belief. Questions of honor (one man insulting another, for example) were still settled on occasion by duels—even though dueling was illegal.

Lincoln Lingo

One's **word of honor** is a promise based on one's personal honor and integrity.

Conversely, violating another person's trust constituted serious personal and societal breaches for which there were severe and longstanding consequences. Failing to keep your word could also get you shot, and that was especially true for soldiers in the early days of the Civil War.

Honor on the Battlefield?

Many people in the nineteenth century relied on the personal integrity of others. One of the best illustrations of this concept is the way in which prisoners of war were treated in the early days of the Civil War. (Of course, conditions for prisoners deteriorated dramatically as the war dragged on, but that's another matter.)

In sharp contrast to the frequent mistreatment of modern-day prisoners of war, early Civil War combatants who were captured during battle were commonly treated with dignity and respect. That practice was in keeping with the personal integrity of their captors and the expectations of a genteel society. But that's not all. Enemy combatants captured in the first months of the Civil War didn't languish in a military prison or prisoner-of-war camp. They were almost always *paroled*.

Lincoln Lingo

Parole is a conditional release of a prisoner who has not yet served his full term. In Civil War times, the term *parole of honor* was synonymous with "word of honor." A Civil War prisoner could be granted freedom simply by promising not to engage in combat until formally exchanged.

To gain freedom, a captured soldier or officer gave captors his solemn word of honor that he would not engage in war activity against the captor's side. The soldier's name and other identification were recorded. And then the prisoner picked up his belongings and walked away.

Sound incredible? Well, what's even more stunning is that nearly every military man who gave such a pledge followed through on the promise. Not only that, but the former prisoners' superiors upheld the parolees' honor pledges. (Even captured and released generals who accepted the terms of parole ceased their involvement in the war effort.)

Beginning around 1862, the parole process became more formalized and included a written agreement acknowledging the prisoner's promise. Still, the contract's effectiveness relied on the parolee's word.

Dishonor's Price

Civil War prisoners who were paroled under these conditions were not permitted to take any action that could be construed as supporting the war effort. A military man who'd been paroled and later betrayed that trust by returning to his regiment was considered dishonorable, even despicable. Both sides shared this view.

Not surprisingly, if a paroled soldier or officer dared enter the battlefield in violation of his word and happened to be captured again by opposing forces, his captors promptly executed him. No questions asked.

Under the Stovepipe

During the Civil War, prisoner parole policies became problematic for both sides. Imagine one side capturing 10,000 men in a single battle and sending them all home, knowing that the former captives would never return to fight another day!

As time passed and the loss of troops became more serious, some people charged wrongful surrenders were being made for purposes of avoiding military service. So military leaders changed parole rules and practices around 1862, to the benefit of military goals—and to the detriment of personal honor codes.

After the military diminished the value and honor of a man's word, Civil War military practices and treatment of prisoners deteriorated to near barbaric levels. It's worth noting that these changes also altered societal behavior and standards of conduct.

Most people in Lincoln's era, regardless of their societal position, revered personal integrity. Folks commonly acted in ways that supported those beliefs—even during wartime, and even with enemy soldiers. So in general, Lincoln's values weren't unusual in his day and time.

But what makes Lincoln a standout even among his contemporaries is that his principles were exceptionally high, and he rarely if ever acted in ways that violated his personal values. For Lincoln, there didn't seem to be much ambiguity between right and wrong. "My great concern is not whether God is on our side—my great concern is to be on God's side," Lincoln said.

Civil Liberties in Wartime

We all know about Lincoln's dedication to the protection of personal freedom. But what's not as well known is that during the national crisis that was the Civil War, Lincoln did take measures to limit liberties. The steps he took were radical in their day and remain controversial even in this one.

Notes and Orations

"I think the constitution invests its commander-in-chief, with the **law of war**, in time of war."

—Abraham Lincoln, letter to James C. Conkling, August 26, 1863

On April 15, 1861, the day after Fort Sumter fell to the Confederates, Lincoln put out his first call for troops—75,000 soldiers to protect the capital city. Concerns about Washington's security grew even more serious when, two days later, Virginia seceded.

Northern militiamen mustered and headed for Washington. Union troops probably didn't expect to be harassed as they passed through what should have been friendly territory, but the people of Maryland hadn't decided whether they'd fight for the Union or not.

When a Massachusetts regiment of about 800 men arrived in Baltimore by way of Philadelphia, a riot ensued. As the soldiers prepared to board trains bound for Washington, an angry mob of about 20,000 Baltimore citizens pelted them with rocks. When the militiamen fired into the crowd, the rioters responded by firing back.

Given the chaos, the death toll was surprisingly low. Four Massachusetts volunteers and 12 civilians were killed in the melee.

The regiment finally made it out of Baltimore. But as the Washington-bound train pulled away from the station, the last thing those soldiers heard was a cheer for Confederate president Jefferson Davis.

Notes and Orations

"To the Commanding General of the Army of the United States: You are engaged in repressing an insurrection against the laws of the United States. If at any point on or in the vicinity of the [any] military line, which is now [or which shall be] used between the City of Philadelphia and the City of Washington, via Perryville, Annapolis City, and Annapolis Junction, you find resistance which renders it necessary to suspend the writ of **Habeas Corpus** for the public safety, you, personally or through the officer in command at the point where the [at which] resistance occurs, are authorized to suspend that writ."

—Abraham Lincoln, to Winfield Scott, April 27, 1861

Lincoln's Wartime Power

For a time after the incident in Baltimore, Washington seemed especially vulnerable. The telegraph lines had been cut, troops weren't arriving when expected, and a southern blockade of the Potomac River south of Washington threatened to keep supply ships away. The Union was advised not to route troops through Maryland at all.

Tensions were high, and fear was rampant. Without an immediate influx of troops, folks feared Washington might fall at any moment. What a prize the capital city would have been for the Confederacy!

When Maryland's governor decided to convene the state's legislature on April 26, 1861—little more than a week after the Baltimore riot—it made everyone in Washington nervous. At first, Lincoln thought he'd wait and see what happened when Maryland legislators gathered.

But on April 27, he had a change of heart. It was time for drastic action. That day, Lincoln suspended *habeas corpus*, the law that enables a person under arrest to be immediately released if a court finds that the arrest and imprisonment did not comply with the law.

Lincoln's suspension of habeas corpus would be the first of many wartime actions that would interfere with rights most Americans had taken for granted.

Lincoln Lingo

Habeas corpus is a Latin phrase literally meaning "you shall have the body." Also known as the "Great Writ," the writ of habeas corpus is an order requiring a person to be released from unlawful restraint, offering protection against imprisonment without cause, a personal liberty guaranteed by the Constitution. Lincoln suspended habeas corpus throughout much of the Civil War, denying citizens this constitutional right. However, Lincoln acted appropriately. The Constitution provides for a suspension of the writ during rebellion.

Curbing Enemy Threats

Although Supreme Court Chief Justice Taney challenged Lincoln's suspension of habeas corpus, the president argued that, as commander in chief, he had the responsibility and authority to enact wartime measures to protect the country. Over the course of the Civil War, Lincoln expanded presidential wartime powers far beyond his predecessors. Congress and later court decisions essentially ratified Lincoln's decision.

His actions unnerved many people. Even today, a few historians charge that Lincoln's exercise of power approached that of a quasi-dictator. Still, his actions weren't inconsistent with those a president might take against a foreign country in war. The unique situation posed by the Civil War was that the "enemy" was already within the country. Many historians argue that if Lincoln hadn't taken strong action, there might not have been a Constitution to defend. What's more, the Constitution itself vested Lincoln with the wartime powers he exercised. Under the Constitution and his presidential oath of office, Lincoln was authorized—and required—to act to protect the Union.

Interestingly, the Emancipation Proclamation is also an example of Lincoln's expansion of presidential power. Keep in mind that in 1863, slaves were considered personal property. When Lincoln proclaimed that African Americans held in the South were "free," he essentially confiscated the property of southern slaveholders and negated their property rights. Neither the president nor Congress had a constitutional right to take away those rights, but in issuing the proclamation, Lincoln exercised his wartime powers. In doing so, he weakened the enemy while doing what he felt was morally right—and constitutionally acceptable.

Wartime presidents who succeeded Lincoln routinely refer to his Civil War decisions when determining the extent of their power as commander in chief. After the September 11, 2001, terrorist attack, President George W. Bush took action (and Congress endorsed) with the temporary suspension of the rights of individuals suspected of terrorist plots against the United States.

Most people in the United States are uncomfortable with what they perceive to be an infringement upon civil liberties. However, like the Union citizens of Lincoln's day, most understand and accept that sometimes national security outweighs individual liberties.

Commander in Chief Redefined

Beyond expanding presidential powers during wartime, Lincoln was also intimately involved in military strategy—perhaps more extensively than any president since Washington.

But few people really understand just how involved Lincoln really was on the battlefield. If you scan records of President Lincoln's daily calendar, you'd be shocked to see how frequently the man visited nearby encampments. He was so close to the action at times that on one occasion, he came under enemy fire—although it's doubtful that the opposing forces realized Lincoln was present at the time.

In addition to making personnel changes, Lincoln was also involved in selecting weaponry, charting out battle plans, and evaluating the offerings of military services vendors—even to the appointment of army mule drivers! Some folks in his administration actually suggested that Lincoln ought to be a field commander!

Presidential Spin

You might believe that framing politicians and political issues in a favorable light began in modern times. But actually, the practice of what's known today as *spin doctoring* began even before Lincoln entered office. (Thomas Jefferson is often considered the original American spin doctor.)

Lincoln knew the power of public opinion and didn't hesitate to communicate with constituents through the media and other means. In his careful style, he crafted evocative, compelling messages designed to educate the public and sway opinion.

The country's extensive telegraph network enabled Lincoln to convey his messages within about 24 hours—extremely fast for that era. He could deliver a speech one afternoon and his remarks would be published in newspapers across the country the very next day. This was a new phenomenon.

Lincoln's successors have further honed his techniques, aided along the way by technological advancements. President Franklin Roosevelt, another wartime president, followed Lincoln's example of rapid communications to citizens during World War II. Radio broadcasts of Roosevelt's patriotic speeches helped rally Americans in favor of the war effort. His frequent audio addresses known as "Fireside Chats" were aimed directly at the public and reassured listeners that the cause of democracy was morally right.

President John F. Kennedy was the first to exploit television as a viable medium of communicating with the American public. Former Hollywood star President Ronald Reagan made excellent use of television to deliver messages to the public—employing oratory skills that were often compared to those of Lincoln.

Throughout history, presidents have used a variety of media to cajole, educate, influence, move, and persuade citizens. They've also employed the same techniques to intimidate and threaten our enemies.

Who can forget the image of President George W. Bush at Ground Zero in 2001, reassuring the American public and vowing retaliation? Sometimes it's not just about "spin."

Executive Powers

We've talked about the extraordinary powers Lincoln exercised as a wartime president, particularly the steps he took that limited some freedoms in the pursuit of expanding freedom. But another important power he exercised was the exclusive right to *pardon* individuals convicted of federal crimes. As you might imagine, there were tens of thousands of presidential pardon requests made during the Civil War.

The ability to pardon a person who's been convicted of an offense against the federal government is a power reserved exclusively for the United States president. What's more, the power is virtually limitless. In recent years, presidents have been criticized for their exercise of this executive privilege. Consider the public outcry over President Gerald Ford's pardon of former President Nixon, who had resigned from office during the Watergate scandal. Or the ridicule President Bill Clinton endured for the pardons he granted to former business associates in his last few days in office because they resembled political favors.

Lincoln Lingo

An official **pardon** is when an executive forgives an offense and reduces or eliminates the convicted person's punishment.

Even Lincoln was not immune to such criticism for the decisions he made. But it is clear that Lincoln viewed pardons as a serious judicial responsibility and not a gift to others. He also approached the task in his own principled way.

Notes and Orations

"In very truth he was, the noblest work of God—an honest man."
—Abraham Lincoln, from the eulogy of Benjamin Ferguson, February 8, 1842

Incredibly, Lincoln personally examined the case files himself, rather than relying on reviews or opinions of advisors. Being a lawyer, he would have felt right at home among all that paperwork!

The individuals and the offenses he deemed worthy of pardon reveal Lincoln's own morality and deep understanding of the nature of people. In making the decision to pardon an individual, he was guided by justice, not simply strict adherence to law. For example, Union sentries were routinely sentenced to death for falling asleep at their posts. Lincoln didn't think the drastic punishment fit the crime. So even though military leaders strongly protested, when given the chance, Lincoln almost always pardoned the convicted soldier in such cases.

He was particularly sympathetic in cases that involved defendants under the age of 18. Lincoln recognized that it was natural for these "boy soldiers" to be homesick and terrified at times, even if their initial ambition was to be courageous in battle.

Lincoln granted so many pardons that he was harshly criticized as a softy. He could be swayed by appeals from a convict's family, especially when delivered by a tearful wife or mother. But he could also be tough. Repeat offenders and individuals who showed a lack of respect for the law didn't obtain presidential pardons.

One thing's for sure: Lincoln did his homework. It was his practice to thoroughly examine case files the way a judge might—carefully weighing circumstances, testimony, the validity of evidence against the defendant, and other factors.

Under the Stovepipe

Several close relatives of Abraham Lincoln's wife, Mary Todd Lincoln, were among the few southerners permitted to visit the White House during the Civil War. When members of President Lincoln's administration balked at the idea, Lincoln stood his ground. He didn't believe banning Mary's family was appropriate solely on the basis of their southern birthplace.

The Least You Need to Know

♦ Abraham Lincoln's personal integrity was above reproach and voters have come to seek this quality in America's leaders.

♦ Lincoln was a hands-on commander in chief, and his successors have emulated his approach to varying degrees.

♦ As a powerful communicator, Lincoln influenced public opinion on important national and international issues—a technique later used by his successors.

♦ President Lincoln tested the limits of constitutional power as a wartime leader, and many of his acts were controversial and highly unpopular with Democrats.

♦ Lincoln redefined presidential pardons and their purpose.

Chapter 10

Leveraging Lincoln's Influence

In This Chapter

◆ How and why Abraham Lincoln's memory is leveraged

◆ Why Lincoln's character and policies continue to be debated today

◆ How and why questions about Lincoln's sexuality became media fodder

◆ How the most common misconceptions of Abraham Lincoln are explained

◆ Why Lincoln scholars are concerned about our sixteenth president's heritage

Abraham Lincoln's star power was established immediately after his death in 1865. As they did then, many people and causes seek to be identified with this true American hero. But celebrity and adoration also carry a price.

Conversely, some seek to topple Lincoln from his pedestal while others search for ways to redefine him. New myths and legends have been created as history is challenged. However, what's amazing is that Abraham Lincoln still makes headlines.

The Lincoln Phenomenon

Lincoln is such a fixture in American history that many people, organizations, and companies choose to use him as a symbol of their position or beliefs—and sometimes merely for recognition in advertising campaigns. Whether this usage is grounded in fact, fiction, or merely symbolism varies widely.

Both major U.S. political parties like to claim Lincoln as their own, and sometimes take credit for having his same views on an issue! Various companies use Lincoln's name or image in their corporate branding. And you can't get through a February without hearing about a Presidents' Day sale! (Remember when both Lincoln and George Washington had their own holidays?) Lincoln's silhouette is so recognizable that his image is often used in company logos and sales flyers.

Lincoln also makes frequent appearances in the high-tech environment of cyberspace! You might not realize this, but there are Internet chat boards—lots of them—in which debates about Lincoln are taking place at this very moment. Some of the issues being discussed are familiar: Lincoln's views on slavery, nineteenth-century economics, and executive power as exercised by Lincoln.

However, other topics being seriously debated in the twenty-first century resemble personal attacks that one might expect to read in a grocery store tabloid. These include charges that Lincoln was a racist, an atheist, and an anarchist. Even Lincoln's sexuality has been challenged. How did we end up on this path?

As heroes, politicians, and movie stars alike will tell you, one of the hazards of celebrity is the public's constant clamor for details and commentary about their idol. The search for the "fresh" and unexpected story is relentless today.

 Splitting Rails _____

Abraham Lincoln is frequently misquoted, and it's also not uncommon for quotations to be incorrectly attributed to Lincoln. Savvy students of Lincoln lore consult the *Collected Works of Abraham Lincoln* by Roy P. Basler. This multi-volume set contains Lincoln's correspondence, speeches, and other writings, and is available in the research section of many public libraries. The material is also available online in a searchable database format, courtesy of the Abraham Lincoln Association. To check a quote or peruse Lincoln's words, go to www.alincolnassoc.com.

Recollected Words of Abraham Lincoln by Don and Virginia Fehrenbacher (Stanford, 1996) is an excellent resource for recollections provided by individuals, and evaluates the credibility of statements attributed to Lincoln.

Continued study, even scrutiny, of past leaders and their decisions is a time-honored American tradition. That's especially true when the subject is an icon such as Lincoln, of whom many people want to increase their knowledge and improve their understanding.

But more than a century after Lincoln's death, folks are still angling for that blockbuster twist, that singular detail seemingly overlooked by everyone—the "hidden truth" that will totally redefine our perception of this beloved American legend. Some historians view the goal of this effort as an attempt to transform history into salacious entertainment. As you might imagine, this isn't particularly popular among Lincoln scholars.

For students of Lincoln and nineteenth-century culture and politics, the old axiom of "buyer beware" applies. Check out claims, quotes, and hot news about our sixteenth president. If a story sounds utterly unbelievable, chances are it probably is.

But remember, too, that historians have been digging through Lincoln's rich past for more than a century. You just never know when someone will turn up a heretofore unknown detail within *Lincolniana* that will provide new insight.

Lincoln Lingo

Lincolniana is a term to describe virtually anything having to do with Abraham Lincoln, including primary and secondary research materials. A few examples are letters, speeches, and other writings; fiction and nonfiction works that feature Lincoln as a key character; and biographies about Lincoln, his family members, and key associates.

History Revisited

One of the challenges faced by anyone who sets out to study a historic person is that the era in which the individual lived must also be clearly understood. Positions held or words spoken in nineteenth-century America can't be interpreted in the context of twenty-first-century beliefs and culture.

For example, one of the most contentious issues surrounding Lincoln's character is his views on race. In his time, Lincoln's pronouncements on racial equality were considered quite radical. But in today's enlightened society more than a century later, some of what he said sounds remarkably racist.

It's important to keep in mind that not only did Lincoln's views on race evolve during his lifetime but the entire country's perceptions were in the process of change. That's said not to excuse the statements, but to put them into perspective. Simply put, the average nineteenth-century American held views we'd consider today as racist. It was part of the culture.

Notes and Orations _____

"There is more involved in this contest than is realized by every one. There is involved in this struggle the question whether your children and my children shall enjoy the privileges we have enjoyed. I say this in order to impress upon you, if you are not already so impressed, that no small matter should divert us from our great purpose."

—Abraham Lincoln, speech to the One Hundred Sixty-Fourth Ohio Regiment, Washington, D.C., August 18, 1864

The steady evolution of Lincoln's thinking on the subject is evidenced by his own words. In his debates with Stephen Douglas in 1858, Lincoln clearly took a strong stand against slavery—a radical position at the time. Mirroring the views of his contemporaries, he stopped short, though, of advocating full equality. At the time, he expressed the opinion that blacks and whites would never be on an equal footing.

But later, as his views matured, Lincoln spoke in support of enfranchisement for African Americans and hinted of his advocacy of full civil rights for blacks. In fact, just days before his assassination in 1865, he suggested that African Americans in Louisiana ought to be given the right to vote. Because John Wilkes Booth was among those who heard Lincoln's opinion, many draw the conclusion that Lincoln's pronouncement—clearly illustrating a decidedly nonracist viewpoint—was so compelling that it triggered his assassination days later.

Here are a few other controversies that have emerged over the years. We offered views consistent with those held by a majority of Lincoln historians. Even so, the topics are worth exploring:

◆ *Did Lincoln engage the South and wage a civil war over the issue of economic tariffs?* From the beginning of America's history, sectional differences on tariff issues led to tensions. But the vast majority of historians agree the evidence clearly shows that Lincoln's goal was to save the Union. Slavery, not tariffs, was the Civil War's immediate trigger.

◆ *Was Lincoln a dictator? Was that his political goal?* As a wartime president, Lincoln certainly stretched the boundaries of executive power. Many of his decisions were unpopular and made a lot of people uncomfortable. But had Lincoln's objective been to establish a dictatorship, he never would have permitted the 1864 presidential election to take place.

Notes and Orations

"It is not merely for to-day, but for all time to come that we should perpetuate for our children's children this great and free government, which we have enjoyed all our lives. I beg you to remember this, not merely for my sake, but for yours. I happen temporarily to occupy this big White House. I am a living witness that any one of your children may look to come here as my father's child has. It is in order that each of you may have through this free government which we have enjoyed, an open field and a fair chance for your industry, enterprise and intelligence; that you may all have equal privileges in the race of life, with all its desirable human aspirations."

—Abraham Lincoln, speech to the One Hundred Sixty-Sixth Ohio Regiment, Washington, D.C., August 22, 1864

♦ *Was Lincoln so unpopular that his own Cabinet members conspired to kill him?* Although this idea may be tantalizing for those who theorize that Lincoln's assassination was the result of a huge government conspiracy plot, there is no evidence to support it.

Notes and Orations

"The will of God prevails. In great contests each party claims to act in accordance with the will of God. Both may be, and one must be, wrong. God cannot be for and against the same thing at the same time. In the present civil war it is quite possible that God's purpose is something different from the purpose of either party; and yet the human instrumentalities, working just as they do, are of the best adaptation to effect [sic] his purpose. I am almost ready to say that this is probably true; that God wills this contest, and wills that it shall not end yet. By his mere great power on the minds of the now contestants, he could have either saved or destroyed the Union without a human contest. Yet the contest began. And, having begun, he could give the final victory to either side any day. Yet the contest proceeds."

—Abraham Lincoln, Meditation on Divine Will (found and preserved by Lincoln secretary John Hay, who said it was "not written to be seen of men"), Washington, D.C., September 1862

◆ *Did Lincoln believe in the paranormal?* Lincoln was an open-minded man, and historians say he and his wife were intrigued but not obsessed by the idea of psychic phenomena. Mary Todd Lincoln believed in spiritualism. Lincoln attended a spiritualist circle with her, but apparently didn't believe in any of it. It's worth noting that interest in mysticism was fairly commonplace in Lincoln's era.

◆ *Was Lincoln an atheist?* Although he reported no personal affiliation with a specific church or organized religion, Lincoln's writings and speeches demonstrate a strong belief in God.

Lincoln Reinterpreted

Affiliation with a highly popular individual helps advance and raise awareness of many causes—from political and social issues to commercial endeavors. Leveraging the public's steadfast interest in our sixteenth president and capitalizing on his reputation have been longstanding practices. Lincoln's name and image have been used to promote everything from Presidents' Day sales to television shows.

Over the years, many people have looked to Lincoln's words and deeds to validate a variety of beliefs and positions. Just as Scripture may be interpreted in a variety of ways, so can the words of Abraham Lincoln. Not all the conclusions that have resulted from an examination of his life are consistent with the facts that are known about Lincoln and the era in which he lived.

And the practice isn't uniquely American.

For instance, Illinois state historian Thomas Schwartz estimates that there are more schools in Cuba named after Abraham Lincoln than there are in Lincoln's birthplace, the state of Kentucky. The reason? Well, in Cuba and other nations which hold similar political views, Lincoln's words and life have been reinterpreted to show him as a revolutionary with beliefs consistent with socialism.

It's gratifying to know that a statue of Abraham Lincoln—one of America's greatest leaders—prominently greets visitors to Havana. But being perceived as a socialist probably wasn't what Lincoln, a defender of democracy and capitalism, hoped would be his legacy.

Similarly, Lincoln would no doubt be amused by challenges to his heterosexuality. Historians must rely on facts and context, not merely modern-day interpretation.

Notes and Orations

"In this connection there is another topic to which I desire to allude. I seldom refer to the course of newspapers, or notice the articles which they publish in regard to myself; but the course of the Washington *Union* has been so extraordinary, for the last two or three months, that I think it well enough to make some allusion to it. It has read me out of the Democratic party every other day, at least for two or three months, and keeps reading me out, (laughter [by audience members]) and, as if it had not succeeded still continues to read me out, using such terms as 'traitor,' 'renegade,' 'deserter,' and other kind and polite epithets of that nature."

"Sir, I have no vindication to make of my democracy against the Washington *Union*, or any other newspapers. I am willing to allow my **history** and action for the last twenty years to speak for themselves as to my political principles, and my fidelity to political obligations. The Washington *Union* has a personal grievance. When its editor was nominated for Public Printer I declined to vote for him, and stated that at some time I might give my reasons for doing so. Since I declined to give that vote, this scurrilous abuse, these vindictive and constant attacks have been repeated almost daily on me."

—Abraham Lincoln, from the first debate with Stephen Douglas, Ottawa, Illinois, August 21, 1858

Some modern observers suspect that Lincoln was "gay" because he shared beds with men—a commonplace practice in nineteenth-century America that had to do with economics, not sexual orientation. What's more, the culture in Lincoln's era didn't sexualize that behavior the way we do today. They had much deeper expectations about emotional intimacy in same-gender friendships than today.

Although there have been attempts throughout the years to show that Lincoln was homosexual, the evidence doesn't support the claim. Still, the controversy continues—and like other unproven theories, it's changing how some people view Lincoln.

What the Future Might Bring

Academic inquiry and vigorous pursuit of research enable all of us to gain insight into the most important people and events in history. What's important to remember, though, is that when history is revised or reinterpreted, we run the risk of losing touch with facts.

Lincoln knew he lived in historic times and was making decisions that would change the course of America's future. Preserving what we know about him will help his legacy live on.

The Least You Need to Know

♦ When examining Lincoln's life, it's important to view him in the context of his own era—not in the twenty-first century!

♦ Since Lincoln's death, many have sought to invoke his name to advance their agendas, and Lincoln's views are quoted—or misquoted—to that end.

♦ News of Abraham Lincoln still draws attention and headlines today.

♦ Theories not supported by facts and context serve to diminish our understanding of Lincoln and his impact on American politics and culture.

Part 4

Lincoln's Personal Liberty and Legal Rights Legacies

Abraham Lincoln's role in abolishing slavery in the United States is familiar to most Americans.

Lincoln's stance against slavery was all the more remarkable considering that the practice was ingrained virtually worldwide in the nineteenth century. But even after his Emancipation Proclamation was enacted, freed African Americans did not enjoy full citizenship. A century would pass before Lincoln's vision of constitutional equality for all Americans became reality. We explore Lincoln's "unfinished business," and how the Civil War factored into his decision-making.

Although Lincoln freed African Americans and set the stage for the Civil Rights movement, that legacy must also be balanced with another, lesser-known fact: While in office, he also enacted laws restricting or suspending personal rights guaranteed by the U.S. Constitution.

Chapter 11

The Abolition of Slavery

In This Chapter

- ◆ Finding the origins of slavery and religion's role in stopping it

- ◆ Viewing how slavery evolved and what Lincoln accomplished in his lifetime

- ◆ Garnering support for his most radical idea: The Emancipation Proclamation

- ◆ Surprising (mis)treatment of black Civil War soldiers and other little-known behind-the-scenes stories

He was known as the Great Emancipator, and Abraham Lincoln's legendary opposition to slavery was nurtured in childhood, but he wasn't a lifelong abolitionist. In fact, he didn't plan on abolishing slavery when he took office in 1861.

As with many Americans of his era, Lincoln's view of blacks evolved and his commitment to free them from the bonds of slavery grew gradually. When his opinions had matured and he had determined the time was right, Lincoln acted decisively. He first proclaimed that all slaves held by rebels were free, then supported the Thirteenth Amendment to abolish slavery throughout the United States. By taking these steps, Lincoln set the stage for full equality.

Slavery's Origins

Slavery was not an American invention. In fact, the practice existed well before Columbus ever set foot in the New World. In fact, one reason it took so long to eradicate slavery in America is that it had been a worldwide practice. When Lincoln spoke of freeing slaves in the nineteenth century, slavery had already been abolished in most of the rest of the world. But he was directly confronting centuries of ingrained societal custom that had involved captives of all color.

Ancient cultures—Egyptians, Mayans, Aztecs, Greeks, Romans, and Babylonians—all kept slaves. Their captives included Jews, Europeans, and Ethiopians. The Bible and the Koran, among other religious texts, mention humans in bondage. Greeks and Romans, in particular, commonly raided the regions now known as Great Britain, France, and Germany and captured humans for the purpose of enslaving them.

In ancient times, slaves were kept to serve their masters as soldiers, laborers, household servants, concubines, and government workers. Some enslaved humans were survivors who happened to find themselves on the losing side of a battle. Others became slaves by virtue of the societal class into which they were born.

But ancient slavery was not race-based or permanent, and the enslaved individuals were not treated as if inhuman. Unlike American slavery, ancient practices also did not involve kidnapping individuals and transporting them—more than 20 million of them – across an ocean!

Lincoln Lingo

Slavery is broadly defined as buying, selling, and/or holding captive another human being for the purpose of forced, unpaid labor. In ancient times, slaves were considered a separate social class of people.

The English word **slave** first appeared in the late thirteenth century and is historically identical to the word *Slav*. Both terms are derived from Old French *esclave*, which means enslaved.

Slavs were a people who inhabited large portions of Eastern Europe and whom Spanish Muslims captured and enslaved in the ninth century. Slavic descendants include Czechs, Poles, and Russians. Family surnames such as those that incorporate the word *slav* or a derivative form—names like Stanislaw, Bohuslav, and Mstislav, for instance—are believed to indicate an ancestral history of European slavery.

A number of societies and kingdoms in Africa also kept slaves in a manner similar to other cultures. Among the African slaveholders were the Asanti, the Kings of Bonny, and Dahomey, and their slaves were used primarily for domestic work and farming.

From the beginning, holding slaves in all cultures—including African—was considered a sign of power and wealth. Slaveholders had overcome their enemies. When battles were fought, victors gained land *and* people. Captured enemies were enslaved and forced to work for their captors.

Slaveholders built wealth and status by possessing many workers—hands engaged in developing land, producing food, and performing other tasks needed to support these ancient societies. And the ability to provide for many slaves was also viewed as an indication of wealth and prosperity.

In these ancient societies and later, some slaves were treated better than others. But even if some masters were kind and benevolent, no human group or individual ever enjoyed captivity.

Commercial Trade

Sultanates of the Middle East were the first to commercialize or traffic in slavery, in east Africa. Slaves of African descent were bought and sold, ending up in places such as Persia and other Middle Eastern countries. They fought in armies as soldiers, worked in households, and produced food, among other work. Female captives were often used as sex slaves.

But not until the fifteenth century did slave trading become an African institution. With the opening of the New World, demand for free labor grew enormously and slavery became big business. In the middle of the fifteenth century, Europeans attempted to kidnap Africans from their homes for the purpose of enslaving them. That approach met with considerable violence. Eventually Europeans learned to offer commodities in exchange for slaves.

Under the Stovepipe

Slavery in the Americas somewhat resembled that of Imperial Russia's nineteenth-century system, which treated its serf class as property that could be bought and sold. Russian serfs were finally freed just two years before Lincoln issued the Emancipation Proclamation!

Because the African slave culture was different from the American version, Africans who collaborated with European traffickers probably didn't realize the cruelty that awaited the captives. Even so, Africans and others established a vast commercial supply network that brought slaves from the continent's interior to the coasts, where Europeans set up trading outposts. Rulers of large tribal communities obtained slaves from less powerful states in exchange for protection or as a show of allegiance. Slaves were traded to the Europeans in competitively negotiated transactions for guns, coins, horses, cloth, salt, and other goods.

By the end of the eighteenth century, it is estimated that more than 70,000 Africans each year were being sold to slave traders and taken against their will to the Americas. Compare that figure to the total current population of Wyoming's most populous city, Cheyenne, at 53,200!

In all, it's estimated that between the fifteenth and nineteenth century, 12 million Africans were enslaved and forcibly moved from the African continent. Only a fraction of them were brought to the American colonies.

Millions in Human Bondage

Africans were purchased and then transported across the Atlantic to toil at their masters' bidding throughout North and South America. About 42 percent of slaves were taken to the Caribbean, to places such as Jamaica and Barbados. Thirty-eight percent were sent to Brazil. Only about five percent ended up in North America. That's how huge the slavery business was. Not surprisingly, entire economies became dependent upon slave labor.

The transatlantic slave trade involved three continents. Traders followed a triangular route, in which ships set out from European ports headed for Africa's western coast. At various African ports, captives were kept in pens like cattle while waiting to be traded into slavery. Traders exchanged European goods for people and loaded the Africans into ships. Many died even before they boarded ships.

The transatlantic journey, or Middle Voyage of the triangle, took six to eight weeks. It was not uncommon for one third of the captives to die due to extremely crowded, unsanitary conditions aboard ship and the lack of food and water. After the Middle Voyage had been completed, the traders off-loaded their human cargo—those who had survived the trip. African people were then sold for cash or exchanged for commodities in the Carribean islands as well as eastern ports along the coasts of North and South America.

Traders returned to Europe in the last leg of the triangular trade route. Their ships were loaded down with goods produced by slave labor, such as sugar, coffee, tobacco, rice, and later, cotton. (After 1800, colonists in the Americas increasingly made direct slaving voyages to the western coast of Africa, cutting out the European market in the bargain.)

In ancient times, slaves in Greece and Rome or even in North Africa might rise to prominence or marry into the ruling class. The plight of slaves in America was completely different. In America, slavery was a permanent condition.

Under the Stovepipe

Before the commercialization of slave trading, many Europeans and some Africans were held as indentured servants—a voluntary form of servitude. Most executed contracts to perform free labor in exchange for passage to the British American colonies. When they had completed their contractual obligation—usually a period of seven years—they were given "freedom dues" that included land and other personal property.

But once in America, indentured servants often decided they'd had enough of the work and escaped. The contracted masters had an extremely difficult time locating runaway servants of European descent. Because their skin color and other physical features matched those of the colonists they served, European indentured servants could instantly vanish into a crowd.

In America as well as by European slave traders, slaves of African descent were viewed as subhuman, seen on the level of livestock. They were despised for the color of their skin and treated with anything from indifference to brutal cruelty. Unlike the ancients, none married their masters. When there were sexually intimate relationships between slaves and their American masters, the encounters were almost always forced upon the slaves. Children who resulted from these encounters remained slaves.

Throughout the Americas, slaves were a commodity; a product to be bought and sold in the marketplace. The slave trade and the free labor it brought enabled slaveholders to accumulate great wealth and prominence. In colonial times, a total of about 500,000 African Americans were held as slaves in North America.

Most American slaves after the colonial period were American- not African-born. By Lincoln's time, there were hardly any African-born slaves in the American South. Yet the rate of increase among American slaves was unprecedented in the history of slavery, comparable to the rate of increase among free workers.

The Seeds of Lincoln's Commitment to Abolition

Although the Founding Fathers—many of whom were slaveholders—undoubtedly shared the ideological ideal of freedom for all, the Declaration of Independence and the Constitution were silent on the issue of slavery. Jefferson's original draft of the

Declaration of Independence included a charge against King George III that the monarch had "waged a cruel war against human nature" through direct involvement in the slave trade.

Although Jefferson shifted the blame from colonists to the monarchy, southern delegates to the Continental Congress were insulted by the document's characterization of slavery as violating the "most sacred rights of life and liberty." Several delegates, most notably South Carolina, refused to endorse the Declaration unless the slavery passage was removed. In the first of many compromises to appease slaveholders, the offending passage was eliminated from the final draft. The result was the perpetuation of American slavery and its expansion into new territories over the next century. Following the American Revolution, the northern United States began to abolish slavery. Vermont was the first territory to do so, in 1777. Pennsylvania was the first state to implement a gradual abolition law in 1780. Massachusetts was the first state to achieve emancipation with a judicial ruling in 1781. In the North and South, abolition came slower wherever slavery was of economic benefit. States such as New York and New Jersey did not stop the practice right away. But by the mid-1820s, almost all slavery was confined to the South.

By the time Lincoln was born, opposition to slavery on the basis of religious belief had just begun to emerge as a force. Lincoln's upbringing included these religious doctrines, and he would later say that he couldn't remember a time when he wasn't against slavery. The practice of holding humans captive repulsed him.

Even so, Lincoln didn't initially believe that there was anything he could do legally—constitutionally—to stop slavery. So early on, it was his fervent hope that slavery would eventually die out all on its own. But when given the chance to make a change, he did.

Notes and Orations

"Whenever I hear any one arguing for slavery I feel a strong impulse to see it tried on him personally."

—Abraham Lincoln's speech to the 140th Indiana Regiment, March 17, 1865

Lincoln's speeches provide perhaps the best historical record of his evolving views on slavery, abolition, and African Americans. They also point to his increasing determination to sway public opinion and convince others that radical change was necessary. The famous Lincoln–Douglas debates give tremendous insight, too.

But in his Cooper Union Address of 1860, Lincoln set out his strongest argument yet against slavery. Grounded in the Declaration of Independence and the Constitution, Lincoln made the case that the Founding Fathers had no intention of allowing slavery to exist here.

Moreover, Lincoln argued that the framers of the Constitution hadn't intended to exclude African Americans from equal treatment under the law. In making such a compelling and well-reasoned argument, Lincoln set the foundation for what he had previously believed was constitutionally impossible: complete emancipation of all African Americans.

But it's also important to know that the issue wasn't just about morality or constitutional law. Most northerners believed slavery was economically unfair. Expanding slavery's reach into new territories competed with the North's free labor system.

Lincoln's Emancipation Proclamation

As mentioned, Lincoln hadn't planned on abolishing slavery when he took office in 1861. But he quickly realized that he'd have to take that step, to save the Union and to do what he felt was morally right.

Immediately after the Union's stunning loss at the First Battle of Manassas (Bull Run) in Virginia, Union senators and congressmen debated the slavery issue in the context of the war's goals. General George McClellan made it quite clear that as long as he was in charge of the Army of the Potomac, his troops would not be used as instruments of emancipation.

Radical Republicans pressed for the immediate emancipation of all slaves in the southern Confederacy. But their aim wasn't just to free African Americans. They wanted to completely reshape the South and change its entire society. The rest of the Union wasn't ready for that, and the radicals didn't have enough votes to push their agenda. So in 1861, Lincoln and Congress decided to affirm that the war's sole mission was to preserve the Union.

Free the Slaves; Disarm the South

But they still had to deal with the pesky problem of Confederates using their slaves to battle the Union. Thousands of slaves had no choice but to serve the Confederate army, some as cooks, laborers, and teamsters—and even soldiers. Slaves helped make up for the South's smaller white male population, which was outnumbered by the North's manpower.

Given that the North could not duplicate the considerable number of slaves working for the Confederacy, something had to be done to reduce the South's advantage. The first step taken to disarm and weaken the Confederate army was to encourage slave rebellions.

In August 1861, Congress passed the Confiscation Act. The act authorized the seizure and liberation of slaves actively involved in the Confederate war effort. Although the act clearly benefited the Union's military aims, it also moved African Americans one tiny step closer to freedom.

Under the Stovepipe

Under the Confiscation Act of 1861, Union soldiers treated slaves as property. When Union soldiers took control of a southern plantation, town, or opposing force, they gathered up all rebel property for use by the Union forces. Slaves were hauled away with the livestock and were considered rebel "contraband."

Contraband slaves were brought to the North, usually to Washington, D.C., where they lived in a makeshift refugee camp.

Meanwhile, religious leaders in the North continued to call for abolition. Some said fighting a war in the South without freeing slaves was like battling hell without disturbing Satan.

Politically, Lincoln stood on a fragile balance beam. He had to appease border states that might immediately secede if the war's stated purpose shifted to emancipation. On the other hand, he might lose the support of northern states urging that bold action immediately be taken and abolition embraced as part of the war's aims. (Out of the fifteen slave states, four—Delaware, Kentucky, Maryland, and Missouri—remained in the Union during the Civil War.)

Under the Stovepipe

By the end of the Civil War, blacks accounted for nearly 10 percent of all Union troops, with nearly 200,000 blacks serving in the Union army and navy. The majority of them were former slaves. About 68,000 black soldiers were killed or lost in combat, and 24 received the Congressional Medal of Honor for extraordinary bravery on the field of battle.

Before the war, tens of thousands of slaves risked their lives to escape their captors in the South, demonstrating their strong desire for freedom. The vast majority headed north. In the beginning of the war, some northerners returned slaves for bounty money or forced them to work for the Union army. Lincoln felt more and more pressure to take a decisive stand on the issue.

By the end of 1861, he left the question of full emancipation for Congress to decide. But recognizing that the antislavery sentiment had begun to take hold in the North, Lincoln also took another step that benefited the cause of African Americans.

In December 1861, Lincoln granted freedom to all fugitive slaves serving in the Union army.

Black Union soldiers, who fought against the Confederacy, did so at great risk. Those who were captured by rebels were either immediately executed or sold into slavery. Lincoln promised to retaliate against such actions.

But during the Civil War, African Americans also faced discrimination within the Union army. They served in separate regiments and received less pay than white Union soldiers—blacks received $10 a month for their service, less $3 for clothing, while whites collected $13 each month plus an additional $3.50 clothing allowance.

Unlike white Union soldiers, blacks did not receive enlistment bonuses. They also drew menial, labor-intensive assignments. Some white officers refused to lead black regiments, and others subjected insubordinate black soldiers to humiliating and cruel punishments that closely resembled conditions under slavery—whippings, for instance.

Nevertheless, blacks kept their goal of freedom in sight, and continued to battle on behalf of the Union. In 1864, black soldiers gained equal pay, and by 1865, they were permitted to hold positions as officers. By the end of the Civil War, more than 150,000 former slaves had served in the Union army.

The Bloodiest Day, the Finest Hour

Lincoln held his Emancipation Proclamation, waiting for the right political moment to unveil it. That day came when the Union army won the Battle of Antietam in September 1862. Robert E. Lee lost a quarter of his men that day. After losing to Lee at Manassas, McClellan and his army must have felt redeemed.

Although the Union was victorious, neither side gained any real ground that day. But Antietam provided the political opportunity Lincoln needed to make the public aware of his preliminary draft of the Emancipation Proclamation.

A few months later, on January 1, 1863, Lincoln transformed the Union's Civil War goals to include slavery's destruction. That day he issued his Emancipation Proclamation, freeing slaves held by rebel southerners. (You can find the complete text of the Emancipation Proclamation in Appendix G.)

Under the Stovepipe

The Battle of Antietam was fought on September 17, 1862, near Antietam Creek in the Maryland countryside near the tiny hamlet of Sharpsburg. By nightfall that day, more than 26,000 soldiers had either lost their lives, been wounded, or gone missing. It remains the single bloodiest day in American history.

The battle at Gettysburg, which was fought from July 1 through 3, 1863, and won by the Union army, marked the turning point in America's Civil War. Although the war dragged on for nearly two more years, the collapse of the Confederacy became inevitable. By 1865, the Union had won.

Finally, Freedom

Before Lincoln's death, Congress proposed to the state legislatures a Thirteenth Amendment to the United States Constitution that eliminated slavery throughout the country.

> Section 1. Neither slavery nor involuntary servitude, except as a punishment for crime whereof the party shall have been duly convicted, shall exist within the United States, or any place subject to their jurisdiction.

> Section 2. Congress shall have the power to enforce this article by appropriate legislation.

Lincoln actively lobbied for the amendment, and the 1864 Union Party platform included an endorsement of the amendment—making the election a referendum on both the war and the end of slavery.

Lincoln didn't live to see the amendment's ratification. On December 6, 1865, the Thirteenth Amendment was declared ratified by majority, after legislators in 27 of 36 states passed the measure. In 1901, Delaware became the last state to ratify the amendment. Mississippi rejected the amendment in 1865 and did not subsequently ratify it—ever.

Many people today believe passage of the Thirteenth Amendment automatically gave former slaves equality. Unfortunately, it did not. Although slaves rejoiced in their new freedom, they would not see full equality for another 100 years.

The Least You Need to Know

- Slavery did not originate in America, but was an ancient practice dating back to Greek and Roman times.

- Millions of Africans were enslaved when Europeans commercialized slavery.

- Lincoln was not a lifelong abolitionist; his commitment to total emancipation grew gradually.

- Union military needs helped speed emancipation, although freeing slaves was a multi-step process.

- When Lincoln issued the Emancipation Proclamation on January 1, 1863, the Union's Civil War goals were expanded to include the eradication of slavery.

Chapter 12

Enfranchisement of Blacks

In This Chapter

- ◆ What happened after the Thirteenth Amendment was passed that interfered with the promise of African American citizenship
- ◆ How Lincoln's vision of racial equality was realized, then dashed
- ◆ How Jim Crow laws triggered the rise of the Black Civil Rights Movement
- ◆ Why Lincoln's legacy regarding black equality endures

Abraham Lincoln's 1863 Emancipation Proclamation was of course a watershed event in the history of personal freedom in America. But two years later, Lincoln made an equally stunning pronouncement.

On April 11, 1865, he told a crowd gathered at the White House that he supported black suffrage in Louisiana. Lawmakers in that state had just been given the constitutional power to give blacks the right to vote. Further, Lincoln implied Louisiana's example of granting full citizenship to African Americans ought to be followed elsewhere.

With all this momentum, why did it take so long for blacks to gain civil rights in America?

A Voice in Representation

Abraham Lincoln knew a constitutional amendment would be required to make the provisions of his Emancipation Proclamation stick—and apply to all slaves. So he pushed Congress for fast action.

The Senate passed the Thirteenth Amendment, which abolished slavery in America, on April 8, 1864. The House approved the measure on January 31, 1865, and the proposal was then sent to the states for ratification.

On December 6, 1865, the Thirteenth Amendment was declared ratified by majority, after legislators in 27 of 36 states passed the measure. In 1901, Delaware became the last state to ratify the amendment. Mississippi rejected the amendment in 1865 and did not subsequently ratify it—ever.

Many federal legislators viewed the amendment's congressional passage as a signal to bring on a much larger, more far-reaching agenda: *enfranchisement* of blacks.

Lincoln Lingo

Enfranchisement is the act of bestowing citizenship rights upon an individual or group. The term originates from the old French *enfranchir*, "to set free." **Suffrage** is the right to vote. In a democracy, a citizen's right to vote is a crucial element of enfranchisement. Accordingly, voting rights and enfranchisement are commonly used interchangeably.

You might think that after slavery was abolished, granting full citizenship to African Americans would be a no-brainer. It was, after all, the next natural step in the process of personal freedom for blacks.

But in the nineteenth century, most folks didn't see it that way. A majority of white Americans—including those in the North—weren't entirely sold on the idea of granting full citizenship to former slaves. Unlike the abolitionist movement, there was no groundswell pushing for African American enfranchisement in the mid-1860s.

However, there was a political group whose federal legislators were pressing their congressional colleagues to make sweeping changes to benefit blacks: the Radical Republican Party. Rather powerful at the time, this political party was separate and apart from the more moderate Republican Party. You might recall that early in Lincoln's political career, he distanced himself from the Radicals.

Lincoln generally believed that the Radical agenda—transforming centuries of southern culture and economics virtually overnight—was a bit too extreme for most Americans. Radicals also called for black *suffrage*.

Many historians believe that America's founders viewed voting as a privilege rather than a fundamental right. The words "right to vote" do not appear in the original U.S. Constitution, and the term was not incorporated until the Fourteenth Amendment was added to the Constitution in 1868. Radicals most certainly lobbied Lincoln in an attempt to gain his support and to get him moving on the issue of black equality, but, for both political and practical reasons, Lincoln preferred to gradually introduce political and social change in America.

However, in the days preceding his assassination, Lincoln's plan for post-Civil War reconstruction was still evolving. He seemed more focused on bringing about a peaceful reuniting of the country than extending civil rights to freed slaves—at least that's how it appeared to the outside world.

The Fifteenth and Nineteenth Amendments to the U.S. Constitution removed race and gender as legal barriers to this citizenship right. The two amendments were ratified and became laws in 1870 and 1920 respectively.

A Stunning Announcement

On April 11, 1865, a crowd of jubilant citizens formed outside the White House, calling for Lincoln to address them on the occasion of the Civil War's end. Two days earlier, Confederate General Robert E. Lee had surrendered to Union General Grant at Appomattox Court House, Virginia. That historic act had followed the Union's capture of Richmond and signaled the end of the American Civil War.

Splitting Rails

Was the great orator Abraham Lincoln uncomfortable speaking without notes? Well, many historians agree that Abraham Lincoln didn't like giving extemporaneous speeches—even short ones. He almost always spoke from a handwritten manuscript and his words were carefully and thoughtfully chosen. Lincoln was also a big believer in revising his work. He tinkered with some speeches—even short remarks—right up to the last minute.

In his 50 months as president, Lincoln addressed the public only around 100 times. That's not very often. Consider how frequently modern-day leaders appear on television each day. Lincoln might not have had the media exposure of today's presidents, but when he spoke, he made sure every word counted.

A group had assembled at the president's home on April 9, also. But Lincoln didn't have time to prepare a proper speech, so he gently sent the folks on their way and indicated he'd speak to them at a later date.

So when a throng of cheering people gathered on April 11, calling loudly for Lincoln to make a few remarks on the occasion of the great Union victory, he was prepared to address them. As always, he'd carefully and thoughtfully crafted a speech and set it out on paper.

Thunderous applause greeted Lincoln as he stepped to an open second-story window to address the immense assembly. He began by acknowledging the crowd's joy, and congratulated the military leaders responsible for the capture of Richmond. Then he called for peace and unity.

But after that, Lincoln's address took a totally unexpected—some might say radical—turn. That night, Abraham Lincoln became the first American president in history to publicly announce that he favored voting rights for African Americans. He specifically recommended black suffrage for "those who serve our cause as soldiers."

This might not seem like such a big deal today. But in 1865, the very fact that Lincoln uttered such an opinion was huge news. Although free blacks had the right to vote in several northern states, most states had prohibited enfranchisement of blacks—slave or free! (Before 1820, free blacks were able to vote in Massachusetts, New Jersey, Pennsylvania, New York, Maine, Vermont, Connecticut, Rhode Island, and New Hampshire.)

Under the Stovepipe

Early American suffrage laws emulated those of Great Britain. Under British parliamentary law in 1430, voting rights were restricted to white male adult landowners whose property generated an annual income of at least 40 shillings. Voting laws in thirteenth-century England also barred certain classes: servants, women, and non-native born persons, for instance.

Colonial and Revolutionary Americans viewed suffrage as a privilege earned by economic independence and civic virtue. They believed an impoverished or otherwise economically dependent person was more likely to be swayed by others—a precursor to political corruption. Colonial societies also withheld voting rights on the basis of religion, race, and residency. Free blacks were among those disenfranchised during that era.

With a few exceptions in the American West and New England, the requirement that a voter be a prosperous landowner stood until the early 1800s.

Lincoln's pronouncement, which followed victory at Richmond and also Lee's surrender, was reminiscent of the timing he chose for the unveiling of his Emancipation Proclamation after the victory at Antietam. It's entirely possible that Lincoln had held this opinion for quite some time—but was waiting for the right historical and political moment to reveal his thinking.

In the crowd that day, listening to Lincoln's address, was John Wilkes Booth. The president's remarks infuriated Booth, a local actor and southern sympathizer. It's said Booth angrily muttered to his friends who stood with him on the White House lawn, "That is the last speech he will ever make."

Three days later, at Ford's Theatre, Booth drew his derringer and shot Lincoln at nearly point-blank range. We'll never know how Lincoln would have carried out his plan for reconstruction or exactly what he had in mind for enfranchisement and racial equality. But his untimely demise proved disastrous for African Americans.

Lincoln's Vision Realized, Then Dashed

To be a government "by the people," individuals must pick their leaders. Without free and fair elections, there can be no democratic society. And without that constant accountability of government officials to the electorate, there can, in fact, be no assurance of any other civil right. The right to vote is not only an important individual liberty, it is the cornerstone of free government.

Until the post-Civil War era, suffrage had always been a matter decided by state constitutions, laws, and local ordinances. Nationalizing the right to vote in America was a completely new idea in 1865, and one not expected to play well in the South. After all, at the heart of the Civil War was a contentious battle between self-governance and federal control.

So it's a mistake to believe that the expansion of suffrage and other citizenship rights to African Americans was inevitable. Every attempt to expand suffrage rights—regardless of the righteousness of the cause—has triggered prolonged and sometimes violent conflict.

What is indeed frustrating about the battle for black suffrage, however, is that at the time of Lincoln's death, the momentum necessary to win the fight had been built. It seemed as though it was only a matter of time before the struggle would be won. But in the absence of Lincoln's open-minded leadership, the drive for black civil rights slowed, sputtered, and then sadly regressed.

Under the Stovepipe

In 1866, Congress passed a Civil Rights Act that declared that any person born in the United States was a citizen, regardless of race, color, or previous condition. Some of these citizen rights include making and enforcing contracts; ability to sue and be sued; and to purchase, sell, lease, and inherit property. President Andrew Johnson vetoed the Civil Rights Act of 1866, but Congress overrode the veto and the measure became law.

However, passage of the act didn't settle the argument. Local laws and the activities of organizations such as the Ku Klux Klan undermined the guarantees of the act and defeated its purpose of granting civil rights to African Americans.

Lincoln's death didn't prevent the Thirteenth Amendment from becoming law. Ratified by the states in 1865, the measure became the law of the land little more than seven months after Lincoln's murder. The Radical Republicans played a role in moving other progressive initiatives along.

But the political climate under Lincoln's successor, President Andrew Johnson, was reactionary and disorganized. Without Lincoln in the picture, the federal government didn't really have a plan in place to reunite the nation.

President Johnson, a Democrat from Tennessee, advocated amnesty for rebels. Under his administration, a southern state that sought readmission to the Union was only required to change its constitution to outlaw slavery and renounce secession. Lincoln would have preferred far stricter requirements.

Lincoln Lingo

After the Civil War ended, southern legislatures enacted laws, collectively known as **black codes,** designed to limit the rights of former slaves and to undermine the intent of the Thirteenth Amendment to the U.S. Constitution. Congress moved to defeat black codes by passing the Fourteenth Amendment to the U.S. Constitution.

As a result of Johnson's lenient policies, plantation owners maintained political power in their home states, and legislative measures that restricted the freedoms and citizenry rights of African Americans were passed. These state and local laws were known as *black codes*.

In 1866, a white mob attacked Louisiana Republicans and their black supporters who had assembled in New Orleans for that party's state convention. Federal troops were called in to restore order after 34 blacks and three white Republicans were killed. Voters outside the South were so outraged by the mob's action that they cast the votes necessary to give Republicans an overwhelming majority in both houses of Congress—enough to override any veto Johnson might attempt.

In 1867, Congress passed the Reconstruction Act, which signaled the period we know as Reconstruction. Under this new act, rebel states seeking readmission to the Union had to register all qualified voters, create new state constitutions, and ratify the newly passed Fourteenth Amendment, which was intended to guarantee African Americans full federal citizenship.

The Fourteenth Amendment to the United States Constitution was ratified in 1868 and made citizenship a national right of all persons born or naturalized in the United States. After the amendment was ratified, and for most of Reconstruction, blacks voted and gained the political power necessary to protect their other rights.

Passage of the Fifteenth Amendment, which was ratified in 1870, was required to ensure voting rights for African American males. (It's important to mention that the Fifteenth Amendment excluded women from its protections, but not all forms of voting. States, for example, could still allow women to vote—and several did during the years before the Nineteenth Amendment was ratified.)

Under the Stovepipe

Despite resistance from many sectors, the first few years following the Civil War's end saw significant progress for many African Americans. In Washington, D.C., for instance, the period from 1865 to about 1885 is known as the Golden Age of Black Washington. You might recall that tens of thousands of former slaves fled to Washington in search of a better life. For a time, African Americans realized Lincoln's vision and flourished in Washington where civil rights were upheld.

Among many progressive steps, the city established a black public school system, and African Americans led a successful drive to establish local black colleges and universities. Former slave and abolitionist Frederick Douglass was appointed to city office and influenced policies.

Elsewhere in the country, 2 blacks became senators, and 20 were elected to the House of Representatives during this era.

In the beginning years of Reconstruction, African Americans tentatively expanded their influence and took initial steps to exert political power. Some took leading roles in the arts, education, and political scenes of many cities—even as a countermovement began, seeking to undermine them.

Southern Outrage

Throughout the Reconstruction period, the federal government maintained troops in southern states, and to a certain extent, that helped the cause for equality. But the presence of Union forces, who had the backing of the Republican-dominated Congress, also infuriated southern whites.

Southerners bristled at the very idea of federal intervention. Resentment smoldered. Even though the Civil War had ended, the county was still deeply divided on the issue of African American equality.

Ultimately, white Democrats in many jurisdictions brought an end to Reconstruction's progressive goals by way of forcibly keeping African Americans from the polls. Discriminatory election laws crippled the ability of African Americans to exert the political power needed to enforce protective laws.

According to the United States Department of Justice, the Ku Klux Klan, the Knights of the White Camellia, and other terrorist organizations used violence and intimidation to prevent the Fifteenth Amendment from being enforced.

A political compromise between the Republican Party and southern leaders of the Democratic Party signaled the end of Reconstruction. The negotiation between the two sides led to the official withdrawal of Union troops from southern states in 1877.

Notes and Orations

"The World has never had a good definition of the word liberty, and the American people, just now, are much in want of one. We all declare for liberty; but in using the same word we do not all mean the same thing. With some the word liberty may mean for each man to do as he pleases with himself, and the product of his labor; while with others the same word may mean for some men to do as they please with other men, and their product of other men's labor. Here are two, not only different, but incompatible things, called by the same name—liberty. And it follows that each of the things is, by the respective parties, called by two different and incompatible names—liberty and tyranny."

—Abraham Lincoln, address at Sanitary Fair, Baltimore, Maryland, April 18, 1864

When the American economy plunged into a recession after 1893, African American civil rights began to seriously decline throughout the country. Employment discrimination flared, and southern states rapidly returned to repressive policies. The North was by no means innocent in this process.

Independent of economic factors was the failure of the Supreme Court to defend the principles of the Fourteenth and Fifteenth Amendments. In 1876, two decisions by the Supreme Court narrowed the scope of enforcement. Together with the end of Reconstruction and the withdrawal of federal troops, a climate was created that allowed violence to be used to suppress black voter turnout and fraud to undo the effect of lawfully cast votes.

Gerrymandering of election districts further reduced black voting strength and minimized the number of black elected officials. In the 1890s, former Confederate states began the process of amending their state constitutions and enacted a series of laws intended to reestablish and entrench white political supremacy.

Poll taxes, vouchers of "good character," and disqualification for "crimes of moral turpitude," were among disfranchising laws. Although these laws appeared to be color blind, they were specifically designed to disproportionately exclude black citizens from exercising voting rights. (Until 1965, federal laws did not challenge the authority of states and localities to establish their own voting requirements.)

Among other initiatives, northern and southern election reformers led a movement to purify the election process by requiring formal literacy tests. But these tests typically evaluated more than simple reading and writing, and were used to prevent blacks from voting. This was especially true in the southern states of Alabama, Georgia, Louisiana, Mississippi, Texas, and Virginia.

Literacy tests often required voter applicants to answer "general knowledge" questions. If black applicants answered just one question incorrectly, they were considered "unqualified" and could be refused the right to vote. Here are a few questions from an Alabama sample test used by civil rights workers to prepare applicants. (Answers appear at the end of this chapter.)

1. If a person charged with treason denies his guilt, how many persons must testify against him before he can be convicted?

2. If a bill is passed by Congress and the President refuses to sign it and does not send it back to Congress in session within the specified period of time, is the bill defeated or does it become law?

3. At what time of day on January 20 each four years does the term of the president of the United States end?

4. In what year did the Congress gain the right to prohibit the migration of persons to the United States?

(Source: Civil Rights Movement Veterans. For more information, visit www.crmvet.org.)

In Alabama, for instance, prospective voters might be required to complete a four-page registration form that requested detailed personal information, including a complete employment history, names and addresses of close associates, military history, and others. The Alabama forms also asked questions designed to uncover civil rights movement activity, such as, "Have you ever seen a copy of this registration application before receiving this copy today? If so, when and where?"

Alabama's literacy test typically consisted of three parts. In Part A, the applicant was asked to read aloud a selected excerpt from the Constitution, then respond orally to questions about the section. Then the applicant was usually required to write a section of the Constitution as it was dictated by a registar. Parts B and C consisted of a written examination. Part B required the applicant to provide written questions based on the Constitutional excerpt in Part A. Part C consisted of "general knowledge" questions about state and national government. Literacy tests were outlawed in 1965 with the passage of the Federal Voting Rights Act. To prevent applicants from studying for the tests, Alabama reportedly created 100 versions.

Discriminatory laws, violence, and exclusionary practices that were pervasive throughout society served to halt—then reverse—the progress African Americans had previously made. The previously overturned black codes were replaced by segregationist laws and practices—known as Jim Crow laws. These laws included restricted access of blacks to public areas, accommodations, water fountains, waiting rooms, courthouse exits and entrances, and theatres. Some jurisdictions set curfews for blacks and employment restrictions.

Under the Stovepipe

African American civil rights emerged as a major national political issue in the 1950s. In 1957, Congress enacted the first federal civil rights law since the Reconstruction period. The act established the U.S. Commission on Civil Rights and authorized the enforcement of voting rights by the U.S. Attorney General.

Additional legislation in 1960 further strengthened the act. Then in 1964, a sweeping Civil Rights Act outlawed racial discrimination in public facilities, and also by unions, employers, and voting registrars. Voting rights of blacks were bolstered in 1965.

As African Americans struggled for their rightful place in society as full citizens, even the U.S. Supreme Court offered little support. In 1896, that court ruled unconstitutional an 1875 act that prohibited discrimination by innkeepers, public transportation providers, and amusement venues. The justices decided that "separate but equal" facilities were sufficient.

Lincoln's Lasting Influence

No real progress to remove segregationist policies and discriminatory laws came until World War II. In actions reminiscent of those taken by black soldiers in the Civil War, African American leaders called for acknowledgement of contributions made by African American military personnel in World War II and protested the military's segregation practices. In 1948, President Harry Truman ordered desegregation of the U.S. military—a year after Jackie Robinson became the first African American to play major league baseball. Civil rights for African Americans then became a major political issue in the 1950s.

What turned the tide, though, was the Supreme Court's 1954 ruling in *Brown v. Board of Education*. That decision overturned the court's 1896 "separate but equal" ruling. In 1954, the Supreme Court held that segregation of public schools denied black children equal protection afforded them under the U.S. Constitution.

Along with other favorable court rulings subsequently issued, *Brown v. Board of Education* provided the momentum needed to renew the fight for African American civil rights. A great movement began that pushed for full equality throughout the country. (Discriminatory laws and racial segregation existed in many northern and western states, not just the southern states.)

As in the Civil War, the twentieth-century fight for African American civil rights did not end until after much debate, bloodshed, and suffering. But in 1965, a century after Lincoln had expressed the view that African Americans should be given the right to vote, Congress finally passed a measure to ensure enfranchisement. The Voting Rights Act of 1965 and subsequent amendments banned all the obstacles that had been intentionally put in place to prevent blacks from exercising this fundamental right.

One of the most memorable images from this era is of the multitude gathered for the March on Washington. That day, civil rights leader Martin Luther King Jr. addressed the crowd from the steps of the Lincoln Memorial. Behind King stood a statue of the man who had likely given King's ancestors great hope for the future: Abraham Lincoln.

Literacy Test Answers: (1) Two; (2) It becomes law unless Congress adjourns before the expiration of 10 days; (3) 12 noon; (4) 1808.

The Least You Need to Know

◆ Lincoln's successor, President Andrew Johnson, circumvented—or attempted to overturn—many initiatives that would have granted former slaves equality.

◆ Although laws were passed that gave African Americans citizenry rights, "black codes" and "Jim Crow laws" effectively defeated the intent of these measures.

◆ The turning point for the civil rights movement came with the Supreme Court's 1954 decision in *Brown v. Board of Education.*

◆ Lincoln's vision of black suffrage was not truly realized until a century after his death, with the passage of the Voting Rights Act of 1965.

Chapter 3

The Freedmen's Bureau

In This Chapter

- What Lincoln envisioned for freed slaves and how the Freedmen's Bureau fit into his overall plan

- How Lincoln's vision for the bureau and for reconstruction got derailed

- How the bureau and other reconstruction initiatives divided post-Civil War America

- What the bureau did—and did not—accomplish

Little more than a month before Lincoln's assassination, he signed legislation enabling the establishment of the Freedmen's Bureau. The bureau's broadly defined purpose was to provide aid to newly freed African Americans and impoverished Civil War refugees. Although the bureau itself was short-lived and never realized many of its key objectives, its impact on America was long term—but not for the reasons you might imagine.

A Head Start on a New Life

Abraham Lincoln began formulating plans for post-Civil War reconstruction as early as 1862. It's a good thing he thought ahead. The president needed a reconstruction policy in place in 1862 because Union troops were in the process of recapturing rebel territory in the Mississippi Valley.

Although abolitionists had long called for the end of slavery in America, few people truly anticipated the practical ramifications of emancipation. What would become of the four million captive African Americans after they'd been set free? How should the nation help newly freed blacks transition from slavery to freedom? Did they really need much help? And should their former masters be required to turn over their lands to these new citizens?

From the early days of the Civil War, the Union military's obligation to newly freed slaves was unclear. Union troops that advanced into the South commonly seized the property of Confederate loyalists, and in many cases, that property included African American slaves.

But Union commanders were confused about what to do with the slaves, generally considered wartime contraband. It was a sticky situation for all, especially because Washington hadn't issued any directives on the subject.

As federal troops advanced, slaves rushed Union lines and encampments to seek protection. They had no money, few possessions, and no place to go. Although they had eagerly awaited the arrival of their liberators, they soon found themselves completely dependent on the mercy and generosity of the federal government.

Most Union forces didn't have the resources needed to care for the African Americans. After all, the soldiers were busy fighting a war—and many of them had signed on to save the Constitution, not slaves.

So in the beginning, some African Americans were simply pronounced "freed" and sent on their way. Others were returned to their masters, whom some soldiers believed were in a better position to shelter and care for them. On a darker note, some Union soldiers went out of their way to return runaway slaves for the monetary reward.

Emancipation for Some, but Not All

The *Confiscation Act of 1862* somewhat clarified the matter for Union field commanders. Under the act, Confederates had 60 days from the time the law passed to surrender to the Union army. Those who did not comply faced the possible loss of their labor force; the act outlined a judicial process that would free their slaves.

Obviously, Confederates did not rush to surrender.

Lincoln Lingo

Congress approved the **Confiscation Act of 1862,** also known as the Second Confiscation Act, on July 16, 1862. It was the first measure to specifically call for emancipation of slaves in rebel states. The act declared that slaves residing in Washington, D.C., as well as slaves in the Confederacy who sought refuge behind Union lines, were to be set free.

However, emancipation under the act was at the convenience of the federal government—the act outlined a judicial process that would free slaves on a cumbersome, case-by-case basis, and the measure offered blacks no civil rights guarantees. A **freedman** was a slave made free.

In hindsight, it appears that Congress couldn't come to agreement about the Confiscation Act's practical effects on African Americans or the Union military effort. It might have been difficult for legislators to truly understand and empathize with the plight of slaves. After all, nineteenth-century beliefs and culture were very different from ours today.

But regardless of the reason, the fact remains: Congress gave *freedmen* no civil rights guarantees at all. In fact, some federal legislators wanted to ship newly freed slaves out of the country—to colonize them elsewhere—against their will. Only after much heated debate was a controversial provision added to the bill requiring consent before any freed black could be emigrated from the Union.

It's also important to know that the act's emancipation provisions applied only to those African American slaves residing in states in open rebellion. And according to the Confiscation Act's provisions, a border state slave (one living in Maryland, for example) who escaped a master loyal to the Union was to be immediately returned. Lincoln and members of Congress didn't want to risk alienating residents in border states, who—if sufficiently irritated—might choose to join the Confederacy.

America's Civil War Refugees

The net effect of the Confiscation Act was that thousands of African Americans already behind Union lines were suddenly freed—though still in many cases homeless and penniless refugees. At the time, no plan was in place to ensure their welfare. They were not given the rights of citizenship. And freedmen who, for whatever reason, didn't want to leave the plantation they served weren't given the option of staying.

As a practical matter, Union field commanders took on the job of devising refugee relief for the slaves they liberated. Often, that involved herding slaves into contraband camps where the Union army generally tried its best to provide food, shelter, and clothing.

Splitting Rails

For centuries, African American captives were viewed under the law as chattel to be bought and sold. Even when a captive's owner died, a slave's status was unchanged. Their master's heirs inherited them just like real estate and any other property that would be handed down. In nineteenth-century America, the status of African Americans as property was considered a permanent condition unless they purchased their own freedom or were voluntarily freed ("manumitted") by their owners. (Slaves did purchase their freedom and manumissions did occur. The numbers were small, but by comparison, more slaves gained freedom in this manner than by running away.)

But the relief fashioned by the military was often insensitive, if not inhumane. Conditions at many of the camps were deplorable. Many freed slaves died from disease as a result of the overcrowded conditions. Few received medical care. Understandably, after the war ended, some freedmen voluntarily returned to plantations to escape these injustices.

In some cases, freedmen were hired out to plantation owners loyal to the Union, where they were given low wages and poor living conditions. In Texas and other regions, freedmen were given the task of cultivating land assigned to them, to provide for their own food.

In northern cities, Freedman's Aid Societies were founded in an attempt to organize a relief effort and begin the transition process in a more humane fashion. Thousands of freed slaves fled to these metropolitan areas, where abolitionists and relief societies provided food, clothing, and education. Before long, these organizations sent volunteers, including teachers, to contraband camps to establish schools and provide medical care. Given the numbers of newly emancipated blacks, the challenges relief workers faced were enormous.

Lincoln was certainly aware of the situation, but he might not have clearly envisioned what would happen after he issued his Emancipation Proclamation in 1863. The issue of caring for newly freed African Americans—feeding, clothing, sheltering, educating, and assimilating them into American society—suddenly became a national crisis.

Under the Stovepipe

Emancipated slaves who fled to Union lines for safety as well as those who joined the Union army did so at great peril. When Confederates found these slaves along the way, they were conflicted about whether these African Americans should be treated as slaves in insurrection or taken as prisoners of war. The South was particularly outraged when the Union army began to recruit black soldiers in 1864.

On April 12, 1864, Confederate forces led by General Nathan B. Forrest prevailed in a battle against the Union's Fort Pillow in Tennessee. After the fort surrendered, Forrest followed Confederate Colonel W. P. Shingler's order prohibiting those in his command from taking black prisoners. That day, Forrest and his men massacred the more than 300 black men, women, and children found inside Fort Pillow.

Imagine four million refugees—the vast majority of whom were uneducated and without resources—suddenly flooding into the United States all at once. That's essentially what happened after Lincoln proclaimed that all American slaves were emancipated.

As you might expect, some freedmen headed north. "Freedman's villages," essentially refugee camps, sprang up overnight. Within the makeshift villages, blacks began to create their own societies. Most remained in the South.

Some freedmen joined the Union army after 1863; others wandered aimlessly, not knowing where to go or what to do. Given that so many African Americans had suffered at the hands of white people, many distrusted offers of help and friendship.

A few freed slaves decided to stay with the status quo and remained with their masters, continuing under their control. For many, it was the only life they knew.

Meanwhile, the Union war department set up the American Freedman's Inquiry Commission, to study methods of dealing with emancipated slaves. The commission ultimately determined that a temporary bureau or agency ought to be created to help ex-slaves become self-reliant as fast as possible.

Based on the commission's recommendation and with Lincoln's strong support, Congress passed a measure calling for the establishment of the Bureau of Refugees, Freedmen, and Abandoned Lands. Lincoln signed the legislation on March 4, 1865.

Lincoln Lingo

The **Freedmen's Bureau,** created with the support of Abraham Lincoln, was the first federal government welfare agency in United States history.

The new act gave the bureau broad jurisdiction: "Supervision and management of all abandoned lands, and the control of all subjects relating to refugees and freedmen from rebel states, or from any district within the territory embraced in the operations of the army." The bureau also had extensive authority to determine rules and regulations under which it would deliver services.

The bureau's mission was to serve "destitute and suffering refugees and freedmen and their wives and children." But because the organization's primary purpose was to provide aid to former slaves, the agency quickly became known simply as the *Freedmen's Bureau.*

The bureau was given the authority to distribute lands confiscated or abandoned during the war. Reminiscent of Union General William T. Sherman's *Special Field Order 15*, the Freedmen's Bureau was given authority to assign every male refugee and freedman up to 40 acres of tillable land upon which to start his new life. After three years of homesteading the land at a nominal rate, the tenant could then purchase the property from the government at 1860s prices.

Lincoln Lingo

As Union General William T. Sherman marched to the sea in Savannah, tens of thousands of freed blacks left inland plantations and followed Sherman's forces. Afterward, Sherman met with a group of black men to determine how to deal with all those people. Reverend Garrison Frazier told Sherman the best way they could take care of themselves was to have land. On January 16, 1865, Sherman responded by issuing **Special Field Order 15,** which set the expectation among freed slaves that each would receive "forty acres and a mule."

Sherman's order distributed abandoned plantations on Charleston's southern coast and the barrier islands of South Carolina and Georgia—40,000 freed blacks settled these lands. Freedmen established a separatist democracy at Georgia's St. Catherine's Island that included a constitution, congress, supreme court, schools, and armed militia. (Lincoln's successor, Andrew Johnson, would undo Sherman's good deed when he ordered that confiscated lands be returned to their former owners.)

Lincoln's Vision

By the time the measure creating the Freedmen's Bureau had been presented to the president for his signature, Lincoln's views on civil rights for blacks had evolved and matured. He was of the view that African Americans should be granted full equality, including suffrage rights. However, Lincoln never publicly advocated extending the right to vote to all African Americans—just those who had served in the military or had been educated.

He had ambitious plans for African Americans. But Lincoln knew he had to tread cautiously. He thought that acting too quickly might interfere with the goal of uniting the country. Establishment of the bureau was but one step in a process that would hopefully lead to the accomplishment of Lincoln's ultimate aims.

Many in government considered Lincoln's approach for restoration of the Union moderate and reasonable. But some members of Congress pushed for more rapid changes and considered the gradual process Lincoln favored far too modest.

Notes and Orations

"Some twelve thousand votes in the heretofore slave-state of Louisiana have sworn allegiance to the Union, assumed to be the rightful political power of the State, held elections, organized a State government, adopted a free-state constitution, giving the benefit of public schools equally to black and white, and empowering the Legislature to confer the elective franchise upon the colored man. Their Legislature has already voted to ratify the constitutional amendment recently passed by Congress, abolishing slavery throughout the nation ..."

"What has been said of Louisiana will apply generally to other States."

—Abraham Lincoln, Last Public Address, April 11, 1865

Lincoln believed the executive branch of government held responsibility and authority to direct the reconstruction effort in the South. Southern states had to comply with a list of required changes before they could be officially recognized as a state. (Virginia was called "Military District No. 1" until its reinstatement.)

Congress disagreed. And that disagreement—as well as the conflict between political parties—might have interfered with Congress' full support of the Freedmen's Bureau.

Sadly, Abraham Lincoln was assassinated a few weeks after he signed that important legislation. The task of establishing the bureau was left to Lincoln's successor, Andrew Johnson. At the time of Lincoln's death, the former senator from Tennessee had been vice president for just 40 days. He immediately became embroiled in a political fight for which he was ill prepared.

Establishment of the Freedmen's Bureau

In 1865, President Johnson chose Major General Oliver O. Howard to head up the new bureau as its commissioner. Howard, who was from Maine, was a West Point graduate and distinguished Civil War veteran who had fought at First Manassas (Battle of Bull Run). He had also led the XI Corps, Army of the Potomac, at Cemetery Hill in the Battle of Gettysburg.

A strong advocate of civil rights, Howard was a deeply religious man with great compassion for the African Americans he was to serve. But although he was a celebrated military leader, he was not a particularly good administrator.

Unfortunately, Congress didn't provide direct funding for the bureau. Howard reported to the secretary of war and had to wrestle funds from that already financially strapped agency. Because the bureau had the authority to sell former Confederate land that had been seized, money wasn't a big problem at first. However, financial funding would later prove difficult.

Under the Stovepipe

Howard University in Washington, D.C., was among the educational institutions that benefited from the Freedmen's Bureau's aid. This nationally renowned university is named for the bureau's commissioner, Oliver O. Howard, who also helped found the college in 1867 and served as the university's third president from 1869 to 1874.

Inadequate manpower was one of the biggest problems the bureau faced right from the beginning. Aside from providing for a commissioner, the legislation called for 10 assistant commissioners to be located in each state under reconstruction. Other positions were not named in the act, so Union army officers filled these jobs.

More challenging, though, was that the act that established the bureau set a strict time limit. Howard had only 12 months to completely change the lives of millions of former slaves and others who had been displaced and impoverished by the war.

Controversy Halts Progress

Southern states viewed the bureau and its work as a huge irritant: a governmental body that stirred up trouble for no good reason. Former Confederate states wanted to return to the old ways. Agents who worked for Howard weren't particularly well trained, and owing to southern opposition, had a difficult time carrying out their mission. Before the bureau could really make much of a mark, time ran out.

Although Tennessee native Andrew Johnson had remained loyal to the Union throughout the Civil War, he shared the same attitudes about race that his fellow southerners held. His sympathy for the South's position on African Americans, as well as the predicament former rebel states now faced, clouded his judgment as president.

Johnson stunned many members of Congress when he reduced the Union's readmission requirements for southern states. The new president also restored lands to southerners whom he had pardoned. That act essentially crippled the bureau's primary funding source and virtually eliminated the land grants promised to freedmen in legislation that established the bureau. No more 40 acres and a mule.

Johnson further antagonized members of Congress—Radical Republicans, in particular—when he voiced his view that *Reconstruction* was unnecessary because the former Confederate states had never really left the Union.

Lincoln Lingo

Reconstruction is the period in United States history that spanned from 1863, as the Union openly dealt with the challenges of managing conquered southern territory, to the final withdrawal of Union troops from the South in 1877. The term is also used to describe the attempt made during this time period to solve social, economic, and political problems that rose from the readmission of the 11 states that had seceded from the Union.

When Howard's first 12 months were spent, Radical Republicans in Congress called for passage of a bill that would extend the bureau's existence and provide the funding it needed. The measure passed both houses. Johnson vetoed the bill in February 1866. He also vetoed a Civil Rights Act proposed by Congress that would have granted blacks full citizenship.

So what was Johnson thinking? Well, you might recall that one of the issues underlying the Civil War was a debate over states' rights. Johnson was strongly against federal government interference. Southern states believed that the bureau's work constituted unnecessary meddling in their affairs—and Johnson agreed.

As you might also remember, these and other actions eventually angered so many people that the United States House of Representatives brought impeachment charges against President Johnson. At his trial in 1868, only one vote prevented him from conviction and removal from office.

Under the Stovepipe

One of the greatest accomplishments of the Freedmen's Bureau was the establishment of more than 1,000 schools for African Americans. In addition, the bureau spent nearly a half million dollars to establish training schools for black teachers. All major black colleges and technical institutes in America were either built by or received supplemental financial support from the Freedmen's Bureau.

Johnson's actions and the controversy he triggered further endangered the Freedmen's Bureau and its life span—as well as its vital work.

Congress passed another bill to extend the bureau and increase its powers a few months later. Predictably, Johnson vetoed that measure, too. However, Congress overrode Johnson's second veto on July 16, 1866, and the bureau was back in business.

Among other provisions, the new law authorized additional assistant commissioners, the sale of land to freedmen at nominal terms, and land grants for African American schools to be established in the South.

A Fresh Start for Everyone?

The failures of the Freedmen's Bureau are more legendary than its great accomplishments. But there are good reasons why the bureau never lived up to the potential Lincoln envisioned. Foremost among these is the fact that when Lincoln died, the course of history was altered.

In what could be termed its second life, the Freedmen's Bureau continued to be mired in controversy and suffered from a lack of funding. What's more, Howard's team—which included about 900 agents, most of them military—became known as a corrupt and inefficient organization.

Some of that reputation could have resulted from southern propaganda. During Reconstruction, strife between the North and South was nearly as contentious as during the Civil War. As southerners awoke to the realities of war's aftermath, they became increasingly agitated and resentful. That might have begun when whites, who would not sign an oath of alliance to the Union, were disenfranchised from the vote—and then watched as their former slaves were given that same right for the first time.

Having been overcome by the Union, the focus of southern anger shifted. In post-Civil War time, blacks and anyone who helped them had become the new enemy. And that group especially included the Freedmen's Bureau.

Under the Stovepipe

Abraham Lincoln's successor, President Andrew Johnson, returned most of the land confiscated or abandoned during the war—a total of nearly one million acres. His decision resulted in lost financial resources for the Freedmen's Bureau. But more importantly, freedmen and refugees didn't receive the land they'd been promised. Only about 2,000 freedmen in South Carolina and another 1,500 or so in Georgia actually received land assignments. That's less than one percent of the four million ex-slaves that populated the South.

Many former slaveholders vigorously fought bureau initiatives that were intended to bring a free labor economy to the South. They were of a mind to perpetuate slavery by changing its form and calling it by a different name: sharecropping.

Without slaves to produce an income, former slaveholders were cash poor and land rich. Conversely, former slaves had no land and no place to live. So freedmen and former slaveholders negotiated a new relationship. At first, sharecropping sounded like a good deal: Landowners lent African Americans a plot of land to work in return for a share of the crops produced. No money was exchanged. Former slaves had the freedom to work independently and frequently got a sizeable share of the crop.

But in addition to farming the land, sharecroppers also had to come up with the cash to buy seed, fertilizers, and provisions to live on until the crop was grown and harvested. To raise the funds needed, sharecroppers borrowed against their share. When the crops were harvested, the loans *and* the crop shares came due, leaving many sharecroppers in debt even after the harvest. Most blacks (as well as poor whites who also sharecropped) ended up in an endless cycle of debt.

For its part, the bureau adjudicated labor disputes and tried to help blacks negotiate fair contracts. Even so, the sharecropping system established by white southerners ultimately became almost as oppressive as slavery.

And finally, blacks who sought to establish lives as free citizens or those who asserted their new civil rights became targets of southern resentment. It was during this time that secret terrorist organizations, such as the Ku Klux Klan, were established.

After years of battling against post-Civil War backlash, the bureau was discontinued in 1869, though its school operations continued until 1872. Congress terminated the organization in response to ongoing hostility and political pressure exerted by white southerners.

By 1877, tactics that included intimidation, dishonesty, and violence returned control of southern state governments to conservatives. However, such tactics were not unique to that region. You'll find the rest of that story in Chapter 12 of this book.

Suffice it say, Lincoln would have been outraged by what occurred. He undoubtedly would have chosen a far different course of action than Johnson took.

Bureau Wins and Losses

Although the bureau's failures became legendary, many of its finest accomplishments live on as part of Lincoln's American legacy.

The 900 bureau officials who were scattered from Washington to Texas provided direct and indirect services to millions of freedmen and refugees. By 1869, more than a half million freedmen and refugees had been treated by bureau physicians and surgeons—and more than 60 new medical facilities had been established.

By 1872, more than a million freedmen had received direct medical assistance. In the first 50 months of operation, the bureau distributed about 21 million free rations—at a rate of 30,000 per day.

By far, the great advances made by the Freedmen's Bureau related to education—and it is in this area that Lincoln would likely be proud. The bureau worked with northern relief societies and local communities to expand educational opportunities to newly emancipated African Americans. Bureau agents helped establish public school systems throughout the South.

Under the Stovepipe

Historically, black colleges in the United States owe their beginnings to the Freedmen's Bureau. In virtually every case, the bureau either founded and staffed these institutions or provided financial support that ensured their survival. The bureau spent nearly a half million dollars to establish technical institutions whose purpose was to train black teachers.

By 1869, more than 3,000 new schools had been established to serve more than 150,000 students. In addition, the bureau served as a catalyst for dozens of new private schools that also served black community members.

In addition, the bureau reorganized and managed judicial systems, revised court procedures to improve fairness, and established improved taxation methods. Agents launched initiatives that served as the beginnings of a free labor system in the South. And even in the face of extreme controversy, strife, and southern resistance, the rights of former slaves increased.

Aside from these other benefits, many of the bureau's programs gave newly freed slaves educational advantages and an understanding of the rights they were entitled to under the Constitution. They (and their descendents) would put that knowledge and experience to good use as the struggle for equality continued.

Under the Stovepipe

Post-Civil War era records that document the federal government's assistance to newly freed slaves—some of the most valuable records of the black experience in the second half of the 1800s—are now being preserved on microfilm by the National Archives and Records Administration.

The project was made possible by congressional passage of the Freedmen's Bureau Preservation Act of 2000, which was signed by President William J. Clinton on November 6, 2000. The act authorized the preservation of more than 1,000 linear feet of field office records of the Freedmen's Bureau, and will make these records more accessible to the public.

The Least You Need to Know

- ◆ Abraham Lincoln signed into law legislation enabling the creation of the Freedmen's Bureau.

- ◆ The bureau became operational under Lincoln's successor, President Andrew Johnson.

- ◆ Post-Civil War backlash, lack of financial support, and internal problems interfered with the bureau's effectiveness and hastened its demise.

- ◆ Despite legendary failures, the bureau also succeeded in many ways—most notably in providing significant educational opportunities for African Americans.

Part 5

Lincoln's Economic Development Legacy

The Civil War brought dramatic changes in American taxation and government financing—largely because of decisions made by our sixteenth president. Lincoln faced the challenge of funding an expensive Union war effort while ensuring the North's economic viability and growth. Confederate President Jefferson Davis faced similar problems, but the two leaders took markedly different approaches.

Lincoln enacted a number of domestic policies that still benefit us today. Among the innovations established during Lincoln's administration is the national banking system—forerunner to the Federal Reserve. The Homestead Act triggered western expansion and encouraged all Americans to become landowners. Transportation legislation also fueled economic growth, even as costly civil war raged.

This part explores Lincoln's wartime policies in the context of his economic legacy—what has become the foundation for America's enviable financial strength.

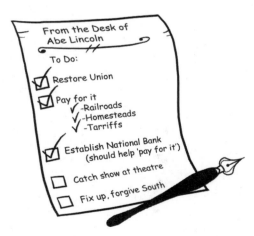

Chapter 14

The Homestead Act

In This Chapter

- ◆ How the Homestead Act figured into Abraham Lincoln's Civil War policies
- ◆ What the Homestead Act offered settlers—and how they fulfilled the requirements for free land
- ◆ Why the Homestead Act ensured economic stability and personal wealth for millions of Americans
- ◆ How Lincoln's vision has enabled the American Dream to be realized for more than a century

Westward Ho!

In 1784, George Washington observed, "The spirit for *emigration* is great." Indeed, America's colonists were brave, adventurous souls who left their homelands to establish new lives in America. Later, many of their descendants (as well as new European immigrants) said goodbye to familiar surroundings in the East and eagerly ventured westward, once again heading into the vast unknown.

Lincoln Lingo

Emigration (from the Latin word *emigrare*, which means "to move") means moving *from* one's country or region to settle elsewhere. **Immigration** means moving *to* a place. **Migration** means the movement of a large group *to* a place.

Many of their descendants continued this wanderlust in the nineteenth century, when many Americans (as well as European *immigrants*) said goodbye to familiar surroundings in the East and eagerly ventured westward into the great unknown. The driving force behind this great *migration* was the hope of a better life at journey's end. Land and its promised riches drew these hardy settlers as strongly as their colonist ancestors.

What to Do with All That Land?

As the United States expanded and acquired land across the continent, the prospects for emigration grew, too. For those who had established their roots in the comparatively crowded confines of the East, the open spaces and opportunities of the western frontier must have seemed limitless.

The 1830s saw designation of much of America's prairie land as Indian Territory, and early settlers heading west accordingly passed over these lands.

After a serious economic recession in 1837, U.S. workers and labor organizations in the North urged lawmakers to open up public domain in the West. They and land reform advocates viewed such a move as a way for workers to escape an unstable and increasingly oppressive industrial society in the East. "The right to labor and the right to soil" became the rallying cry of jobless workers.

Virtually every federal lawmaker back then agreed that western expansion was needed for economic reasons. But the western territories also became a crucible for the slavery issue and the question of whether these new territories would be slave or free became an overriding concern for both sides of the debate. Officials couldn't decide how to encourage large groups of people to immigrate to the West without angering special interests. When the idea of distributing publicly owned lands to settlers was introduced, a raging debate ensued in Congress that continued for more than two decades.

Numerous initiatives had been attempted, but none triggered the influx of people needed to establish U.S. presence in the western territories. Some legislators were convinced that the only way to compel folks to move westward was to give public land away, so they introduced a bill to do just that. Over the years, several versions of the Homestead Act were introduced, but most never made it off the floor of Congress.

Businessmen in the Northeast vehemently opposed legislation that provided free land to settlers. They believed it was bad for business. Industrialists in particular feared that the proposed giveaway would trigger massive emigration from the industrial East by members of the labor class. The loss of so many workers, they speculated, would drive up labor costs and dramatically reduce profits. Others were convinced that property values—and revenue derived from real estate holdings and sales—would plummet if a homestead measure passed.

Southern plantation owners worried the measure would interfere with their slave-based economy, too, by weakening northern demand for raw materials. Later, as the abolitionist movement strengthened, southern slaveholders also realized that western homesteading would hinder their ability to expand their business interests and might even instigate an end to slavery. If territories were admitted to the Union as free states, it could tip the balance of American political power (especially in the Senate) away from slavery—to the South's disadvantage.

Gradually, federal legislators from the North were able to garner enough support for compromise versions of the Homestead Act. Three of these passed the House of Representatives in 1852, 1854, and 1859—only to be rejected by the Senate.

Another attempt was made in 1860, just before Lincoln took office. However, interest groups remained staunchly opposed to homesteading, and prevailed. President James Buchanan vetoed the bill.

Efforts to revive the act seemed doomed, especially in light of the South's growing concerns about the North's aims to end slavery. That is, until the Civil War began.

While the Cat's Away ...

Abraham Lincoln had been in office just a few months when the 37th Congress convened on July 1, 1861. The Union was reeling from the fall of Fort Sumter, the first battles of the Civil War, and most recently, the secession of three more states: Tennessee, North Carolina, and Arkansas.

Senators and congressmen arrived in Washington that summer to see an unfinished Capitol building and an armed encampment protecting the city. In the time that had passed since Lincoln's inauguration, he had suspended a few constitutional rights. The nation was in an uproar.

So which pressing matters do you think the U.S. House and Senate took up first?

Well, in this most dire time, the United States Congress decided to address three crucial domestic issues: the creation of land grant colleges, the transcontinental railroad, and homesteading.

Surprised? Well, the timing couldn't have been better. By July 1861, 11 southern states had seceded and withdrawn their representatives from Congress. With the primary opposition out of the picture, it was the perfect time for the president and his allies in Congress to hammer out and pass legislation that addressed all three acts.

That meant the Homestead Act was back on the table. And Lincoln and the 37th Congress had only to negotiate among friends.

1,400 Words That Opened Up the West

Even in the absence of southern representatives, passing the Homestead Act wasn't a done deal. One of the chief opponents to the Homestead Act was Senator Justin Morrill, a Vermont Republican who was far more interested in the land grant college proposal he sponsored than the Homestead Act. Morrill argued that the Homestead Act would give away government-owned land better suited for use by land grant colleges.

He thought the government was giving away land needed to shore up the nation's flagging credit, while his proposed land grant college bill would increase the land's value. But his colleagues convinced him that the country needed settlers in the West as well as colleges. (Morrill's bill ultimately passed Congress, perhaps with a *quid pro quo* negotiated.)

The Homestead Act—"To Secure Homesteads to Actual Settlers on the Public Domain"—was finally crafted and passed by Congress on May 20, 1862. Lincoln signed the measure that day and it took effect on January 1, 1863, the same day he issued the Emancipation Proclamation.

After 20 years of congressional bickering, it's unbelievable that the Homestead Act consisted of only about 1,400 words. Just imagine how lengthy the same measure might have been in the hands of today's legislators!

The offer made to prospective settlers was simple: One only had to stake a claim, submit an application at a land office, and pay a $10 filing fee and $2 commission fee to the land agent. In return, the homesteader received a grant of 160 acres of virtually untouched, publicly owned land in the West.

But homesteaders had to meet a few pesky requirements.

The Fine Print

After the equivalent of a title search was completed, the homesteader was given a temporary claim to the land—and was required to reside on the property continuously for a period of five years. During that span, the homesteader was required to "improve" the land. At a minimum, that meant constructing a 12-by-14 residential dwelling, soil cultivation, and crop production. Absentee landlords need not apply!

Applicants were also required to attest that they did not already own more than 320 acres of land within the United States. Folks who had previously abandoned other land in the same state or territory were ineligible.

The residency requirements and the limitations on land ownership virtually eliminated land-development companies and big-time speculators from participating in the program. Beyond that, however, the beauty of the program was its extremely broad eligibility standards.

There were no restrictions regarding gender, race, or financial status—except that applicants had to possess the means to pay the meager filing fees required. For America's labor class, who couldn't afford to buy land in the East and likely saw no way to do so in the future, the Homestead Act offered a once-in-a-lifetime opportunity. Finally, workers could become property owners.

What's more, the Homestead Act opened up land ownership to blacks and women. Any single person or head of household who was at least 21 years of age was eligible for the program. All applicants had to be citizens of the United States or profess intent to become one soon, and they had to be loyal to the Union. Anyone who had ever taken up arms against the Union was barred from the program. (Confederates were absolutely excluded.)

Civil War veterans who were honorably discharged would be able to deduct from the five-year residency requirement one year for every year served in the Union army. Widows and children of fallen Union soldiers also got a break on the residency requirements. These provisions made the Homestead Act a powerful recruitment tool.

After an applicant had established the homestead and fulfilled the five-year residency and other requirements, the federal government transferred the land's title to the homesteader—free and clear. From that day forward, the homesteader owned the property and its improvements forever.

Simple as the conditions seemed, some folks resorted to trickery and bribery rather than meet those requirements. Some claimants even took advantage of the legal loophole created when authors of the act failed to define whether the 12-by-14 dwelling size meant inches or feet! However, it's believed that the vast majority of homesteaders were honest, hardworking people who earned every square inch and foot of their land.

Home Sweet Home

After a homesteader arrived at the claimed property, one of the first tasks was construction of a residential shelter. Under the Homestead Act, the term dwelling was rather generously applied to all manner of construction. That was probably a good thing, too, because most homesteaders had little to no money when they started out.

Some of these new settlers were fortunate enough to be granted forested land. They had the raw materials to build sturdy log cabins that most anyone of the era would have been proud to own.

However, creativity was required for those who settled the prairie, where trees were scarce. The most consistently available construction material on the American prairie was, of course, dirt and grass, or sod. (The few scarce trees were used for more important purposes, such as construction of wagons, tools, and other necessities.)

Homesteaders who settled the Plains had no choice but to build houses made of sod. What's a sod house look like? Picture landscaping sod piled together to form the sides and roof of a hut with the roots intact, Buffalo grass swaying in the near-constant wind. Yep, that's how the American dream of home ownership began.

Sod homes were inexpensive and environmentally friendly—not that conservation was a top concern at that time! The thick dirt provided relatively good insulation, too. But living inside a sod home was just plain icky. Spiders and other insects were the settlers' frequent roommates. Rain caused lots of problems. In addition to leaks, storms would sometimes cause snakes and other critters that lived in the grass overhead to drop into the hut. And just imagine watching the walls of your home crumble into a muddy mess after a pounding rain. The little sod huts were no match for hailstorms, tornadoes, or prairie fires. And they didn't provide much protection against blizzards or the occasional Indian attack. On the plus side, repairs could be made cheaply and quickly—there was always more sod!

Notes and Orations _____

My name is Frank Bolar—an old bach'lor I am,
I'm keeping old batch on an elegant plan,
You'll find me out West in the County of Lane,
Starving to death on my government claim.

My house it is built of the national soil;
The walls are erected according to Hoyle;
The roof has no pitch but is level and plane,
And I never get wet 'til it happens to rain.

Then Hurrah for Lane County, the land of the free,
The home of the bedbug, mosquito, and flea;
I'll sing loud her praises and boast of her fame,
While starvin' to death on my government claim.

—Excerpt from a well-known nineteenth-century American folk song written about the difficulties of life on a government claim in Lane County, Kansas

Grow Food or Starve

Like the pilgrims who colonized America and the pioneers who settled the upper Midwest in the early 1800s, homesteaders needed to establish a productive farm—and they had to be quick about it or they'd starve to death. Many brought horses that could pull plows, but the work was just as backbreaking as it was for Lincoln in his youth.

Erratic and sometimes violent weather worked against homesteaders. Pounding rain tore up tender seedlings. Drought and summer heat withered strong, maturing crops. Lightning often set off blazes that consumed crops, undoing a homesteader's entire effort.

In the East, 160 acres would support a fine farming operation, but that wasn't the case in the western territories. In many instances, original homesteaders found that 160 acres of dry prairie and scarce natural vegetation wouldn't sustain much of anything. What the harsh climate and weather didn't kill off, the insects ate!

Under the Stovepipe _____

Abraham Lincoln's support of the Homestead Act benefited America by enabling many people to fulfill their dreams. For instance, the daughter of one homesteader was so moved by her experience on the prairie that she decided to share her story with the world.

Author Laura Ingalls Wilder wrote a series of books about growing up on homesteads in Kansas, Minnesota, the Dakota Territory, and Wisconsin. The well-known television series _Little House on the Prairie_ was inspired by Wilder's books, which accurately describe what life was like in that harsh environment.

As if all those challenges weren't enough, homesteaders also had to contend with constant danger and the loneliness wrought by living in virtual isolation. With relatives, friends, and the rest of civilization so far way, the endurance test required of settlers was an emotional as well as physical one.

Under the Stovepipe _____

A diverse group of Americans took advantage of the opportunity offered by the Homestead Act. Here are just a few of the people who personally gained—and from whom America benefited—as a result of Lincoln's legacy.

George Washington Carver, homesteader—inventor and educator

Virgil Earp, homesteader—Wells-Fargo shotgun guard, deputy marshal, and brother of Wyatt Earp

Walter Knott, homesteader—farmer, agricultural entrepreneur, restauranteur, and founder of Knott's Berry Farm

William McKnight, son of homesteaders—businessman, industrialist, and head of 3M Corporation

Forest Ray Moulton, son of homesteaders—astronomer and mathematician

Willa Cather, daughter of homesteaders—Pulitzer Prize-winning author

Thomas Kleppe, son of homesteaders—mayor, congressman, and secretary of the interior

Jeannette Rankin, daughter of homesteaders—first woman elected to Congress and a peace advocate

Steve Owen, son of homesteaders—All-Pro football player and coach of the New York Giants

Jewel Kilcher, granddaughter of homesteaders—singer, author, and actress

All in all, life for homesteaders was cruel, requiring extreme fortitude, resilience, and incredible luck. Despite the allure of free land, some settlers simply called it quits. They either returned to their homeland or moved on to another western state to begin homesteading a new claim.

Others, of course, hung on and completed the requirements. After five years of toil and hardship, the homesteader was required to find two friends or neighbors willing to sign a "proof" document attesting to the homesteader's improvements and continuous five-year residency. After this document was submitted, along with another whopping $6 fee, the homesteader was given a permanent, free-and-clear patent (another term for land title) to their land. This process was known as *proving up*.

The patents homesteaders received were proudly displayed in their dwelling, attesting to five years of grueling work. They were truly fit survivors.

The American Way

The Homestead Act of 1862 had a dramatic impact on the nation's demographics. Prior to the westward expansion sparked by the act, the nation's population was heavily centered along the eastern seaboard. Homesteaders spurred a prolonged period of economic development, railway and transportation expansion, and a dramatic increase in the nation's agricultural interests.

Homesteaders who held out long enough were rewarded with opportunities for wealth and happiness. New railroads eventually brought easy transportation to western settlers, and access to much-needed provisions such as barbed-wire fencing, weapons, and even houses that could be ordered from a catalog.

Leading the group of westward immigrants were people such as Daniel Freeman, who the U.S. Department of the Interior recognizes as the first person to take advantage of the Homestead Act. Freeman, a Union army scout on furlough, was scheduled to depart Gage County, Nebraska Territory, on January 1, 1863, to report for duty in St. Louis. At a New Year's Eve party the night before, Freeman convinced a local clerk to open the land office just after midnight so he could file his claim.

At the land office in Brownville, Nebraska, 10 minutes into the new year (the day the Homestead Act went into effect), Freeman submitted his claim for 160 acres of land along Cub Creek at Beatrice, Nebraska, near the Kansas border. He was among the more than 400 people who filed claims that first day. You can see Freeman's homestead application, his proof document, and his certificate of eligibility online at the National Archives website.

It's not clear whether Freeman remained in Nebraska or went on to St. Louis to serve his army stint. But according to his 1868 "proof," Freeman constructed an 11-by-20-foot, one-story home that was partially built of logs and featured two windows and two doors, a shingle roof, and board flooring. His *affiant* went on to comment that Freeman's was "a comfortable house to live in." Freeman had also made other permanent improvements since staking his claim in 1863. He'd built a stable, a sheep shed, a corn crib measuring 100 feet in length, and had planted 40 apple trees and about 400 peach trees.

Lincoln Lingo

Affiant is a legal term used to describe a person who swears under oath as to the truth of certain facts, usually in the form of a written legal document known as an affidavit.

Today, the site of Freeman's homestead is the home of the Homestead National Monument of America, operated by the National Park Service.

Many other pioneers followed in Freeman's footsteps and populated the land. Towns and schools sprang up to serve the new residents, and the vast territories eventually become states in the Union.

Opportunity for All

A significant legacy of the Homestead Act was its lasting impact on personal freedom and property rights. In 1862, when the Homestead Act went into effect, the concept of a woman (except widows) or African American owning property was uncommon—and in some cases prohibited by law.

For centuries, property ownership had been restricted to white males, and possession of large tracts of land was typically reserved for those of wealth. The social, economic, and political advantages that came with owning property were simply not accessible to members of the industrial working class or to most people of color.

Homesteading gave former slaves, who had once been considered property themselves, the opportunity to own their own spread and reap the rewards of their hard work. Single women (even single moms) could prove their mettle as homesteaders and establish places of their own. Immigrants were given the chance to begin life in a land where possibilities were limitless.

No wonder two million people applied for these land grants. What may be more surprising is that the Homestead Act remained in effect until 1986. (Modern claims were made in Alaska.)

> **Under the Stovepipe**
>
> Between 1862 and 1986, more than two million people applied for and received patents for land under the provisions of the Homestead Act. Of those two million people, about 783,000 (roughly 40 percent) were successful in meeting all the government's requirements to earn title to their property. Somewhere between 8 and 10 percent of the land in the United States was settled under the Homestead Act.

The Last Homesteader

Although passage of the Federal Land Policy and Management Act of 1976 repealed the Homestead Act in the 48 contiguous states, the measure granted a 10-year extension to claims in Alaska. The last person to take advantage of the Homestead Act's provisions was Kenneth Deardorff.

The challenges that last American homesteader faced weren't all that different from what his nineteenth-century counterparts endured. Deardorff, a young Vietnam veteran and native Californian, filed a homestead claim on 80 acres of land on the Stony River in the southwestern Alaskan wilderness in 1974. Over the next 10 years, he and his family lived on and worked the land—virtually isolated from civilization.

Battling temperatures that dipped as low as 65 degrees below zero, Deardorff constructed his home and other buildings from white spruce trees that grew on the property. To feed his family, he farmed, fished for salmon, and hunted moose and other wild game.

Deardorff met homestead requirements in 1979. He received title to his claimed land in 1988, thus signaling the end of an extraordinary era.

Today, Lincoln's legacy lives on through the descendents of extraordinary people who sought a fresh start in the West—and in the American ideal of home ownership.

The Least You Need to Know

♦ Virtually anyone 21 years or older and the head of a household was eligible to obtain almost free land from the government.

♦ Many people who would never have otherwise owned property benefited from the Homestead Act.

♦ The Homestead Act spurred westward emigration and a shifting of the nation's population center.

◆ The need for workers on the transcontinental railroad and elsewhere generated an increase in foreign immigration.

◆ The Homestead Act likely promoted racial and gender equality.

Chapter 15

Taxation and National Banking Systems

In This Chapter

- ◆ Why most people distrusted paper money before the Civil War era
- ◆ What motivated Lincoln to sign legislation that established federal currency
- ◆ How the creation of a network of national banks aided the war effort
- ◆ How the national banking system was established and why
- ◆ How the graduated income tax originated and deductions for extraordinary expenses

When the Lincoln one-cent coin was introduced in 1909, it marked the first time a portrait had ever appeared on a United States coin. But Abraham Lincoln's ties to money and our banking system go much deeper than that honor.

As president, Lincoln stepped up to the significant challenge of Civil War financing and ensuring the stability of the country's monetary system. He signed into law measures that established federal currency and the creation of a network of national banks, the forerunner to the Federal Reserve

System. Many innovations of the Lincoln administration remain today—including the concept of a graduated income tax!

Financing America's Civil War

Certainly at the start of the Civil War, the Lincoln administration believed it could quickly quell the southern rebellion and get back to business. In fact, the very idea of a long, protracted war didn't even occur to most Washingtonians in 1861.

To illustrate the point, consider that Washington politicians and socialites turned out to watch the first major battle of the Civil War, the Battle of Bull Run (First Manassas), armed with picnic baskets. The naïve "audience" approached the event as an opportunity for a pleasant lunch in the countryside, an afternoon's idle entertainment! Imagine their surprise when Confederates overwhelmed ill-prepared Union forces and captured a senator among the picnickers.

Similarly, the question of how to finance the Civil War effort didn't become an issue until folks realized its seriousness and possible long-term nature. What's more, the war didn't only involve combatants. Private property was destroyed; at times the ravages of battle engulfed entire towns.

Warfare required not only funding for troops, but also finding entirely new approaches to government financing and economics. Financial survival hinged on innovation. But addressing the issue also required leaders on both sides to review history.

Notes and Orations

Chicago, September 13, 1857

Dear Jesse K.

Several persons here keep teasing me about you and the Bank commissioners not enforcing the banking laws. In my stupidity, I do not believe I quite understand what the ground of complaint is; but it appears to me to be this; that the stocks which the banks have on deposite [sic] have depreciated; that in such case, it is your duty to make the banks deposite [sic] additional stocks, or, in default, wind them up; and that you do not perform this duty. Now how is this? Write me plainly enough to make me understand; and write soon too, for I am annoyed about it a good deal.

Your friend as ever,
A. Lincoln.

Source: *The Collected Works of Abraham Lincoln* by Roy P. Basler, courtesy of the Abraham Lincoln Association.

"Not Worth a Continental"

Early in America's history, money's value was measured by its material worth. For instance, coins were equal to the value of the material from which they were cast. But when coins became scarce, as in the early colonial days, the lack of money restricted trade.

The Massachusetts Bay Colony issued the first paper money in 1690, in response to this financial crisis. In some ways, the paper could be considered more of a promissory note, which could be exchanged for gold or silver when those precious metals were available. However, in practice it didn't work that way. Because not everyone accepted the paper, its value quickly depreciated.

Since that time, changes in our monetary system have almost always been triggered by national crises. To fund the Revolutionary War, Congress authorized paper currency notes with no backing in silver or gold reserves. The notes were given in anticipation of future tax revenues that would be generated after the war had ended—and only if the colonies gained independence from Great Britain.

The newly formed American Congress authorized the first federal paper money in 1775 to help fund the Revolutionary War. Some of the currency was printed from plates engraved by Paul Revere. Known as Continentals, the paper featured pictures of colonial minutemen and bore the words "The United Colonies." Without solid backing, Continentals soon became worthless. Even George Washington grumbled about the currency and its utter lack of value.

A new form of paper money was created after the Declaration of Independence was signed. Like the Continental, the money's worth was derived from its purchasing power rather than its intrinsic value. To help add credibility this time, well-known men of the era put their signatures on the new money in hopes of wide public acceptance.

But given the experience with Continentals, even the signatures of Revolutionary War heroes didn't convince people that the paper held any worth. Coins remained the money of choice.

Raising Funds for the Civil War

In 1861, the nation faced another financial crisis instigated by war. The Confederacy approached financing the war with loans and limited taxation. The Union, under Lincoln's leadership, took more innovative approaches.

First of all, the North was industry-based and that helped the overall economy. But perhaps even more important was that the Union already had an established Treasury department.

One of the first steps Lincoln and Congress took to finance the war effort was to pass the Revenue Act of 1861. The act reinstated excise taxes on certain purchases and also, for the first time, instituted a tax on corporate and personal income. Previously, the country had relied on excise taxes and customs duties to support government expenses.

The 1861 system wasn't exactly fair to lower-income Americans; it treated those of modest means the same as the wealthy. Republicans set out to level the field by recommending a system that more accurately reflected a taxpayer's ability to pay.

On July 1, 1862, Lincoln signed into law sweeping tax legislation that expanded excise taxes and reformed corporate and personal income tax provisions that were set in place in 1861. Tax was collected on a wide variety of items, particularly those considered luxuries. These included playing cards, whiskey, pianos, billiard tables, and ships. Surprisingly, though, the measure also taxed leather, gunpowder, certain medicines, and telegrams.

Republicans prevailed on the issue of making personal income tax fair for all citizens. Republican Justin Morrill of Vermont, chairman of the House Ways and Means Subcommittee, was the chief architect of the tax reform legislation. The 1862 Revenue Act, as signed into law by Abraham Lincoln, allowed for a two-tier, graduated tax rate based on income level. Those earning $10,000 or less paid a 3 percent tax rate, while those who earned income above that amount were taxed at 5 percent. A standard deduction was added, exempting the first $600 in earnings from taxation. Other deductions were also offered to taxpayers.

Congress tinkered with the tax rates twice more in 1864, when the Union's wartime debt rose to a stunning rate of about $2 million a day. Income taxes for citizens rose, too. Income of between $600 and $5,000 was taxed at 5 percent; income between $5,000 and $10,000 was taxed at 7.5 percent, and income of more than $10,000 was taxed at a maximum rate of 10 percent. The new tax rates outraged many people.

As if that weren't enough, Congress also passed an emergency tax bill later in 1864 that extracted an additional whopping 5 percent of all income of more than $600. For Union taxpayers, 1864 wasn't a very good year!

Under the Stovepipe

The 1862 tax measures signed by Abraham Lincoln included wide-ranging reforms to the 1861 personal income tax system. Today's tax codes reflect many of the innovative features of the tax laws Lincoln enacted in 1862. Some of these include the following:

- ◆ Personal income tax "withheld at the source" by employers, to ensure timely collection
- ◆ A two-tiered tax rate structure that allowed for a person's ability to pay, and established percentages based on certain levels of income earned
- ◆ A standard deduction for all taxpayers
- ◆ Other deductions could be taken to offset taxes, including extraordinary losses, other taxes paid, and rental housing costs
- ◆ Established the Bureau of Internal Revenue, forerunner to the IRS

The Legal Tender Act

Even with changes in taxation, the Union still faced mounting debt and a shortage of money in circulation. Sound familiar? These were the same problems that plagued Revolutionary War-era colonists nearly a century before.

Many in Lincoln's administration called for the issuance of paper money, and in 1861 Lincoln authorized the creation of *demand notes*. The notes were like today's checks, and were used to transfer money. But Secretary of the Treasury Salmon Chase was among many who distrusted the idea, given what had happened during the American Revolution.

Chase greatly preferred gold to paper money. He and many other wealthy men took comfort in knowing that gold was literally moved from the Treasury to pay government debts.

Lincoln Lingo

Printed in $5, $10, and $20 denominations, **demand notes,** called "greenbacks" because of their green color, were the first paper money issued since the Continentals. Only about $10 million worth were issued, and most that remain today are in the hands of collectors. Unlike Confederacy currency, any Union currency issued from 1861 forward is still considered valid and can be redeemed for cash at face value.

Chase had considered taxation and borrowing the best ways to finance the war. But the Civil War, the shortage of coins, and the threat of inflation had created a nearly insurmountable financial crisis. The Union needed to take swift action.

Ultimately, Chase saw the need for some creative financing. A war bond effort was quickly established. Chase asked prominent Philadelphia financier Jay Cooke to administer the program. Cooke's massive campaign involved promoting the bonds to the wealthy and middle class. He used newspaper advertisements and a sales force of more than 2,000 war bond agents. An incredible amount of money was raised—reportedly approaching several billion dollars.

Under the Stovepipe

The war bond effort initiated by the Lincoln administration established the blueprint for future war bond efforts. Techniques used by the Union during the Civil War to boost bond sales among ordinary people were later used to fund modern-day wars.

For Cooke's war bond program to be successful, citizens needed a currency supply. So in February 1862, Lincoln signed the Legal Tender Act, which authorized the issuance of legal tender notes. Unlike demand notes, this new national currency could be used to pay virtually any public or private debt.

What's more, the Treasury Department backed legal tender notes. Confidence in the new currency was high because the notes could be redeemed for coins if the holder chose to do so. (The redemption practice was eventually halted during the war to conserve gold and silver supplies, but resumed in 1879.) With the flow of money assured, the North's economy stabilized and bond sales soared.

Under the Stovepipe

Even after the issuance of legal tender notes in 1862, Union citizens continued to hoard coins. That activity, coupled with the use of metals to cast weapons, further increased the nation's already severe coin shortage.

To bridge the supply gap, the Lincoln administration issued "paper coins"—fractional currency that was physically smaller in size than legal tender notes or even today's currency.

The paper coins came in denominations ranging from three to fifty cents. Union soldiers often lined their worn-out boots with fractional notes, earning paper coins the nickname of "shinplasters." Like other Civil War-era currency issued by the Union, fractional currency is still valid today and redeemable for modern-day cash at face value.

The Confederate currency didn't do so well. That government relied on the belief that their notes would be redeemable after they'd won the war. However, it's important to know that the North helped reduce the value of Confederate money. The Union printed counterfeit bills and circulated the fake money throughout the South. By the end of the Civil War, Confederate notes were so worthless folks used them as wallpaper.

National Banking System

All the financial innovations during the Civil War were separately introduced but linked together by a common goal—to finance the war effort. So given the centralized taxation system and the issuance of national currency, a national banking system was probably the next logical step for the Lincoln administration. After all, wouldn't a nationwide system of banks make it easier to sell government bonds?

In February 1863, Lincoln signed the National Banking Act. Its primary purpose was to enable the government to more efficiently sell those war bonds. The federal government regulated the system of banks, but each institution was to be privately owned.

Each bank was required to have adequate cash reserves on hand at all times and could issue notes of its own—known as national bank notes. As enticement for acceptance and to ensure stability, the bank notes were backed by government bonds. Plus, unlike greenbacks, which carried only the guarantee of the government's declaration of their value, national bank notes could be exchanged for their face value in gold.

The unstated purpose of this act (and others that followed in 1864 and 1865) was to drive the state banks out of business.

Credit extended to bank customers helped keep money circulating within the North's economy. The use of national currency ensured uniformity and wide acceptance of legal tender notes.

Banks within the system were also required to accept and redeem notes issued by any other national bank. A federal official, the comptroller of the currency, was named to oversee the banks and ensure their compliance with federal regulations.

Under the Stovepipe

The Union's wealthiest citizens provided the tax base necessary to fund the government's war effort. This group supplied 75 percent of the total revenue paid to the government during the Civil War. What's more, the Union generated about 20 percent of its war funding through taxation. In contrast, taxation accounted for only about 5 percent of the South's war revenues.

This "free banking" system granted national charters to state banks in existence at the time. When some of these institutions failed to take advantage of the offer, Congress included provisions in a subsequent banking act in 1864 that imposed a 10 percent tax on state bank notes.

That move effectively put state banks out of business. But it paid off for the Union. By the end of the Civil War, the 1864 tax provision resulted in a tripling of national banks and a quadrupling of the purchase of United States bonds.

By 1865, the nation had a coordinated system of private banks regulated by the federal government in Washington. This system replaced President Andrew Jackson's state-chartered program that had been in existence since 1836.

The Bottom Line

Following the end of the Civil War, the need for federal revenue sharply declined. Most of the wartime taxes imposed by Congress were swiftly repealed. By 1868, the bulk of all federal revenue was derived from taxes on liquor and tobacco.

Income tax provisions, which were extremely unpopular even during the Civil War, remained in place for a time. But in 1872, income tax was abolished. All of America must have celebrated wildly the day Congress abolished those taxes! However, the freedom from taxation was short-lived.

Another Crisis, New Tax Laws

When the country faced a new financial crisis at the end of the nineteenth century, Congress tried to reestablish a flat income tax. But the Supreme Court ruled the proposed flat rate program unconstitutional in 1895. Without a tax base derived from income, a War Revenue Act had to be passed in 1899 to fund the Spanish–American War. The act taxed virtually everything in sight—including chewing gum and recreational facilities used by workers.

In 1913, a few years before the U.S. entered World War I, a constitutional amendment was ratified that allowed the federal government to again impose taxes on an individual's income. Like the income tax provisions authorized by President Lincoln, the first rates imposed were graduated. Tax rates began at 1 percent of "lawful" income and rose to a high of 7 percent for those individuals whose income exceeded $500,000. The infamous Form 1040 was introduced as part of the 1913 package, but less than 1 percent of the U.S. population actually filed or paid any tax. As the tax code and enabling legislation were refined, more and more people filed taxes.

Over the years, numerous changes in the tax code have been implemented and additions made, including provisions for Social Security and even privacy. When the 1913 tax law was enacted, there was no mandate that required the government to keep tax returns confidential.

Today, we all know the occasion marked by April 15 and do our civic duty to help fund government-backed programs. However, the basic tenets of the income tax system still carry many of the hallmarks of the Lincoln administration.

The Federal Reserve System

The year 1913 also saw the establishment of the Federal Reserve System. Until that time, the provisions of the National Banking Act served as the basis of America's banking system. A banking panic in 1903 served as the catalyst for the Fed, whose responsibility is to foster a healthy economy and oversee the nation's banking system.

The provisions of the 1913 Federal Reserve Act called for a central national bank to regulate the flow of money and credit—crucial factors impacting the country's economic stability and growth. The following year, the Federal Reserve issued its own currency: Federal Reserve notes. The new notes replaced national bank notes as the country's paper money.

Today, the 12 nationwide Federal Reserve banks serve the needs of specific regions of the country and answer to a Board of Governors located in Washington, D.C. Federal Reserve notes comprise virtually the entire supply of currency in use.

The bottom line? Although Lincoln may have had some awkward first steps with his Cabinet when he took office, he proved to be a master at selecting the right people when it came to financial matters. All in all, the plan to finance the Union's war effort was a brilliant one. Above all, Lincoln's financial strategies helped build a solid economic foundation that benefits all Americans.

The Least You Need to Know

- ◆ Abraham Lincoln signed the first U.S. legislation that enabled taxation of personal and corporate income.

- ◆ Government bonds were sold to raise money for the Union's Civil War effort, and many of the same sales techniques are still used today.

- ◆ Following the Civil War, income tax was abolished—but was reinstituted in 1913.

◆ Lincoln helped establish the national banking system, the forerunner to today's Federal Reserve System.

◆ Changes in government funding measures and monetary systems have frequently been triggered by national financial crises, especially wars.

Chapter 16

Tariff Legislation

In This Chapter

◆ How tariff forms influence trade and economics

◆ How tariffs have been applied since America's founding

◆ How a dispute over federal tariffs and states' rights almost started a civil war in 1832

◆ Why Lincoln approved of pre-Civil War tariff hikes

◆ Why the North immediately moved to pass tariff legislation after southern states seceded

◆ How high tariffs helped preserve the Union

Tariff legislation was as politically controversial in Abraham Lincoln's time as it is today. So perhaps it's not surprising that a few historians have vigorously promoted the concept that it was a sectional dispute over tariffs, not slavery, that triggered the American Civil War.

In this chapter, we will touch on this academic debate and do our best to objectively describe the origins of the dispute, what's generally known about Lincoln's beliefs, and how tariffs were used to support the Union war effort.

Be American, Buy American

Two days before Abraham Lincoln's inauguration in 1861, outgoing President James Buchanan signed into law *tariff* legislation that the South had unsuccessfully fought to block. The few southern legislators who were left—because seven states had seceded by this time—argued that the tariff unfairly protected northern interests at the expense of southern citizens. But in the end, the Morrill Tariff Act of 1861 gained congressional approval.

Lincoln Lingo

A **tariff** is a form of government tax levied on raw or manufactured goods as they move in or out of a country. The term tariff is synonymously used with customs tax or duty. Tariffs are commonly collected by the government of the country importing goods but can also be applied to exported as well as local goods.

Even when southern legislators were fully represented, they'd been outvoted. Indeed, the battle over tariffs and state challenges to the federal government's authority to impose the taxes had begun nearly a century before. Most scholars agree that conflicts between the North and South on slavery and states' rights led to the American Civil War. But some historians claim that Lincoln needlessly instigated the war to protect northern industries and the Union's interest in the money derived from tariffs. Could that actually be true?

To examine the role tariffs may or may not have played in the Civil War and their influence on Lincoln's wartime policies, we need to delve into the history behind these tax measures. Admittedly, the subject matter—economics—is a bit dry and not nearly as entertaining as stories about Lincoln's debates with Stephen Douglas, the colorful origins of Lincoln mythology, or how Lincoln changed education in America.

Notes and Orations

"It is true that in the organization of the Republican party this question of Slavery was more important than any other; indeed, so much more important has it become that no other national question can even get a hearing just at present. The old question of tariff—a matter that will remain one of the chief affairs of national housekeeping to all time—the question of the management of financial affairs; the question of the disposition of the public domain—how shall it be managed for the purpose of getting it well settled, and of making there the homes of a free and happy people—these will remain open and require attention for a great while yet, and these questions will have to be attended to by whatever party has the control of the government."

—Abraham Lincoln, speech at New Haven, Connecticut, March 8, 1860

But knowing a little bit of the history behind these tax measures and how they shaped America will give you a greater understanding of the economic issues Lincoln faced as president. Moreover, you'll gain insight into why Lincoln's wartime decisions still affect us today.

Tariffs Explained

Tariffs represent one of the oldest forms of government taxation in the world. The earliest export tariffs date back to ancient Greece. Also known as customs taxes or duty taxes, tariffs draw a distinction between domestically produced goods and those produced by foreign countries.

Economists generally classify tariffs as either "revenue producing" or "protective." Revenue-producing tariffs generate tax income for government. Protective tariffs tend to safeguard domestic companies or financial interests by imposing taxes that make foreign goods—or even some types of domestic goods—less affordable.

As you might imagine, this is a greatly simplified explanation and these basic concepts can be applied in many ways, often blurring the distinction between the two forms of tariffs. However, the bottom line is that imposition of tariffs can have profound effects on a nation's—or a region's—economy.

Protective and revenue-producing tariffs are further defined as *import*, *export*, and *transit*. Import tariffs are levied as foreign goods entering a country. Generally, the purpose of such taxes is to generate government revenue. However, adjusting the rates of import tariffs can alter trade practices. As demand for foreign goods rises, a country that wants to encourage trade and importation will keep import tariffs low. Conversely, to reduce imports and protect certain industries, a government will increase the tax rates charged for imported goods. The higher taxes result in higher prices for consumers, which tend to make imported goods less desirable. Import tariffs are the most common form of customs tax.

When a government taxes domestic goods as they leave the country, the tax is called an export tariff. Although duty taxes levied on outbound goods result in revenue for the government, export tariffs are also imposed to protect a country's domestic supplies.

For instance, to reduce the export of grain when supplies are low, export taxes might be applied to make sure the country's citizens don't starve. The export taxes would increase the cost of grain to foreign countries, reducing foreign sales and ensuring that more grain remained at home. Export taxes can also be applied to encourage domestic investment. When export taxes are high, foreign investment doesn't pay off as quickly as it might without the tariff. So in that event, investors are more likely to support domestic business. (Are you with me so far?)

Notes and Orations

"And this reminds me that Mr. Lincoln told you that the slavery question was the only thing that ever disturbed the peace and harmony of the Union. Did not nullification once raise its head and disturb the peace of this Union in 1832? Was that the slavery question, Mr. Lincoln? Did not disunion raise its monster head during the last war with Great Britain? Was that the slavery question, Mr. Lincoln? The peace of this country has been disturbed three times, once during the war with Great Britain, once on the tariff question, and once on the slavery question. ("Three cheers for Douglas." [chanted the audience]) His argument, therefore, that slavery is the only question that has ever created dissension in the Union falls to the ground."

—Stephen A. Douglas, seventh and last debate with Abraham Lincoln at Alton, Illinois, October 15, 1858

Transit tariffs, rarely if ever applied today, are a little more complicated. When goods are exported from Country A to Country C and pass through Country B along the way, Country B may tax the goods. It might help to think of a transit tariff as a kind of highway toll—a tax imposed while the goods are in the process of traveling to their destination.

Finally, it's also important to know that regardless of the type of tariff, customs taxes can also be applied selectively. Selective taxes on certain goods might be imposed to encourage their domestic production, to raise revenue on high-demand imports, or to protect a country's home industries.

States: "Me, First!"

Long before Lincoln took office, tariff legislation was a divisive factor between the North and South.

The administration of President George Washington imposed the first national tariffs in 1789, primarily to generate revenue for the new government but also to promote and protect America's fledgling shipbuilding industry. The new law established that goods transported to and from the United States by American-built vessels would receive favorable tax treatment.

Under the Stovepipe

In addition to the 1789 Tariff Act's 10 percent tariff reductions for shipments arriving in the United States by way of American-made vessels, subsequent navigation-related legislation offered further financial incentives that benefited American industry. Foreign-built and/or foreign-owned vessels were charged 50 cents per ton when they entered a U.S. port. In contrast, American-built and owned vessels were charged just six cents per ton.

By 1795, 92 percent of all imports and 86 percent of all exports were transported by American-built and owned vessels. American shipbuilding revenues soared—from just under $6 million in annual earnings in 1790 to more than $40 million in 1807.

The 1789 Tariff Act would seem to have been good for all of America, and for a while it was. Northern shipping grew at a phenomenal rate and southern agricultural ventures expanded to meet foreign demand. The U.S. Treasury benefited, too.

But one of the factors that made federal tariff legislation so divisive and politically charged was the separatist nature of the states. Although the colonies joined together to form the United States of America, each state considered itself to be self-governing and self-interested. That philosophy wouldn't have been so problematic except for an undeniable reality: the needs of the South's *agrarian* economy and the North's rapidly evolving *industrial* economy were completely different.

Lincoln Lingo

Agrarian means relating to or promoting the interests of agriculture, land, or farmers. The term is also used to define ownership of rural property or the division of land.

Industrial relates to companies involved in the manufacture and/or distribution of products.

Early tariff legislation nurtured New England enterprises but failed to protect the agrarian economies of southern states. Even though demand for southern crops was high, the cost of exporting those goods was also high. Worse, tariff legislation ultimately increased prices southern citizens paid for manufactured imports—goods often produced using the South's own raw materials. These costs reduced profit margins for southern plantation owners, even though crop production was dependent on slave labor.

After President Washington signed the first tariff and navigation acts, northern capitalists rushed to create northern ports. Shipbuilders scrambled to set up shops and build vessels, and shipping companies formed. All sought to take advantage of the favorable trade legislation, and these shipping interests quickly expanded with the intent of dominating U.S. foreign trade.

However, in the South, the focus remained on building an agricultural economy. Southern ports and shipping industries developed far more slowly than those in the North.

Shoring Up the Borders

To take full advantage of the nation's protectionist tariffs and navigation laws, the New England-based shipping industry created triangular shipping routes to capture the southern shipping market, too. With the South's ports posing little to no competition and foreign shipping operators pushed out of the equation, the North's shipping industry gained a virtual monopoly.

As a result, the South's economy became dependent on northern shipping businesses to transport goods to customers overseas. What's more, the South also grew dependent on the North for imported manufactured goods and, later, much of its food. (Southern farmers began to put all their land into cotton and tobacco, pushing out the less profitable food crops.)

Here's how the basic U.S. export route worked: American ships bound for Europe departed from rapidly growing northern ports such as Boston and New York. But instead of taking the direct route to England, they sailed down the eastern seaboard to southern ports. There the ships loaded up with cotton and other crops before heading for Great Britain and other overseas ports. In addition to the revenue derived from freight charges, shipping companies boosted income by charging for loading and unloading cargo, insurance, commissions, and a host of other fees. Talk about easy money! Costs charged by northern shipping companies could pull up to 40 cents from every dollar paid for cotton. Add in customs duties and other surcharges and you can see why the federal government and northern industrialists liked this scenario.

The net effect was a huge windfall for northern companies and losses for the South. And because government investments focused on northern port development, the South's shipping industry never really took off. Instead, New York, Boston, and Philadelphia became the major international seaports.

Under the Stovepipe

The North's dominance in the shipping industry was already evident by the 1850s, when nearly 75 percent of all import shipments from foreign countries entered the United States by way of the port of New York. To further illustrate, consider that in 1851, the South Carolina port of Charleston handled just about 100,000 tons of import cargo. Compare that to the nearly 1.5 million tons handled by New York's port the same year.

Boom, Then Bust

As federal legislators came to understand the significant impact tariffs could have on industries and trade, they quickly politicized tariffs. Keep in mind that up until the start of the Civil War, tariffs provided the only tax revenue collected by the federal government. (Income tax was not introduced until 1861.)

The commercial shipping boom triggered by the 1786 tariff came to an abrupt halt in 1807 when tensions flared between the United States and Great Britain. The War of 1812 and the British blockade followed. International trade ended. Demand for manufactured goods rose and led to the establishment of the U.S. manufacturing industry—which, of course, was founded in the already commercialized and capital-rich New England region.

Locked out of foreign markets, southern growers had no choice but to send their raw materials north. Among other cash crops, cotton fed New England's fledgling textile mill industry. In 1815, when the war with Great Britain ended, the United States reopened international trade. Britain responded by flooding the American marketplace with less expensive and far superior manufactured goods.

Great Britain's action didn't do much harm to the South's economy, but it threatened to bankrupt northern manufacturing interests. So to protect the North, in 1816 the federal government enacted the first *major* protective tariff act. That move helped insulate northern manufacturers from foreign competition. But the tariffs made it more difficult for southern ventures to survive.

Under the Stovepipe

Part of the economic controversy between the North and South involved competing economic theories that emerged early in U.S. history. Alexander Hamilton and U.S. Senator Henry Clay were among proponents of the "American System." This theory held that the new nation could not be fully independent unless it became completely self-sufficient economically.

Others, including Thomas Jefferson and later the Confederate States of America, believed the United States should develop as an agrarian nation based on a plantation economy.

In 1819, the nation's economy collapsed. Even though a protective tariff had been enacted in 1816, the North blamed the government's previous inaction and lack of support. Northern industrialists vowed they'd never allow themselves to be placed in such a vulnerable position again.

Business and Patriotism

In the absence of a cohesive, national view of economic needs and direction, federal legislators almost always voted to the benefit of their home districts, often to the exclusion of the rest of the country.

Keep in mind that in Lincoln's time, loyalty to one's state was often a higher priority than loyalty to the country. Consider Virginian Robert E. Lee. Lee and his family shared a long history of American patriotism, but when Lincoln asked him to lead the Union army after Virginia seceded, Lee refused. His first duty was to his home state, and he could not bring himself to take up arms against the Commonwealth. Lee was honor-bound to defend Virginia against all external threats, including those posed by the Union.

Accordingly, proposals to change tariff laws triggered political squabbles and worsened sectional rifts. For instance, a new tariff, the Tariff of 1828, was first proposed when New England textile manufacturers complained about unfair foreign competition. Northern manufacturers charged that British woolen goods manufacturers were selling their products in the American marketplace in huge numbers at artificially low prices.

As Congress moved to respond to New England's economic threat, western legislators supported the inclusion of a tariff increase to limit importation of raw materials. The South wanted nothing to do with protectionism and vigorously objected to the entire proposal as it interfered with plantation profits.

Notes and Orations

"To comply with your request to furnish extracts from my tariff speeches is simply impossible, because none of those speeches were published … In 1844 I was on the Clay electoral ticket in this State (*i.e.*, Illinois) and, to the best of my ability, sustained, together, the tariff of 1842 and the tariff plank of the Clay platform; still it is not in print, except by inference … The papers show that I was one of a committee which reported, among others, a resolution in these words: 'That we are in favor of an adequate revenue on duties from imports so levied as to afford ample protection to American industry.'"

—Abraham Lincoln, letter to James E. Harvey, October 2, 1860

Had this dispute taken place today, it's possible that Congress would have worked more diligently to reach a compromise to benefit all regions. But the interests of the North and West overwhelmed the South's objections, and the proposal became law.

In the end, the 1828 Tariff Act didn't please anyone. In fact, the measure was so unpopular that it became widely known as the "Tariff of Abominations."

Following the 1828 Tariff Act, Great Britain complained that American cotton prices were too high and threatened to take its business elsewhere. Understandably, that greatly alarmed the South. Signs of civil unrest began to emerge from South Carolina's citizens, who were outraged by what they viewed as federal interference in their local affairs.

In 1832, new tariff legislation was passed to bring duties back to a more modest level. But the new tariff act didn't appease South Carolina, whose crop growers were still stinging from the effects of the Tariff of Abominations. They decided to take a stand for states' rights.

Notes and Orations

"I believe yet, if we could have a moderate, carefully adjusted, protective tariff, so far acquiesced [sic] in, as to not be a perpetual subject of political strife, squabbles, charges, and uncertainties, it would be better for us. Still, it is my opinion that, just now, the revival of that question, will not advance the cause itself, or the man who revives it. I have not thought much upon the subject recently; but my general impression is, that the necessity for a protective tariff will, ere long, force it's [sic] old opponents to take it up; and then it's [sic] old friends can join in, and establish it on a more firm and durable basis. We, the old whigs, have been entirely beaten out on the tariff question; and we shall not be able to re-establish the policy, until the absence of it, shall have demonstrated the necessity for it, in the minds of men heretofore opposed to it."

—Abraham Lincoln, letter to Dr. Edward Wallace, October 11, 1859

South Carolina Rebels

On November 24, 1832, South Carolina passed a Nullification Ordinance, declaring the 1828 and 1832 tariff acts unconstitutional and ordering that no federal taxes be collected. State legislators then passed laws enforcing the new ordinance—including appropriations for an armed military force. President Andrew Jackson viewed these actions as treasonous and immediately sent warships to Charleston.

South Carolina fully expected other southern states to join their insurrection, but support never materialized. Instead, other states in the South agreed with Jackson and urged South Carolina to rescind its action.

The crisis ended after congressional leaders from both sides crafted and passed compromise tariff legislation in 1833. The new tariff act called for the gradual reduction of rates over time, so that customs taxes would eventually return to 1816 levels. Its demands satisfied, South Carolina backed away from its secessionist-style threats and eventually overturned the ordinance. But no one ever forgot the trouble brought about by a single state's resistance to federal authority.

In response to South Carolina's ordinance of nullification, Congress passed the Force Bill in 1833. The measure authorized President Jackson to use military force to enforce federal law, including tariffs.

In 1846 and 1857, the South gained further tax relief when Democrats controlled the U.S. House and Senate and passed new tariff acts that were decidedly advantageous to the South's economy. The 1857 Tariff Act, in particular, created a free trade market that worked against northern industry. An economic panic occurred not long after the tariff reductions took effect. But when government revenues plummeted by a staggering 30 percent, Republicans—who had long supported northern industry—called for higher tariffs.

Prelude to Civil War

At the 1860 Republican Convention in Chicago, delegates crafted and passed a platform that included, among other planks, a call for the abolition of slavery and a strengthening of the nation's import tariffs. In addition, the party also favored the creation of national policies on a variety of issues related to labor, agriculture, and commercial enterprise.

Notes and Orations

"In the days of Henry Clay I was a Henry Clay-tariff-man; and my views have undergone no material change upon that subject. I now think the Tariff question ought not to be agitated in the Chicago convention; but that all should be satisfied on that point, with a presidential candidate, whose antecedents give assurance that he would neither seek to force a tariff-law by Executive influence; nor yet to arrest a reasonable one, by a veto, or otherwise. Just such a candidate I desire shall be put in nomination. I really have no objection to these views being publicly known; but I do wish to thrust no letter before the public now, upon any subject. Save me from the appearance of obtrusion; and I do not care who sees this, or my former letter."

—Abraham Lincoln, letter to Dr. Edward Wallace, Springfield, Illinois, May 12, 1860

Abraham Lincoln—an outspoken opponent of slavery on moral grounds and an advocate of northern industry—gained the Republican Party's presidential nomination that year in Chicago. Southern plantation owners likely bristled at the very thought of what might happen next.

As Lincoln campaigned, Vermont Representative Justin Morrill's proposed tariff measure was being debated in Congress. Seven states had already seceded over the issue of slavery. Although outnumbered, the remaining southern legislators argued against Morrill's proposed rate increases on the basis of fairness.

By 1860, the South's cotton crop represented 57 percent of all U.S. exports. Southern lawmakers charged that when compared to northern industries, the South paid a disproportionately higher share of customs duties. Import taxes were especially punitive to the South. But worse, they said, the funds raised through customs duties were helping fund northern states almost exclusively.

When the Morrill Tariff was enacted in 1861, it reversed the South's previous gains. Combine deep sectional divisions on the issues of slavery and states' rights to the already volatile, long-standing trade and tariff battles between the North and South, and you have the ingredients for civil war.

Notes and Orations

"Permit me to express the hope that this important subject may receive such consideration at the hands of your representatives, that the interests of no part of the country may be overlooked, but that all sections may share in common the benefits of a just and equitable tariff."

—Abraham Lincoln, speech at Pittsburgh, Pennsylvania, February 15, 1861

Winning the Economic War

As Lincoln took office and the Civil War began, the necessity of financing the Union's war effort was of paramount importance. Raising tariff rates was just one of several financial strategies.

The Morrill Act's rates were increased twice in 1861, nearly doubling import taxes from 1857 levels. These two measures were just the beginning of a series of tariff rate increases that Congress would pass during the Civil War.

Lincoln had gained a reputation for support of protectionist tariffs, but the purpose of virtually all the tariffs enacted during his time in office was to raise funds for the Union's war effort. In 1862, for instance, tariff rate increases approved by Lincoln were designed to generate revenue rather than build northern business. Tariff revenues complemented other domestic taxes that were imposed strictly for purposes of financing the Union's war chest.

Some of the beneficiaries of the rate increases included construction of a transcontinental railroad line, establishment of agricultural colleges, and federal land grants. The new rates established in 1862 increased customs duties by an average of about 37 percent more than 1861 rates. Customs taxes also helped raise funds needed for bold initiatives that would enable the United States to remain independent and strong.

Under the Stovepipe

By 1864, Union tariff rates were at an all-time high. Even though the bill worsened the already high cost of living for the North's citizenry, most accepted the increases as the only way to win the war. Still, customs duties brought in only about $75 million a year, a fraction of the amount needed to finance the Union's Civil War effort. But as the saying goes, every penny counted!

As battles raged and financial pressures continued to mount, the need for additional revenue persisted. Along with other financial strategies, the Lincoln administration repeatedly increased tariff rates throughout the Civil War. In June 1864, Lincoln approved a new tariff bill that further increased rates—from 37 percent to more than 47 percent!

Lincoln's wartime tariff policies helped advance loyalty for domestic goods, a concept that prevailed for decades. And although protection of the Union's industrial base wasn't Lincoln's primary goal, the North's industries—including some commercial farmers—nevertheless reaped short- and long-term benefits.

Ultimately, Lincoln's approval of revenue-producing tariffs strengthened the Union treasury and helped ensure the North's victory. Tariffs also provided funding for other Lincoln-era initiatives that safeguarded America's economic future for decades to come.

When the Civil War ended, so did the Union's severe financial crisis. By 1872, postwar tariff reforms reduced rates on many manufactured goods. The downward revisions generally continued until the late 1890s, when the McKinley administration ratcheted rates back upward—with some items being taxed as high as 57 percent! As the long history of tariff legislation shows, rates and trade policies have constantly changed, and probably always will.

From our nation's earliest times, tariffs have provided a key mechanism for government funding as well as growth and prosperity for American businesses and consumers. Lincoln recognized the power of tariffs to achieve these goals. However, the fundamental problem of how to apply these taxes to benefit the greatest number of people without unduly penalizing others has never really gone away.

This form of government taxation is fluid and continues to be the subject of intense debate and controversy, and tariff legislation is just as volatile today as it was in Lincoln's day. Tariffs can have dramatic and long-lasting effects on virtually every aspect of personal finance and our nation's economy—from domestic investments and homeland business growth to international relations and world trade. In deciding what's best, we would do well to look to the past as a guide.

So about the nagging question posed at the beginning of this chapter: Did the North go to war over tariffs?

Well, recall that when Lincoln was elected president, he vowed to keep the country united and the western territories free from slavery. These two objectives were uppermost in his mind as events unfolded during his first months in office.

Most historians agree that although there were other areas of strong disagreement between the states, slavery was the primary cause and the immediate trigger of the American Civil War.

Notes and Orations

"We have, as all will agree, a free Government, where every man has a right to be equal with every other man. In this great struggle, this form of Government and every form of human right is endangered if our enemies succeed. There is more involved in this contest than is realized by every one. There is involved in this struggle the question whether your children and my children shall enjoy the privileges we have enjoyed."

—Abraham Lincoln, from remarks to the 164th Ohio Regiment, August 18, 1864

The Least You Need to Know

◆ The first American tariff legislation was signed by George Washington as a means of funding the government and protecting the new country's fledging industries.

◆ Almost from the beginning of America's history, the needs of the South's agrarian economy and the North's rapidly evolving industry-based economy were very different.

◆ Sectional disagreements over tariffs and their effects on local economies began in the late 1700s and were ongoing—South Carolina threatened secession in 1832 for this reason.

◆ Abraham Lincoln generally supported tariff legislation that protected American industry.

◆ During the Civil War, Lincoln approved tariff rate hikes to help finance the Union's Civil War effort and to fund initiatives designed to strengthen the country's postwar infrastructure.

Chapter 17

Transportation Legislation

In This Chapter

- ◆ Why the transcontinental railroad was so slow in pulling away from the station
- ◆ Why Lincoln was so motivated to expand the nation's railroads
- ◆ How the fates of railroads and economic and population growth were intertwined
- ◆ Why today's entire transportation network owes thanks to Abraham Lincoln

Despite struggling to keep what remained of the Union together, President Abraham Lincoln still managed to find time to sign into law the Pacific Railway Act. Lincoln would not live to see the day the two railroads met at Promontory Summit, Utah, on May 10, 1869, but in approving the measure, he provided the accelerant needed to propel the nation's fledgling rail service forward.

The dramatic events that took place between the time Lincoln enacted the law and the day a golden spike was driven into the track in Utah's high desert changed the nation forever. In this chapter, we examine the history of the transcontinental railroad and its role in "how the West was won," and also explore how the coming of the railroad triggered a permanent change to all the lands it touched.

Faster Than a Wagon Train

As early as 1840, Abraham Lincoln was eyeing the nation's infrastructure and formulating ways to modernize transportation. Lincoln called these "internal improvements," and he was specifically interested in making changes to improve the nation's system of railroads and canals.

In the 1850s, Lincoln's interest in and knowledge of railroad transportation increased. As a young Illinois attorney, he represented railroad companies in legal cases and began to see the strategic value railroads offered. Lincoln had seen the impact himself—commerce and population sprouted up wherever a station was built. He imagined the possibilities of a railroad system that extended across the as-yet unsettled western territories of the United States.

We've Been Workin' on the Railroad

Of course, Lincoln wasn't the first to consider railroad expansion. In 1818, when Lincoln was still a young boy, Senator Thomas Hart Benton of Missouri wrote several editorials in his local newspaper, the *St. Louis Enquirer*, promoting the idea of building a series of canals and railroads between the Columbia and Missouri Rivers. Benton predicted the benefits of such a construction project spreading trade over more of the continent. He even speculated that the benefits might also extend to increasing international trade, attracting more commerce with Europe—even China and Japan.

The federal government also recognized the possible benefits. The cost of mail delivery would be significantly reduced, and the transportation network would make the army's designs to control Indian populations simpler.

But even though so many people agreed that an improved transportation system was advantageous, little progress was made. As Lincoln entered adulthood in 1830, only 23 miles of railroad track existed in the United States.

In 1850, President Millard Fillmore signed into law the Railroad Land Grant Act, which encouraged the development of railroads, especially in the South and West, in hopes of increasing the nation's tax base and unifying the nation as it grew. Railroad development increased, but primarily as an improvement to existing trails in the East. This served to modernize the existing infrastructure, and shortened shipping times along established routes.

Horse-drawn wagons were replaced in many instances by the "Iron Horse," capable of carrying much greater loads more quickly. But expansion to new routes in the sparsely populated West had not yet begun. To prepare preliminary plans for a westbound railway, Jefferson Davis, then U.S. Secretary of War, asked army engineers to determine the five best routes westward for the railroad. (Yes, that's the same Jefferson Davis who later served as president of the Confederate States of America.)

As you might imagine, there was considerable debate over the most desirable route for the railroad to take. The issue was an economic one. Towns located near the railroad would undoubtedly grow and prosper, while those bypassed would almost surely wither away. The most contentious debate surrounded where the railroad's eastern terminus should be, given that wherever was chosen would unquestionably become a major hub for commerce of all types. Ultimately, Council Bluffs, Iowa, just across the Missouri River from Omaha, Nebraska, was given this honor.

Despite the best intentions, however, the railway project couldn't get moving.

In 1859, Abraham Lincoln laid some preliminary groundwork for promoting the westward growth of the railroad. That year he happened to meet railroad engineer and surveyor Granville Dodge in Council Bluffs, Iowa. Lincoln grilled Dodge about what he knew about the land to the west. He told Dodge at the time that he felt there was nothing more important to our nation than building a railroad to the Pacific Coast.

Dodge would later rise to the rank of brigadier general during the Civil War through his skill at rebuilding southern railroads damaged during combat. Eventually, he became the chief engineer of the transcontinental railroad project.

But up until the start of the Civil War, the federal government's support of the railroad's expansion had been only marginally successful. By 1860, there were 30,000 miles of railroad track across the eastern United States, where population continued to grow. (Between 1861 and 1865, some 800,000 European immigrants came to the United States, most of whom settled in the northeast.)

Stitching the Union Together

When Lincoln took office in 1861, he passed a number of legislative measures designed to get the country moving while supporting the Union's war effort. Many of these initiatives were those he had first contemplated in his early days as a young politician in Illinois.

After the Homestead Act was passed encouraging westward emigration, establishing a railroad into the West was viewed as crucial. Lincoln and others in his administration wanted to promote western expansion to strengthen the economy—and to further establish the Union.

The territory of Nevada and two states—California and Oregon—were so physically distant and unreachable they might as well have been located on another continent. With California contemplating secession, and with the Union desperately needing California's wealth to help finance the Civil War, connecting the coasts seemed imperative.

Men of vision were already seeking ways to expand the railroads. And they intended to get rich while doing it. An enthusiastic and ambitious railroad engineer named Theodore Judah had long tried to solve the problem of finding a viable route over California's rugged Sierra Nevada Mountains. He finally believed he found the way through Donner Pass, north of Lake Tahoe.

Under the Stovepipe

Donner Pass was infamous, remembered as the location of a tragic story about a doomed wagon train of American pioneers. In April 1846, nine wagons carrying the families of George and Jacob Donner left Springfield, Illinois, and headed west for California. As they traveled, other wagon trains joined them, increasing the Donner party's numbers.

In July, the 81 emigrants in the Donner party took a shortcut through the mountains to shave off about 400 miles of their journey. Near the crest of the Sierra Nevadas in November 1846, they encountered immense snow. The party was trapped there for months. Food supplies dwindled quickly and many in the party died. As desperation increased and starvation loomed, they were forced to resort to cannibalism to survive. Rescue of the last survivors didn't occur until April 1847.

After meeting Judah, Sacramento merchant Collis P. Huntington decided to invest heavily in the transcontinental railroad enterprise. Huntington brought in three additional investors—Charles Crocker, Mark Hopkins, and Leland Stanford. Together, they formed the Central Pacific Railroad Company. These nineteenth-century power brokers were known as the "Big Four."

When Lincoln arrived in Washington to assume the presidency in 1861, seven states had already seceded, and four others were preparing to do so. Although the situation Lincoln faced was a national crisis in no uncertain terms, members of Congress also saw a unique opportunity.

Southern senators had been *filibustering* against proposed laws that might expand the railroad. With these senators now absent, Congress seized the chance to push the stalled railroad legislation through. In addition to improving infrastructure and helping the country expand, Lincoln believed railroads were strategically important to the Union's war effort.

Lincoln took his first steps to improve the Union's railway system in December 1861. In his annual message to Congress that month, Lincoln proposed that Congress fund, as a military measure, a railroad to serve Union loyalists in western North Carolina and Tennessee. The new tracks were to link with existing rail lines to the north.

Lincoln Lingo

A **filibuster** is an activity designed to prevent a legislative body from taking action on proposed legislation. The activity usually involves prolonged speechmaking and refusing to yield the floor to a fellow member of Congress.

Safer Than a Horse and Buggy

After much anticipation, Lincoln signed into law the Pacific Railway Act on July 1, 1862.

The key provisions of this sweeping legislation established the Union Pacific Railroad Company and permitted that firm to construct westbound railroad tracks from Omaha, Nebraska, to the western border of the Nevada Territory. The act endorsed the Central Pacific Railroad Company's intent to build a railroad east from California's Sacramento Delta—a commercially viable waterway that extended from just outside Sacramento to the Pacific Ocean. The Central Pacific was to construct track until it met up with the line laid by the Union Pacific. The race to Promontory, Utah, was on!

Under the Stovepipe

On July 1, 1862, President Abraham Lincoln signed two landmark legislative measures designed to support the Union's war effort and strengthen America's future—the Internal Revenue Act and the Pacific Railway Act. Each stroke of the pen had lasting effects that continue to influence Americans to this day.

The Pacific Railway Act's Provisions

The Pacific Railway Act of 1862 had 11 sections. Among its most important provisions:

- ◆ Established the Union Pacific Railroad Company. It was granted sole authority to construct a railroad and telegraph line from latitude 100 west between the Republican and Platte Rivers to the western boundary of the Nevada Territory.

- ◆ Granted the transcontinental railroad access to a swath of public land 200 feet to either side of the track's route, and promised to "extinguish as rapidly as may be the Indian titles to all lands falling under the operation of this act." Under the act, the railroad company was also allowed to take whatever raw materials it might wish from the right-of-way to assist in the construction of the railroad.

- ◆ Gave railroad companies every other *section* of land for 10 miles on either side of the tracks for the entire length of the railway. (These land grants excluded mineral rights but included timber rights.)

Lincoln Lingo

A **section** of land is a unit of measurement in real estate parlance equal to 640 square acres.

- ◆ Directed the U.S. Treasury to issue 16 bonds in the amount of $1,000 for each 40-mile section of track, effectively establishing the first mortgage for the railroad.

- ◆ Authorized the Leavenworth, Pawnee, and Western Railroad Company of Kansas to construct a railroad line in Kansas and Missouri, to connect with the proposed transcontinental railroad.

- ◆ Authorized the Central Pacific Railroad Company of California to construct a railroad line from the Pacific Coast to the eastern border of California. And in another section of the act, extended this authority east to the Missouri River. This overlap of the two efforts ensured that each company would have the authority to build track as far and as quickly as possible until they met up at some point in between.

- ◆ Included an "adjustment" that allowed doubling of bond issuance for extra challenging sections of the railroad—generally defined as foothills—and triple the amount of bonds issued for especially difficult sections, primarily in the Sierra Nevada Mountains of California and Nevada.

The passage of the Pacific Railway Act granted the railroad companies an astonishing 64,000 acres of land for every mile of track laid, and up to $48,000 in government bonds for each mile of track, as well. The companies had to prove their mettle first, though, by laying 40 miles of track before any bonds would be released.

The government also withheld 20 percent of the bond value until the entire railroad line was completed. And if the companies didn't finish the entire project within 12 years, all company assets were forfeited to the government. So you can see that the railroad owners were plenty motivated to move quickly!

Under the Stovepipe

Although the act that Lincoln signed into law was known as the Pacific Railway Act, it had a major effect on another industry as well. The act established telegraph lines heading westward along the railroad as well. Messages that would formerly take weeks or months to reach the West Coast now arrived in mere hours.

Expanding "instant" communication to the West had the effect of equalizing many conditions between the East and West coasts. News traveled much, much faster. Who knew that building the railroad would also usher in the earliest stages of the Information Age?

The Rails Must Get Through

After Lincoln set things in motion by signing into law the Pacific Railway Act, he returned his attention to the Civil War. Meanwhile, the individuals now heading federally authorized railroad companies set about the yeoman task of making the railroad happen. These powerful men saw as much opportunity for profit in constructing the railroad as in operating it after its construction.

The challenges facing the railroad project were daunting. Both companies had to find ways to overcome labor and material shortages. But they also faced some rather mighty physical challenges, two major mountain ranges to cross: the Rocky Mountains of Colorado and Wyoming, and the Sierra Nevadas of California and Nevada. The combination of elements conspired to make the railroad undertaking an incredibly arduous one.

These weren't the only challenges faced by the railroads. Because the Union was engaged in the Civil War, materials and labor were in short supply. Most able-bodied men were already soldiers. For the West Coast-based Central Pacific Railroad, crucial items were not readily available, such as railroad cars, locomotives, and even spikes.

Meeting the labor requirements to undertake this massive project required ingenuity. The bulk of the early railroad workforce was Irish immigrants. After the project reached Utah, another group broadly represented among the railroad workers were Mormons. Not until 1864, when Central Pacific Railroad director Charles Crocker suggested hiring some Chinese laborers, did this demographic begin to shift.

Chinese laborers began arriving in California in large numbers in 1850, seeking to escape poverty in their homeland and to pursue rumors of the "Mountain of Gold" that was the California Gold Rush. Many took on five-year contracts to work the mines before setting out on their own as prospectors or laborers. The Chinese immigration created a labor glut in some areas, and prejudice against the Chinese immigrants began to rise.

Laws were enacted making it more difficult for Chinese to find work. Leland Stanford, a director of the Central Pacific Railroad Company, announced in his inaugural address as governor of California in 1862 that he would protect the state from "the dregs of Asia." Stanford apparently later had a change of heart—or priorities—as he hired thousands of Chinese to work on his railroad project.

Changing How and Where America Lives

Many railroad laborers gained well-deserved reputations as heavy drinkers and ruffians who were extremely rowdy when not at work. Despite the possible hazards this bad behavior posed, towns and encampments formed almost spontaneously along the railroad construction route to provide services to railroad workers. Such "services" were readily available and often included liquor and prostitutes. When the work took the men near existing frontier communities, the residents were frequently terrorized. Violence often ensued.

Lincoln Lingo

The term **Hell on Wheels** grew out of the rowdy behavior of some of the workers on the railroad construction project. Because the men usually rode into town via railroad tracks on a wheeled car, they were often described as "Hell on Wheels."

During this era, the Cheyenne, Wyoming, newspaper had a standing column titled "Last Night's Shootings." It's no wonder that when railroad workers entered a community, townspeople often whispered anxiously, "Here comes *Hell on Wheels.*"

Nonetheless, Lincoln's vision of growth and expansion was quickly realized. Growth, although painstakingly slow by today's standards, would have seemed meteoric to someone living along the new railroad line!

In addition to transporting people, the railroad brought a key ingredient needed to populate the western territories: construction supplies. Previously, transporting commercial quantities of timber and other homebuilding supplies could only be accomplished by wagon—an impractical and oppressively expensive means. But with the railroad line in place, lumber could be shipped farther and much less expensively.

Towns fortunate enough to be located along the railroad line, particularly those where stations were established, generally thrived. New towns were created to support the railroad, and they often prospered, too—especially if they were situated at or near the junction of another transportation thoroughfare—a wagon trail or a navigable river, for instance.

Under the Stovepipe

Towns in existence before the railroad but unfortunate enough to have the route of the railroad pass them by often perished. Similar to the nineteenth-century railroad phenomenon, twentieth-century interstate highway routings frequently signaled the demise of entire towns. The destiny and fortunes of many communities often shifted as one highway route replaced another.

The many diners, gas stations, and hotels that opened in the West to support travelers along Route 66, "the Mother Route," thrived for decades. But when high-speed freeways were built, often taking travelers along another route, many businesses lost customers and had no choice but to close their doors.

As Lincoln might have conceived, many of the folks who headed west on the railroad ended up establishing themselves in communities along the route. Intending to proceed to California, many people stopped along the way, perhaps to see the sights or visit kin who'd settled in the area. Some folks decided to put down roots right where they hopped off the train. Why move to a more distant locale if all you needed— shipping, communications, transportation, and more—could be found in that very spot?

Some towns that grew up along the transcontinental railroad and remain today include the following:

California	Nebraska	Nevada	Utah	Wyoming
Auburn	Grand Isle	Elko	Ogden	Cheyenne
Colfax	North Platte	Reno		Laramie
Truckee	Omaha	Winnemucca		Rawlins
	Sidney			

Getting There Today

Lincoln would be pleased to know that today, railroad lines criss-cross all North America. Although many other transportation options exist, railroads are still crucial to our nation's economy and represent one of the most cost-effective means of transporting goods and people.

A few things have changed. Although many large towns continue to thrive along the rail lines as they have for decades, being located at or even near a rail station is no longer essential for—or a guarantee of—economic viability. But even today's most prosperous communities know it's wise to be situated on a major transportation route such as a major highway or near an airport.

Transportation hubs that arose from the railroad boom set the stage for America's future. The transportation network and today's technology allow an individual to build a home—or for an entire community to be established—almost anywhere in the country.

When our country was growing, really expanding, the railroad was the only means of getting people and raw materials any distance across the country. Prior to the railroad's growth, major commerce and trade hubs were restricted to ocean ports or ports along major navigable rivers such as the Mississippi or canal systems such as the C&O. From those ports of call, the railroad then became a natural extension to parts more distant from those ports.

In our day and age, long-haul trucks seem to be everywhere as they transport many of our goods and materials. But the railroad is still a major factor, particularly in long-distance shipping. Looking at a transportation map, you can see that many roadways emerge from railroad lines such as a hub. If railroads served as extensions to seaports, highways serve as extensions to rail lines.

In the early days of the railroad, the train was *the* way to get from Point A to Point B for any great distance, particularly cross country. The stagecoach certainly played its own crucial role, but to an extent, the stagecoach lines became an extension of the railroad. Stagecoaches transported people to places where the demand wasn't strong enough to warrant the great expense of a railroad.

Amtrak

Today those major rail lines don't carry nearly the percentage of travelers they once did. Although commuter rail lines exist—and are in some cases even expanding their track—the long-haul transportation of passengers is now basically restricted to *Amtrak*.

Once an elegant, sophisticated, and relaxing means of travel, by the 1940s the railroads were losing business—lots of it—to airlines and private automobiles. By the 1960s, people were staying away from passenger trains; trains were increasingly run-down, missed schedules, and were just no longer fun.

Amtrak was formed in 1971 after passage of the Rail Passenger Service Act of 1970. This legislation was created when all the private railroad companies stopped carrying passengers because they were losing money on the deal. The government viewed passenger rail travel as an important part of the entire transportation system. And in many regions of the country, taking the train was an option few were willing to relinquish.

Lincoln Lingo

Amtrak, whose real name is the National Railroad Passenger Corporation, is a quasi-governmental agency that operates passenger rail service throughout the United States and parts of Canada. All Amtrak's stock is owned by the federal government, through the U.S. Department of Transportation.

In many ways, the government's involvement with Amtrak is just continuing the tradition of intimate government involvement in the railroad industry that began in 1862.

A Lasting Legacy

The foresight of Abraham Lincoln and others caused the railroad to push westward and greatly expand our national transportation network. When you consider telegraph lines that were constructed alongside the railroad, you can see that Lincoln's transportation legacy influenced communications networks, too.

Railroads already in existence in Lincoln's era benefited from the Pacific Railway Act. Formerly short-line tracks serving small point-to-point routes became connected to a coast-to-coast railroad line. Our world started getting a little smaller when that took place.

Today there are more than 500 freight railroad carriers in existence. Seven major U.S. carriers earn 92 percent of the industry's revenue. In 2002, freight trains carried more than 31 million carloads of cargo in the United States. Amtrak carried more than 25 million passengers in 2003 to 2004.

The concept of a transportation network growing outward like spokes from the hub of a wheel was certainly part of the doctrine in the design of the transcontinental railroad. Check out a local map and chances are you'll see that same pattern—connecting the various forms of transportation available in your locale.

The next time you see a train consisting of dozens of cars speeding off into the distance, remember that Abraham Lincoln had the vision and the fortitude to push for the railroad's expansion. And he boldly made that decision even during the difficult days of our nation's Civil War.

Finally, if you still think railroad transportation is old-fashioned and out of date, consider this: The food on your table, the car you drive, the materials with which your house was built, the paper used in the book you hold in your hands—some or all these items almost certainly traveled by train before they reached you. All aboard!

The Least You Need to Know

- Lincoln had long been a proponent of transportation infrastructure improvements.

- As a lawyer, Lincoln represented several railroad companies and earned his biggest fees from them.

- Motivation for building the transcontinental railroad was not just to promote westward growth, but to gain access to California's wealth to help finance the Civil War.

- Although expansion of the railroad network was dependent on wealthy investors, it was also heavily subsidized by the government through cash and extensive land grant incentives.

- Today's ground transportation network remains largely dependent on the initial routes and hubs established by the transcontinental railroad.

Part 6

Lincoln's Societal Legacies

Convinced he could restore the Union, Abraham Lincoln frequently had his eye on the future and reconstruction—or "restoration," as he called it. This part discusses some key measures he enacted to ensure America's future after the Civil War was won.

Lincoln tested some reconstruction hypotheses in Louisiana. We share how his ideas and innovations played out in post-Civil War America. International policy also emerged as an issue during the Civil War, and you learn about the European challenges Lincoln faced.

We also show how Lincoln's background moved him to establish the United States Department of Agriculture, and how his lack of formal education inspired him to enact legislation that established the land grant college system, enabling America's citizens—including farmers—to be among the most educated and productive in the world.

Mr. Lincoln, I think your constituents will really get behind your "Land Grant College", but I really think we should reconsider your "Rail Splitting University" and the "Stovepipe Hat Academy"...

Chapter

18

Establishment of Land Grant Colleges

In This Chapter

- ◆ Why President Lincoln—unlike his predecessor—supported the Morrill Act

- ◆ How land grant colleges helped reconstruct the South

- ◆ How the dream of an affordable education for all Americans was later expanded and strengthened

- ◆ How Lincoln's legacy lives on through millions of land grant college students and alumni nationwide

- ◆ How the "Land for Learning" investment has paid off for America

What do Penn State, Cornell, Purdue, Ohio State, Clemson, and the University of Minnesota have in common?

In addition to delivering academic excellence, all six universities are land grant colleges. They're among the original 70 institutions of higher learning created as a result of legislation signed by Abraham Lincoln in 1862 known as the Morrill Act. That bill is probably the most important public education measure in the history of the United States.

The act has changed the lives of millions of students who, like Lincoln, were passionate about learning but found college totally out of reach financially—or geographically. What's more, we're still reaping the benefits of this groundbreaking legislation more than 150 years after Lincoln signed the measure.

Never heard of it? Don't worry. In the following pages, you'll learn all about nineteenth-century education, the Morrill Act of 1862, and the land grant college system. (You'll also find out why there are 105 land grant colleges today.)

Free Land for Learning

Imagine living in a nation where schools were scarce and, by modern standards, a significant number of adults were uneducated. That was the reality of early to mid-nineteenth-century America—the time of Abraham Lincoln. Even in relatively heavily populated areas, most school-aged children attended classes just long enough to learn how to passably read and write. Moreover, they attended school only if they weren't needed at home.

Back in the 1800s, kids labored alongside adults, planting and harvesting farmland and performing other household chores. Some children, particularly those who lived in the Midwest like Lincoln, never had the chance for much formal education because no schools existed in their communities. For pioneer children, often the only educational opportunities were to teach themselves. Lincoln's lack of a formal education was no anomaly.

Notes and Orations

"Mr. Clay's lack of a more perfect early education, however it may be regretted generally, teaches at least one profitable lesson; it teaches that in this country, one can scarcely be so poor, but that, if he will, he can acquire sufficient education to get through the world respectably."

—Abraham Lincoln, eulogy of Henry Clay, July 1852

As you might predict, the number of people who actually made it to college in the early nineteenth century was pretty puny—just a tiny fraction of all Americans. And unless you were born into the wealthy leisure class, you probably couldn't afford a college education even if the institution was located nearby. Back then, there were no college loan or tuition savings programs. Students either had the money or not.

In addition to the problem of financing tuition, sending a boy to college posed other risks. Most nineteenth-century families were engaged in farming or other labor-intensive endeavors and they needed every hand available. The loss of a strong young man, even temporarily, could jeopardize the entire family's welfare. Because colleges rarely imparted knowledge viewed as useful for farming, many parents seriously questioned the investment and sacrifice required. Colleges of the era prepared males for careers in teaching, law, religion, and medicine. Period.

So it's easy to see why most people in Lincoln's era viewed a college education as an impractical luxury. Education's inaccessibility and perceived irrelevance also meant that America was on the path of recreating European aristocratic society. There, universities existed to serve and perpetuate the upper classes. Education was reserved for the idle rich, government leaders, and members of white-collar professions.

That educational system philosophy didn't mesh at all with democracy's principles—which is one reason Abraham Lincoln latched on to an idea that would revolutionize education in America.

Under the Stovepipe

Until the rise of the abolitionist movement and the involvement of women in that cause, educational institutions prepared girls for future roles as wives and mothers. Coursework commonly consisted of religion, singing, dancing, and literature. Female seminaries educated women for teaching, the only socially acceptable female occupation at the time—limited to unmarried women only.

The first two women's colleges to be chartered in the United States were Georgia Female College (now Wesleyan) in 1836 and Mount Holyoke Female Seminary (Mount Holyoke College) in 1837. The first women's institution to provide a full collegiate course of study was Vassar College, founded by Matthew Vassar at Poughkeepsie, New York, which opened in 1865. (North Carolina's Salem College began as a girls' academy in 1772, but was not chartered as a women's college until 1866.)

Georgia's Spelman College, founded in 1881 as Atlanta Baptist Female Seminary, was the first black women's college in the United States. The school opened in the basement of a Baptist church.

From the mid-1860s into the twentieth century, full-fledged women's colleges were the only educational institutions in the United States where females were taught science, mathematics, law, and philosophy—subjects previously reserved for men.

Enter Jonathan Baldwin Turner

By the mid-1800s, newspapers, agricultural organizations, and others in many states were clamoring for scientific education—including the establishment of colleges where students could study agriculture. The existing educational system's curricula catered to students who either pursued classical studies or planned to enter those professions.

Demand for what amounted to an American education revolution led some educators to speak out on the issue. Illinois professor and former farmer Jonathan Baldwin Turner was one of the most prominent among the early campaigners. He had some rather radical thoughts about higher education.

The Yale graduate believed universities weren't teaching subjects that were appropriate for a growing nation such as the United States. Turner said America would be best served if college students learned about agriculture and mechanics (engineering and so forth) in addition to liberal arts. What's more, he argued that the government should help pay for college education.

Turner's idea, embodied in an 1850 document entitled "Plan for a State University for the Industrial Classes," included proposals such as experimental research to improve agricultural endeavors and other innovations. Conducting scientific research designed to improve crops, for example, hadn't been done before. Science was just gaining acceptance back then.

A pivotal point was reached when Turner introduced his plan for educational reform on November 18, 1851 at the Putnam County Farmers Convention in Illinois. Predictably, farmers liked Turner's ideas.

Notes and Orations

"The old general rule was that *educated* people did not perform manual labor. They managed to eat their bread, leaving the toil of producing it to the uneducated. This was not an insupportable evil to the working bees, so long as the class of drones remained very small. But *now*, especially in these free States, nearly all are educated—quite too nearly all, to leave the labor of the uneducated, in any wise adequate to the support of the whole. It follows from this that henceforth educated people must labor. Otherwise, education itself would become a positive and intolerable evil. No country can sustain, in idleness, more than a small percentage of its numbers. The great majority must labor at something productive."

—Abraham Lincoln, address before the Wisconsin State Agricultural Society, September 30, 1859

After the convention, Turner made more speeches to promote his plan, and he later lobbied Abraham Lincoln and Stephen Douglas when they ran against each other for Congress in 1858. Both men had backgrounds in farming, and they liked what Turner had to say. Eventually, Turner met Vermont Congressman Justin Smith Morrill, another influential politician who also saw a need for improved education.

Here's the Catch ...

Together, Turner and Morrill created proposed legislation that embodied their ideas. But Morrill's plan to fund state colleges was especially novel.

Morrill proposed that the federal government give public land to every state in the Union to finance the colleges. States could sell the land to bring in money, but the proceeds had to be used to establish and maintain colleges that taught agricultural and mechanical sciences as well as liberal arts. The schools would be affordable and open to students from all walks of life—including women and African-Americans.

Morrill's bill sailed through both houses of Congress, but on February 26, 1859, President James Buchanan vetoed the measure. Buchanan said Morrill's bill violated federal government policy, as education was a state matter. What's more, Buchanan didn't believe agriculture and mechanics belonged in the college curriculum. (Buchanan, you may recall, was college educated and born to a well-to-do Pennsylvania family— probably as far away from farm life as one could get.)

Morrill's land grant college bill was dead on arrival.

Education Finds a Friend

Buchanan's veto greatly disappointed Morrill and Turner and dashed the hopes of a lot of potential college students. But after Lincoln became president, Turner and Morrill (who was then a U.S. senator) seized the opportunity to present the legislation to a friend of agriculture. They made some minor modifications to the proposed legislation—known as the Morrill Act—and then rallied the bill's supporters for a second try.

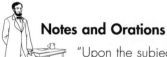

Notes and Orations

"Upon the subject of education, not presuming to dictate any plan or system respecting it, I can only say that I view it as the most important subject which we as a people can be engaged in."

—Abraham Lincoln, first political announcement, March 9, 1832

What may have further ensured the bill's swift passage was a provision Morrill added that required all students to receive training in military tactics. In the midst of the Civil War, the Union couldn't find all the well-trained military officers it needed.

Once again, Congress quickly approved the measure, and the proposed legislation arrived on Lincoln's desk for his signature. Lincoln met Professor Turner while on the 1858 campaign trail and was favorably influenced by his ideas. The act gave students educational opportunities and access to learning that Lincoln could only dream about when he was a young man. It's probably safe to say that he also thought federal funding for higher education would have many short- and long-term benefits for America.

When he considered the future impact of the Morrill Act, Lincoln might have been looking forward to the reconstruction of the South, too. After his efforts to bring an end to slavery were realized, white southerners would need new education to rebuild their economy, which was predominantly agriculturally based. The people who actually performed the work—African Americans—held the most extensive practical knowledge of crops and farming in the South.

On July 2, 1862, Lincoln signed the bill into law—changing America's public education system forever.

Notes and Orations

An Act donating Public Lands to the several States and Territories which may provide Colleges for the Benefit of Agriculture and the Mechanic Arts.

Be it enacted ... that there be granted to the several States, for the purposes hereinafter mentioned, an amount of public land, to be apportioned to each State a quantity equal to thirty thousand acres for each senator and representative of Congress ...

... proceeds thereof applied to the uses and purposes prescribed in this act, and for no other use or purpose whatsoever ...

... to the endowment, support, and maintenance of at least one college where the leading object shall be, without excluding other scientific and classical studies, and including military tactics, to teach such branches of learning as are related to agriculture and mechanic arts, in order to promote the liberal and practical education of the industrial classes in the several pursuits and professions in life ...

—From the Morrill Act of 1862, signed by Abraham Lincoln on July 2, 1862

Lincoln's Educational Dream Expands

The Morrill Act of 1862 is responsible for the establishment of 76 original land grant colleges (sometimes simply referred to as "land-grants") located across the country. But Lincoln's educational legacy doesn't end there.

The Hatch Act of 1887, a measure sponsored by Missouri representative William Henry Hatch, appropriated additional funds for much-needed college textbooks and other learning tools. What's more, Hatch's bill gave land grant colleges the financial means to conduct original agricultural and rural life research—including experiment stations, investigative tools, and the like. The 1887 Act enabled Morrill's original vision to be realized.

In 1890, the Second Morrill Act was passed to bolster federal funding for the original land-grants. Provisions in the 1890 measure required each state to prove that race or color was not an admissions criterion at its land grant colleges. Without providing that evidence, the state could lose federal funding of its land grant colleges.

The South, which was segregated at the time, responded to the 1890 Act's nondiscrimination mandate by creating colleges for African Americans. Today these schools number 17 and are known collectively as the "1890 Land-Grants." Alabama's Tuskegee University and Florida A&M University are just two examples.

But Wait, There's More ...

In 1914, the Smith–Lever Act increased federal funding for the original land grant colleges and created the Cooperative Extension System. The act called for cooperative agricultural extension work between the land grant colleges and the United States Department of Agriculture. The system has county, state, and federal components, but its purpose is direct and single-minded: Expand education's reach into the general community.

Under the Stovepipe

In Lincoln's address before the Wisconsin State Agriculture on September 30, 1859, Lincoln told the assembled crowd: "Every blade of grass is a study; and to produce two, where there was but one is both a profit and a pleasure."

This collaboration between government and higher education is charged with ensuring wide public dissemination of college level information about agriculture and home economics. No matter where you live in the United States, chances are an Extension Bureau is nearby. There you can obtain information on virtually any topic related to local agriculture and home economics—and the information reflects the latest research from the land grant college closest to you.

The 1914 legislation certainly honors Lincoln's lifelong pursuit of learning. Anybody can obtain knowledge on gardening, beekeeping, farm crops, home food preservation, and so much more—without ever setting foot in a college classroom. Best of all, most of what's offered to the public is free of charge. Check it out!

The Equity in Education Act of 1994

As you've probably realized by now, there have been numerous pieces of legislation since 1862 that have continued to add to the Morrill Act's educational power. Could Lincoln have envisioned this when he signed that bill?

Not all the various laws and regulations since 1862 have been mentioned here. (We didn't even mention that the District of Columbia received a $7.24 million college education endowment in lieu of a land grant in 1967!) But we think one more measure is worth special note: the Equity in Education Land Grant Status Act of 1994. (Yes, we've jumped ahead to recent history.)

In the 1994 Act, Congress designated 30 Native American tribal colleges as new land grant colleges. The institutions benefit by the appropriation of federal funding for education, including nonformal education and community outreach. For reasons that should be obvious, no actual land grant or sale of property was necessary in 1994. (Is there anyone out there that doesn't know that the Native Americans were the first guardians and stewards of the land now known as the United States of America?) The Feds handed over cash for learning.

Now that you've come to the end of this section in the chapter, here's your pop quiz question: How many land grant colleges exist today? (For the answer, see the list coming up.)

Today's Land Grant Colleges

The original mission of land grant colleges under the 1862 Morrill Act was to teach agriculture, military tactics, and mechanic arts—but not to the exclusion of classical or other professional studies. The idea was to provide members of the working class a broad range of educational opportunities. Think classical liberal arts education on extra-strength, multivitamins with minerals.

These schools weren't set up simply to teach plowing and mechanical trades. Morrill's intention—which was supported by Lincoln—was to create colleges that provided working-class students the opportunity to explore the entire world ahead of them and to obtain any and all instruction needed to fulfill their dreams.

Land grant colleges were also never considered trade schools. In fact, a school risked the loss of funding if degree offerings narrowed in that way. Instead, new courses of study were added to what was considered standard curriculum for the era—and that step served to broaden the scope of education for all college students. Ultimately, the Morrill Act positively impacted primary and secondary education, too.

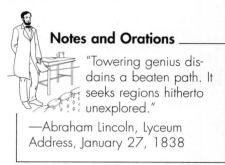

Notes and Orations

"Towering genius disdains a beaten path. It seeks regions hitherto unexplored."

—Abraham Lincoln, Lyceum Address, January 27, 1838

The colleges created under the Morrill Act of 1862 were planned to prepare young people for the profession of *life*, and students were given the chance to define their own path. The study of classics was included in the curriculum. Students who preferred to study philosophy rather than engineering were and still are warmly welcomed.

From the beginning, land grant institutions are institutions of higher learning that provide wide-ranging educational opportunities for all people.

Following is a list of America's land grant colleges. (*) indicates 1890 land grant institution, and (**) indicates 1994 tribal college land grant institution:

- **Alabama.** Alabama A&M University* (Normal, AL); Auburn University (Auburn, AL); Tuskegee University (Tuskegee, AL)

- **Alaska.** University of Alaska Statewide System (Fairbanks, AK)

- **American Samoa.** American Samoa Community College* (Pago Pago, AQ)

- **Arizona.** Navajo Community College** (Tsaile, AZ); University of Arizona (Tucson, AZ)

- **Arkansas.** University of Arkansas, Fayetteville (Fayetteville, AR); University of Arkansas at Pine Bluff* (Pine Bluff, AR)

- **California.** D-Q University** (Davis, CA); University of California System (Oakland, CA)

- **Colorado.** Colorado State University (Fort Collins, CO)

- **Connecticut.** Connecticut Agricultural Experiment Station (New Haven, CT); University of Connecticut (Storrs, CT)

- **Delaware.** Delaware State University* (Dover, DE); University of Delaware (Newark, DE)

- **District of Columbia.** University of the District of Columbia (Washington, DC)

- **Florida.** Florida A&M University* (Tallahassee, FL); University of Florida (Gainesville, FL)

- **Georgia.** Fort Valley State College* (Fort Valley, GA); University of Georgia (Athens, GA)

- **Guam.** University of Guam (Mangilao, GU)

- **Hawaii.** University of Hawaii (Honolulu, HI)

- **Idaho.** University of Idaho (Moscow, ID)

- **Illinois.** University of Illinois (Urbana, IL)

- **Indiana.** Purdue University (West Lafayette, IN)

- **Iowa.** Iowa State University (Ames, IA)

- **Kansas.** Haskell Indian Nations University** (Lawrence, KS); Kansas State University (Manhattan, KS)

- **Kentucky.** Kentucky State University* (Frankfort, KY); University of Kentucky (Lexington, KY)

- **Louisiana.** Louisiana State University System (Baton Rouge, LA); Southern University System* (Baton Rouge, LA)

- **Maine.** University of Maine (Orono, ME)

- **Maryland.** University of Maryland at College Park (College Park, MD); University of Maryland Eastern Shore* (Princess Anne, MD)

- **Massachusetts.** Massachusetts Institute of Technology (Cambridge, MA); University of Massachusetts (Amherst, MA)

- **Michigan.** Bay Mills Community College** (Brimley, MI); Michigan State University (East Lansing, MI)

- **Micronesia.** Community College of Micronesia (Kolonia, Pohnpei, FM)

- **Minnesota.** Fond Du Lac Community College** (Cloquet, MN); Leech Lake Tribal College** (Cass Lake, MN); University of Minnesota (Minneapolis, MN)

- **Mississippi.** Alcorn State University* (Lorman, MS); Mississippi State University (Mississippi State, MS)

- **Missouri.** Lincoln University* (Jefferson City, MO); University of Missouri System (Columbia, MO)

- **Montana.** Blackfeet Community College** (Browning, MT); Dull Knife Community College** (Lame Deer, MT); Fort Belknap Community College** (Harlem, MT); Fort Peck Community College** (Poplar, MT); Little Big Horn College** (Crow Agency, MT); Montana State University (Bozeman, MT); Salish Kootenai College** (Pablo, MT); Stone Child College** (Box Elder, MT)

- **Nebraska.** Nebraska Indian Community College** (Winnebago, NE); University of Nebraska System (Lincoln, NE)

- **Nevada.** University of Nevada, Reno (Reno, NV)

- **New Hampshire.** University of New Hampshire (Durham, NH)

- **New Jersey.** Rutgers, The State University of New Jersey (New Brunswick, NJ)

- **New Mexico.** Crownpoint Institute of Technology** (Crownpoint, NM); Institute of American Indian Arts** (Santa Fe, NM); New Mexico State University (Las Cruces, NM); Southwest Indian Polytechnic Institute** (Albuquerque, NM)

- **New York.** Cornell University (Ithaca, NY)

- **North Carolina.** North Carolina A&T State University* (Greensboro, NC); North Carolina State University (Raleigh, NC)

- **North Dakota.** Fort Berthold Community College** (New Town, ND); Little Hoop Community College** (Fort Totten, ND); North Dakota State University (Fargo, ND); Standing Rock College** (Fort Yates, ND); Turtle Mountain Community College** (Belcourt, ND); United Tribes Technical College** (Bismark, ND)

- **Northern Marianas.** Northern Marianas College (Saipan, CM)

- **Ohio.** The Ohio State University (Columbus, OH)

- **Oklahoma.** Langston University* (Langston, OK); Oklahoma State University (Stillwater, OK)

- **Oregon.** Oregon State University (Corvallis, OR)

- **Pennsylvania.** Pennsylvania State University (University Park, PA)

- **Puerto Rico.** University of Puerto Rico (San Juan, PR)

- **Rhode Island.** University of Rhode Island (Kingston, RI)

- **South Carolina.** Clemson University (Clemson, SC); South Carolina State University* (Orangeburg, SC)

- **South Dakota.** Cheyenne River Community College** (Eagle Butte, SD); Oglala Lakota College** (Kyle, SD); Sinte Gleska University** (Rosebud, SD); Sisseton Wahpeton Community College** (Sisseton, SD); South Dakota State University (Brookings, SD)

- **Tennessee.** Tennessee State University* (Nashville, TN); University of Tennessee (Knoxville, TN)

- **Texas.** Prairie View A&M University* (Prairie View, TX); Texas A&M University (College Station, TX)

- **Utah.** Utah State University (Logan, UT)

- **Vermont.** University of Vermont (Burlington, VT)

- **Virgin Islands.** University of the Virgin Islands (St. Thomas, VI)

- **Virginia.** Virginia Polytechnic Institute & State University (Blacksburg, VA); Virginia State University* (Petersburg, VA)

- **Washington.** Northwest Indian College** (Bellingham, WA); Washington State University (Pullman, WA)

- **West Virginia.** West Virginia University (Morgantown, WV)

- **Wisconsin.** College of the Menominee Nation** (Keshena, WI); Lac Courte Oreilles Ojibwa Community College** (Hayward, WI); University of Wisconsin-Madison (Madison, WI)

- **Wyoming.** University of Wyoming (Laramie, WY)

Source: National Association of State Universities and Land-Grant Colleges, Washington, D.C.

The Return on Lincoln's Legacy

Abraham Lincoln's support of the Morrill Act of 1862 has enriched America's democratic way of life—as well as benefited millions of students and alumni who chose to pursue their educational goals at land grant colleges. This educational legacy also pays big dividends for state, regional, and local economies.

According to the National Association of State Universities and Land-Grant Colleges (NASULGA), land grant colleges return $5 for every $1 of state investment. In addition to providing a well-educated workforce, the colleges generate jobs, attract and help create new high-tech businesses, and increase state tax revenues.

An average of $284 million in annual spending makes land grant colleges major players in the cities and towns in which they are located. University employees, visitors, and students pump another $393 million a year (on average) into the regional economy. That's about $138 for every $100 of university spending! The average land grant college employs about 6,000 full-time workers. For every job on campus, another 1.6 jobs are generated beyond the campus.

Land grant colleges also represent significant value for students. Current annual tuition and fees for full-time undergraduate students who meet in-state residency requirements typically remain well below $5,000 per school year, with average room and board charges slightly above that figure. That makes lots of parents extremely happy.

But the value of land grant colleges is clearly not a one-way deal. Studies show students give back to the community almost immediately. Two out of three students remain in the state where they received their degrees for a significant period of time after graduation. These newly minted grads immediately become a part of the state's educated, taxpaying workforce.

Together with other state-funded colleges and universities, land grant colleges are among the top 50 percent of universities in federal spending on research and development in science and engineering. This group of schools has educated about half the members of Congress and nearly 50 of America's Fortune 100 corporate CEOs.

What a great deal for everyone!

Lincoln couldn't have imagined the impact he'd have on higher education when he signed the Morrill Act, but we bet he'd be pleased with the result.

The Least You Need to Know

- Abraham Lincoln signed the Morrill Act of 1862, which established the land grant college system.

- The act (and subsequent legislation) opened access to higher education for all Americans.

- The U.S. Department of Agriculture teamed up with land grant colleges to create the Cooperative Extension System to share the latest in agricultural and home economics knowledge with everyone!

◆ There are 105 land grant colleges located in the United States and its territories. Land grant colleges return $5 for every $1 of state investment.

◆ Because land grant colleges are affordable and provide practical and liberal arts curricula, millions of students have benefited from Lincoln's educational legacy.

Establishment of the U.S. Department of Agriculture

In This Chapter

◆ Taking a historical perspective of agriculture in America, including pioneer farming and plantation life

◆ Understanding agriculture's role in building a stronger America through Lincoln's background

◆ Knowing what farmers and consumers needed most from the federal government

◆ Creating the U.S. Department of Agriculture

◆ Impacting today's consumers and American farmers with Lincoln's agricultural legacy

When Abraham Lincoln took office in 1861, farmers made up more than half of America's labor force. Most had little formal education, and as a group, they had virtually no representation in federal government—agencies, bureaus, and so forth.

Agricultural science education didn't exist. Agricultural research hadn't even been attempted yet. Tractors hadn't been invented. Still, America's farmers held the weighty responsibility of producing food for the entire nation—a population of more than 31 million people back then.

Given the demands of the Civil War, Lincoln could have decided that he just didn't have time to deal with farmers and their plight. Instead, he took steps that honored and revolutionized American agriculture. Even though Lincoln did not personally enjoy the farming lifestyle (in fact, he hated it!), he viewed the interests of U.S. farmers as "the most worthy of all."

The Most Worthy of All

When European explorers first set foot on the land that would become the United States, they weren't scouting for a place to put up skyscrapers and houses and industrial plants. They weren't searching for a new vacation spot, or planning big land deals with developers. And they had no interest whatsoever in land conservation or in preserving nature's wonders.

What caught the attention of explorers was a vast abundance of fertile soil that could be exploited agriculturally.

From the beginning of civilization, a society's ability to endure has hinged on its ability to feed its people. Great societies were dispersed—or perished completely—solely because they lacked adequate food for their citizens. Acquiring and cultivating land to produce crops and hearty livestock was—and still is—essential to a community's survival.

Lincoln Lingo

The term **agriculture** is derived from ancient Greek and Latin words meaning "related to the land." It is the science, art, and business of farming, generally for purposes of producing food.

Farming is not limited to growing and harvesting crops like grain and corn; it is a huge industry that includes diverse pursuits with a common goal: sustaining society.

A few examples are raising livestock, domesticating honeybees, harvesting fish, tending orchards, making hay, and producing dairy foods like eggs and milk. Farmers also produce nonfood products such as flowers, cotton and wool, straw, and shade trees, to name a few. An agriculturally based economy is one that is dependent on farming.

Think about where we'd be without farmers. Today, little thought is given to the work involved to bring a loaf of bread to the grocery shelf, but in Abraham Lincoln's time, virtually everyone was aware of or engaged in farming activities. More than just a source of income, agriculture is the basis for survival.

Pioneer Farming

As you'll recall, Abraham Lincoln's father and grandfather were both pioneer farmers. To establish a farm in the early nineteenth century, a prospective landowner purchased property from an earlier settler, or more commonly in the frontier, staked a claim to the property by cultivating the land and establishing a homestead, a dwelling with adjoining buildings and land occupied as a principle residence.

The average family farm in the early nineteenth century varied widely depending on region, but generally consisted of about 200 acres. Few farmers were able to cultivate the entire plot. What little farming equipment existed was scarce—the Industrial Revolution didn't even begin until the middle of the century.

In his youth, Abraham Lincoln helped his father, Thomas, clear land and plant crops on the family farm. Pioneer farmers such as Thomas Lincoln usually had some sort of farming background, but most were unaccustomed to breaking or working previously forested prairie sod. Pioneer farmers quickly figured out that the wood- or iron-faced plows they'd previously used weren't suitable. So virtually all the work was done by hand, without the assistance or benefit of machinery.

Beginning a farm was backbreaking labor. After Thomas Lincoln selected the land for his farm in Indiana, for example, he first constructed a basic shelter—a simple log cabin. Like other pioneer farmers, his next priority was to clear trees from the tillable land so crops could be planted.

Under the Stovepipe

Plowing was a job accomplished almost exclusively by hand until 1837. That's when John Deere of Moline, Illinois, figured out a way to manufacture large numbers of smooth, steel-bladed plows that were specifically designed to be pulled by oxen or horses—making the equipment affordable.

The new Deere plow ripped through dense sod to uncover thick black soil, and farmers didn't tire as quickly because strong animals powered the equipment. With the new plow, farmers could prepare land for planting faster than ever before. What's more, the Deere plow enabled farmers to greatly increase the number of acres they cultivated.

Clearing involved stripping bark from trees (to kill them) and cutting away under-brush. Then the trees were either chopped or burnt down. The first land clearing usually began in the spring or early summer, and usually freed up only about three to ten acres.

After the field was clear, farmers plowed the soil, planted the first crop, and hoped for an early and bountiful harvest. Pioneer families rarely brought enough food supplies to sustain them much longer than a few months. If the land proved to be infertile, the farmer had no choice but to move and find another piece of property that was more suitable for farming. You might remember that Thomas Lincoln had to do just that when he discovered that his first Kentucky farm was unsuitable.

Imagine how awful it must have been to put in all that hard work only to find out that crops wouldn't grow! You'd have to start all over again—find new land, uproot your family, and then clear and plow and plant the new fields as fast as possible.

Understanding the basic science behind soil and crops and how to determine the best place to set up a farm would have come in handy. But little knowledge of those issues existed at the time. Farming was essentially a guessing game. Very few farmers would have understood the concept of crop rotation or of putting nutrients back into the soil after harvest.

Under the Stovepipe

Midwestern pioneer farmers like Abraham Lincoln's father commonly planted a mixture of crops that consisted of vegetables and grains intended for home consumption and market. These crops typically included wheat, corn, barley, rye, oats, and potatoes, in addition to other vegetables and fruits. (More wheat than corn was grown because wheat typically brought higher income.)

Farmers who raised livestock also kept part of their land in grass, an inexpensive source of food for cattle, dairy cows, pigs, sheep, and other animals. In the winter, livestock benefited from the farmer's crop harvest and were fed surplus grains and corn.

Lincoln's Perspective on Farming

Even though he lost the U.S. Senate race to Stephen Douglas in 1858, Lincoln was a sought-after speaker. His most memorable speech on the topic of agriculture was delivered in an address he gave to the Wisconsin State Agricultural Society in 1859, a year before he would be elected president.

In his speech to those Midwesterners, Lincoln indicated his interest in agricultural reform. He endorsed broad-based education for those who worked the land to produce the nation's food supply. Interestingly, he suggested a need for scientific inquiry that might help farmers increase crop yields.

All this is to say that Lincoln's support of agriculture goes way back. So it comes as no surprise that, even though the country was in the midst of a civil war, Lincoln decided it was high time somebody helped out the nation's farmers. Lincoln had experienced farming firsthand and undoubtedly remembered his father's farming troubles and all the fieldwork he'd performed in his youth. He knew what was involved in establishing and operating a farm, and he had endured many pioneer farming hardships. Agriculture couldn't have hoped for a more informed and sympathetic advocate.

Notes and Orations

"But farmers, being the most numerous class, it follows that their interest is the largest interest. It also follows that that interest is most worthy of all to be cherished and cultivated—that if there be inevitable conflict between that interest and any other, that other should yield."

—Abraham Lincoln, address before the Wisconsin State Agricultural Society, September 30, 1859

The Civil War Connection

Agriculture wasn't merely one of Lincoln's special interests, however; he simply knew that, just like ancient societies, the Union's population needed a steady food supply to endure. Agriculture was the single most important economic activity in the United States from the time of its founding. If farmers had problems with crop yields or difficulties with pest control or soil fertilization, those troubles directly affected their ability to produce food for the nation. If the food supply dwindled, it affected the Union's economy, the war's outcome, and maybe even the survival and future of democracy itself.

Hungry soldiers did not make good warriors. Moreover, hungry and impoverished citizens typically rebelled against their government. In fact, very soon the starving conditions in the South caused a violent protest now known as the Richmond Bread Riot of 1863. Lincoln wanted to make certain that the Union's future was secure.

And though certainly not as pressing as these factors, we also should acknowledge that Lincoln was a politician. Farmers represented a huge constituency: More than two million American farms were in operation in 1860. Farmers represented nearly half of the entire U.S. population, and 58 percent of the workforce was involved in agriculture.

American farmers were also a powerful economic force, and U.S. agriculture had become the envy of the world. In 1860, farm products represented 82 percent of the country's exports. In addition to producing food for the country, agriculture provided raw materials and the impetus for a variety of other American industries, too—transportation, textiles, and manufacturing.

Under the Stovepipe

Aside from demand for farm goods and products, developments in farm technology fueled agricultural expansion in the United States. Eli Whitney's cotton gin (short for "engine") revolutionized the cotton industry, and the invention of the animal-powered plow was among the greatest pre-Civil War advances for farmers. But many other labor-saving innovations were invented in the nineteenth century that slowly but dramatically improved farm efficiency and productivity.

Oxen and horses pulled or powered most of these newfangled implements, including grain drills, corn and cotton planters, threshing machines, and cultivators, to name a few. The time savings and production increases that resulted from these inventions was nothing short of remarkable.

Take wheat, for example. In 1800, it took 56 man-hours to grow and harvest one acre of wheat. Using new farming equipment in 1840, that same acre of wheat took only about 35 man-hours to plant and harvest. The time savings allowed farmers to expand their farms and grow more crops.

So it wouldn't have been smart to disregard the needs of the very folks who literally ran the economy, especially while the nation was at war. However, folks in government who lacked farming experience erroneously believed that growing crops was a function of nature—about as complicated as taking a breath. Agriculture's booming success served to validate that unfortunate opinion.

Lincoln had to have been aware of farmers complaining bitterly about the government's help in manufacturing and industry while leaving farmers without strong advocacy or resources within government. Given farming's political power and importance to the Union, Lincoln made improving agriculture and the lives of farmers the top priority in his administration. After the initial shock of civil war had passed, he suggested to Congress that it was time to create an agricultural bureau to benefit farmers.

Notes and Orations _____

"Agriculture, confessedly the largest interest of the nation, has, not a department, nor a bureau, but a clerkship only, assigned to it in the government. While it is fortunate that this great interest is so independent in its nature as to not have demanded and extorted more from the government, I respectfully ask Congress to consider whether something more cannot be given voluntarily with general advantage."

"While I make no suggestions as to details, I venture the opinion that an agricultural and statistical bureau might profitably be organized."

—Abraham Lincoln, [first annual] message to Congress, December 3, 1861

Let's Grow!

Congress responded to Lincoln's request by passing legislation to create a broadly defined governmental arm to serve the country's agricultural interests. On May 20, 1862, President Lincoln signed the bill and established the United States Department of Agriculture (USDA). (Coincidentally, Lincoln also signed the act creating land grant colleges on the very same day!)

As you might imagine, lots of folks wanted to be appointed as the department's first commissioner. (The position would become a cabinet-level appointment in 1889.) According to USDA history records, Lincoln received much unsolicited advice about who ought to lead the new department. Some urged the appointment of a distinguished scientist, while others stressed the need for an outstanding man with strong practical experience and knowledge. Editorials appeared in the farming press that also expressed opinions about who Lincoln ought to appoint.

Ultimately, Lincoln decided to appoint a Pennsylvania farmer who shipped fresh butter to the White House each week. The man's name was Isaac Newton.

No, not *Sir* Isaac Newton. *He* lived from 1642 to 1727, and was a brilliant English scientist and mathematician—in fact, he was the most influential scientist who ever lived. But he's not the Isaac Newton who served as the United States Department of Agriculture's first commissioner.

The USDA's First Commissioner

Isaac Newton, an American dairy farmer, was born in 1800 in Burlington County, New Jersey. After completing his common-school education, Newton married and then carried on the family tradition by establishing a farm in Delaware County, Pennsylvania, near Philadelphia. Newton was known as a progressive, knowledgeable farmer and his techniques became models for other farmers in his state.

> **Splitting Rails** _____
>
> Before the USDA was formed in 1862, agriculture was a fragmented industry, with standards and regulations that varied from one locale to another. By 1825, both the U.S. House of Representatives and the U.S. Senate had established agricultural committees.
>
> In 1838, farmers formed the American Society of Agriculture. In addition to sharing agricultural knowledge, the organization's chief goal was to "elevate the character and standing of the cultivators of American soil."
>
> President George Washington was the first to propose a national board of agriculture in 1776, but the idea didn't take hold.

Newton frequently served as a delegate to meetings of the United States Agricultural Society, and he vigorously promoted the idea of urging Congress to establish a national department of agriculture. He'd lobbied four of Lincoln's presidential predecessors, but none had taken action.

Over the years, Newton and his family built a close relationship with the Lincolns. (Sending that tasty butter to the White House every week probably didn't hurt.) Newton had to have been ecstatic to learn that Lincoln had signed the bill establishing the USDA.

Choosing Newton to lead the USDA was probably a no-brainer for Lincoln. The Pennsylvania farmer was known for producing high-quality products and earned the respect of other farmers by operating an efficient and extremely productive farm. He knew the value of the USDA to America's farmers—and the department's potential to improve agriculture nationwide. Newton was perfect for the job.

Powerful Resources for Agriculture

Newton organized the new department and defined its first objectives, many of which were contained in the act signed by Lincoln.

1. Collecting, arranging, and publishing statistical and other useful agricultural information.

2. Introducing valuable plants and animals.

3. Answering inquiries of farmers regarding agriculture.

4. Testing agricultural implements.

5. Conducting chemical analyses of soils, grains, fruits, plants, vegetables, and manures.

6. Establishing a national professorship of botany and entomology.

7. Establishing an agriculture library and museum.

Lincoln's selection of Newton served the country well. Newton ran the department in much the same orderly, efficient way as his farming operation. He held the office until his death in 1867, two years after Lincoln's assassination.

He made real progress in his five years as commissioner and set the standard for his predecessors.

Building an Agricultural Powerhouse

In addition to working with farmers to share knowledge and best practices, the USDA set out to improve food safety. In particular, nineteenth-century meat was risky. Few people knew how to preserve meat properly and many became sick or died from eating meat that *looked* perfectly fine.

The USDA pushed for meat inspection laws, and the first of these were passed in 1890. From that time on, USDA inspectors had the right to inspect slaughterhouses to ensure cleanliness.

In 1906, Congress passed the Food and Drug Act, and the USDA embarked on an aggressive campaign to educate the public about proper food handling and preparation. In 1933, controls on marketing and crops were introduced. New Deal legislation from the early 1930s to 1940s increased government involvement in agriculture and strengthened the USDA's power and influence.

To ensure adequate food supply during World War II, the USDA helped set price controls and established a fair system of rationing. During this same period, the department established the National Victory Garden Program, which encouraged families throughout the country—even city folk—to grow their own fruits and vegetables. The program helped the agricultural industry focus on feeding U.S. troops.

In the 1950s and 1960s, the USDA managed a farm food surplus program that fed the world's needy. Within the last 30 years, marketing regulations have eased somewhat, and today agriculture responds to changes in demand from the consumer marketplace.

Under the Stovepipe

Today's U.S. consumers spend roughly 9 percent of their income on food compared with 11 percent in the United Kingdom, 17 percent in Japan, 27 percent in South Africa, and 53 percent in India. Farmers and ranchers provide food and habitat for 75 percent of the nation's wildlife. The average farm consists of 417 acres, compared to less than 100 acres in 1860.

Although only 15 percent of the U.S. population is employed in farm or farm-related jobs (compared to 58 percent in 1860), productivity continues to rise. In 1960, it was estimated that one U.S. farmer could produce enough food to feed about 25 people. That figure rose to 100 in 1990. Today, one farmer feeds about 129 individuals. Individuals or family corporations operate almost 90 percent of all U.S. farms.

Source: Agriculture Council of America

The Farmer's Perspective

After the Civil War, agriculture continued its rapid expansion. The transcontinental railway's establishment and western migration helped fuel that trend. Thousands of settlers moved across the country to new western territories and states—and many of them established farming operations.

Armed with education and scientific knowledge, farmers dramatically improved soil conditions and crop yields. New machines such as steam tractors, reapers, and harvesters enabled farmers to utilize larger plots of land. Production and efficiency soared. But no matter how hard they worked, most farmers didn't enjoy prosperity.

Under the Stovepipe

By 1916, nearly 900 million acres of U.S. land was being farmed. That same year, America was home to more than six million farms.

As producers of raw material, farmers gradually ended up on the losing end of the trade-exchange equation. The cost of the products they efficiently produced lowered—while the prices farmers paid for manufacturing equipment steadily rose. Many farmers responded by increasing farmed acreage, and squeezing more productivity and yield from their operations.

As farmers gained more knowledge, agriculture settled into regional specializations. Farmers didn't stop growing other crops—they learned that some agricultural ventures simply brought better results than others, depending on local conditions. Those high-yield, high-quality ventures were the ones they pursued as priority crops.

Great Plains farmers, for instance, found that wheat grew especially well in that region. Dairy farming suited upper Midwestern states such as Wisconsin and Michigan. Farmers in Rocky Mountain states raised cattle and sheep as well as sugar beets and alfalfa. Washington and Ohio became top producers of apples, peaches, and pears—as well as wheat. Idaho, of course, grew potatoes. The South continued to specialize in cotton and tobacco.

But then, in postwar 1920, deflation set in—causing agricultural prices to plummet. With efficiency at its maximum, many farmers suffered. Worse, production continued to outpace demand. The number of farms in the United States declined.

Congress passed a series of measures that were intended to help farms survive. Farmers responded with even greater efficiency and productivity, especially when manufacturers introduced gasoline-powered tractors and other machinery. U.S. consumers and manufacturers reaped the benefits. Farmers didn't do so well. Financial margins for agricultural operations further tightened. One bad year could put a farmer out of business.

Keeping in mind that agriculture is key to a society's survival, Congress passed the Agricultural Adjustment Act in 1933, to supplement prices of agricultural commodities, encourage soil conservation, and subsidize exports. Along with other initiatives, programs created by the act remain in place to ensure the future of America's agricultural industry.

Notes and Orations

"Population must increase rapidly—more rapidly than in former times—and ere long the most valuable of all arts, will be the art of deriving a comfortable subsistence from the smallest area of soil. No community whose every member possesses this art, can ever be the victim of oppression of any of its forms. Such community will be alike independent of crowned-kings, money-kings, and land-kings."

—Abraham Lincoln, address before the Wisconsin State Agricultural Society, September 30, 1859

Agriculture Today

At the dawn of the twenty-first century, new trends in agriculture continue to emerge. The demand for organic food has renewed interest in farming. Farmer's markets are enjoying a renaissance as consumers seek out food grown without pesticides or other chemicals.

Although the number of farms has steadily declined since the early 1900s, the average acreage farmed by each operation has more than doubled in recent decades. Today's farmers have access to wireless technology, sophisticated weather stations, and other innovations such as satellite guidance systems that help steer tractors in a straight line.

Even farmers with small, remotely located farms can obtain agricultural education via the Internet—and can also use that technology to market their goods to wholesalers and consumers. Aided by research made possible by the USDA and land grant colleges, farmers have access to more scientific information than ever before.

Under the Stovepipe

The agricultural revolution that began with Abraham Lincoln's support of the U.S. Department of Agriculture greatly improved crop yields. Today's farmers are able to bring forth more food in less space.

For example, one acre of land (an area roughly the size of a football field) can produce 45,000 pounds of strawberries, 24,000 heads of lettuce, 36,000 pounds of potatoes, 14,000 pounds of sweet corn, or 37.1 bushels of wheat.

Source: Chenango County Farm Bureau, Norwich, New York

And all this innovation started with Abraham Lincoln.

The USDA in the Twenty-First Century

Today's USDA continues Lincoln's legacy by serving all of us. Although its primary role has remained steady, the agency's mission has significantly expanded since 1862.

The department is the largest conservation agency in the country, encouraging voluntary efforts to protect soil, water, and wildlife. It manages the nation's 192 million acres of national forests and rangeland through the Forest Service, and also helps ensure open markets to U.S. agricultural products. The USDA provides food aid to needy people overseas and leads federal antihunger efforts with programs such as school lunches and food stamps.

Consistent with its beginnings, the USDA is an agricultural research leader, conducting studies that range from human nutrition to crop technologies. The agency helps further support farmers by bringing housing, modern communications systems, and safe drinking water to rural America.

Although farming declined rapidly in the twentieth century, the U.S. agricultural industry continues to be the most efficient and productive in the world. The legislation that Lincoln signed in 1862 transformed American farming—a revolution that continues to this day.

The Least You Need to Know

- ◆ Abraham Lincoln is responsible for the establishment of the United States Department of Agriculture.

- ◆ Agriculture was the top economic force in America from its earliest beginnings until the early twentieth century.

- ◆ America's agricultural industry is the most efficient and productive in the world.

- ◆ Today's United States Department of Agriculture is a dynamic organization that provides leadership and management on issues related to food, agriculture, natural resources, and more.

Chapter 20

Lincoln's Louisiana Experiment

In This Chapter

- What the first plans for reconstruction entailed

- How the Union seized New Orleans about 13 months after the Civil War began

- Why Louisiana remained under military rule until 1868

- How the gradual process of emancipation and freedom in Louisiana occurred

- How Civil War reconstruction in Louisiana compares to reconstruction in twenty-first-century Iraq

In 1862, in the early stages of the Civil War, the Union captured New Orleans and indeed the entire state of Louisiana. A military government was put into place, and provisions were made for bringing former combatants and "belligerents" back into the Union fold. Even some measure of emancipation was taking place, and means of dealing with free blacks—some of whom were slaveholders themselves—were developed.

Lincoln viewed Louisiana as a testbed for the eventual reconstruction of the South. His grand experiment—like so many—had both successes and failures. Examining what took place in Louisiana provides insight into Lincoln's vision for reconstruction. Sadly, his death intervened, so there was no other state that developed quite like Louisiana. However, the lessons learned from the Louisiana Experiment proved valuable in the massive reconstruction effort that took place in the aftermath of the Civil War. We'll examine what those lessons were, and what we might still be learning from them today.

A Controversial Hypothesis

Strategies for reconstruction were already being formed by members of Lincoln's administration and northern legislators as early as 1861. But debate over the issue of slavery as a factor in the war and reconstruction continued.

The Crittenden-Johnson resolution passed by Congress that year proclaimed that the Civil War was being fought solely to preserve the Union. Slavery as an aim of war was specifically excluded. That resolution, sponsored by Senator John Crittenden of Kentucky, and Senator (later Vice President and President) Andrew Johnson of Tennessee, was crafted carefully, with the intent of keeping in the Union the key slaveholding border states of Maryland, Kentucky, and Missouri. Keeping Maryland in the Union was especially crucial: If that state seceded, Washington would be completely surrounded by Confederate states.

With the needs of border states in mind, Congress's initial reconstruction plan was to return to status quo as quickly as possible. Readmission would be granted and slavery would continue where it had been legal before the war. The legislators subscribed to the belief that slavery would naturally disappear over time. Once gone, it could then be outlawed.

As the war continued, though, the goal of abolishing slavery gained momentum, and it became inextricably linked with reestablishing the Union. But the forum in which abolition would begin, and the manner in which the idea would be introduced to the white majority would have to be carefully orchestrated.

New Orleans Is Captured

In May 1862, Union ships surrounded the Confederate port city of New Orleans, Louisiana. Union Admiral Farragut now took command of the city from a resentful mayor. General Benjamin Butler, in charge of the 15,000 men of the Massachusetts Volunteers, occupied New Orleans. He was now the military commander of the city, but he and his men were treated with contempt as they walked through town.

Butler soon captured a rebel who had torn down the Union flag flying at the U.S. Mint. The rebel was tried, convicted, and sentenced to execution. The order was carried out, despite pleas of many citizens, including the rebel's wife and children, to spare his life. Butler became known as "the Beast."

Under the Stovepipe

As Union forces occupied New Orleans, one of the challenges with which they had to contend was that of the southern woman. Unlike the southern male, she could not be threatened, cajoled, or manhandled for making insulting comments or provoking Union soldiers. Sensibilities of the South afforded a great deal of protection for the "gentle sex."

So General Butler devised a General Order of a particularly devious nature to receive proper respect from southern females:

> "As the officers and soldiers of the United States have been subjected to repeated insults from the women (calling themselves ladies) of New Orleans, in return for the most scrupulous noninterference and courtesy on our part, it is ordered that hereafter when any female shall, by word, gesture, or movement, insult or show contempt for any officer or soldier of the United States, she shall be regarded and held liable to be treated as a woman of the town plying her avocation."

In other words, a woman who showed disrespect to a Union soldier could and would be treated as a common prostitute. Needless to say, this was *not* a popular edict with southerners of either sex!

Butler allowed as much normal activity as was possible to maintain good order and discipline. Food was distributed to the destitute, and token jobs were given to the unemployed to clean the streets and canals. General Butler started gathering a group of Union sympathizers who were fairly well-to-do to form a new government for the city, and required loyalty oaths from them.

When people wanted to use certain governmental services, Butler began requiring them to take loyalty oaths, too. Resentment grew over these requirements, but Butler started threatening those refusing to take the oath with confiscation of property.

Under the Stovepipe

After the Civil War, General Benjamin Butler became a Republican congressman, representing Massachusetts. He was a very vocal critic of President Andrew Johnson, and in fact authored the tenth article of impeachment against Johnson. Butler became the lead House prosecutor of Johnson in the Senate. He was generally regarded as having done a rather poor job, and his performance in that role is often considered a main reason for Johnson's acquittal.

Butler ran for governor of Massachusetts five times before winning the office in 1882. He became a presidential candidate in 1884, representing the Greenback-Labor and Anti-Monopoly parties, and won less than 2 percent of the popular vote.

The Plan for Reconstruction

Lincoln's plan for reconstruction was based on the premise that it wasn't the *states* that had seceded, but rather the disloyal *leaders* of those states who had committed the treasonous act of secession. Therefore, if those disloyal persons were replaced with individuals loyal to the Union and committed to its preservation, then a major step toward reconstruction would have been made.

Lincoln steadfastly refused to believe that the desire for southern secession and dissolution of the Union was widespread. He believed it was an agenda pushed by a select few in office, and that by reaching the masses, he could bring disaffected states back into the Union. There were four basic components of Lincoln's plan:

- ◆ First, states that left the Union should be brought back into the fold, either through force or enticement. Lincoln hoped to convince loyalists in southern states that the model demonstrated in West Virginia—returning to the Union by seceding from a secession state—was a sound one.

- ◆ Second, he focused on winning the war. Defeating the Confederate army would of course hasten reconstruction, but it would also allow Lincoln to be in control using military force, and putting in place military governors as needed (as in Louisiana).

- ◆ Third, the Constitution supported Lincoln's management of the process through his authority as commander in chief. Keeping things in the hands of the military allowed Lincoln, as commander in chief, to remain in charge. That minimized congressional interference and the in-fighting that would naturally result. Reconstruction as a wartime policy kept matters directly in Lincoln's hands.

◆ Fourth, Lincoln worked to gain the support of Congress and the people at large. He had to delicately advance his own antislavery agenda while not promoting anything radical enough to alienate any other group.

Under the Stovepipe

"The Bonnie Blue Flag" was a highly popular southern tune—a rallying cry for the Confederate cause. When Union General Butler took over the city of New Orleans, he fined any citizen—man, woman, or child—caught singing, whistling, or playing the music on any instrument. Then Butler went a step further and had the publisher of "The Bonnie Blue Flag" arrested and the sheet music destroyed. The tune's composer, Harry McCarthy, was fined $500 for creating the music.

One could say (and many have) that Butler was a naturally argumentative man. But it might also be said he understood the powerful undercurrents that could make or break his army's ability to maintain control over an angry citizenry.

The Reconstruction Laboratory

Louisiana would be a fine proving ground for Lincoln's theories, a test that would later be applied to the entire South when the war had concluded. Although the outcome of the war was far from certain in 1862, people from both sides were closely watching Louisiana to see how things would work out. Many recognized that if the Union prevailed in the war, then Louisiana represented what the rest of the South might look like in its aftermath.

There were stronger pockets of Union support in the port city of New Orleans than most places in the South: New Orleans' citizenry was far more cosmopolitan and international than that of most southern cities. That isn't to say Union supporters constituted a majority, and even supporters held many different views. Some wanted the Union preserved along with slavery, others wanted to see slavery abolished. Lincoln had to forge and maintain uneasy coalitions among the various loyalist groups. A particularly delicate challenge for Lincoln was dealing with free blacks in Louisiana. Some 11,000 free blacks lived in this city of 140,000. Although this presented an opportunity for Lincoln to demonstrate the ideals of equality, he also had to consider the sentiments of the white population, which was largely representative of whites throughout the South. Racial fears and prejudices were rampant, and relations would be sorely tested.

Under the Stovepipe

About 25,000 blacks lived in New Orleans, and the 11,000 free blacks among them were hard to categorize. Many owned property; a few even owned slaves.

Some of the African Americans in New Orleans had fought with the Confederacy or served in a militia to guard against slave rebellions. After the North occupied New Orleans, many offered their services to the Union army. These offers were rebuffed until the summer of 1862, when Butler became desperate for assistance. He then formed the Africa Corps, which eventually had 25,000 Louisiana blacks in its ranks.

The free blacks would have little influence on their collective future, however. Lincoln wanted to assure the white males that giving blacks the right to vote wouldn't cause whites to lose dominance politically or economically. Power remained with the white males, and the military government would interdict Louisiana slave uprisings and return runaway slaves to their "owners." Meanwhile, Congress was passing acts that authorized freeing slaves of proven rebels and allowing blacks to serve in the Union army. These evolving treatments of blacks were subtly changing relationships in Louisiana. Lincoln's feelings about slavery, and slavery's likely future, were becoming increasingly obvious. Despite his best efforts to play both sides, the Emancipation Proclamation and other indications made Lincoln's position abundantly clear. Within a month after issuing the Emancipation Proclamation, Lincoln was urging Louisianans to hold elections to install a loyal Union political body. The days of the "old way" were clearly numbered.

Reconstruction Begins at Home

In fact, Brigadier General John Phelps of the military government in Louisiana expressed his opinion that the best way to ensure stability in Louisiana was to free African Americans. Phelps also sought their inclusion in the military. Among other benefits, Phelps believed military service and education would elevate and improve the status of African Americans while bringing stability to the region. He aggressively recruited blacks into the army.

Phelps's philosophy and the actions he took infuriated many Louisiana whites. Phelps was challenging the status quo, and was being far more blatant about it—and speedy—than was Lincoln. Ultimately, General Butler elicited Phelps's resignation.

Notes and Orations

"It seems the Union feeling in Louisiana is being crushed out by the course of General Phelps. Please pardon me for believing that is a false pretense. The people of Louisiana—all intelligent people every where—know full well, that I never had a wish to touch the foundations of their society, or any right of theirs."

"With perfect knowledge of this, they forced a necessity upon me to send armies among them, and it is their own fault, not mine, that they are annoyed by the presence of General Phelps. They also know the remedy—know how to be cured of General Phelps. Remove the necessity of his presence."

—Abraham Lincoln, to Reverdy Johnson, July 26, 1862

Less than a month after the May 1862 Union occupation of New Orleans, Union loyalists held a meeting and founded the Union Association of New Orleans. The members of this group became the New Orleans city government. Courts soon reopened for business, and in December, two congressmen were elected in Louisiana and sent to Washington.

That same month saw the replacement of General Butler, "the Beast," with Nathaniel Best. Butler's hardline approach had served its purpose; now, Lincoln felt, a softer touch was needed. Although Lincoln and Union supporters were installed as political appointees, Best worked hard not to upset the apple cart too quickly.

After he became convinced that enough progress had been made to ensure sympathetic candidates would be elected, Lincoln worked toward holding free elections in Louisiana. He was shaping rights for blacks at the same time.

Although there were proponents for enfranchising blacks, no one in a truly influential position was actually proposing giving that right to them. Freeing them from slavery seemed radical enough for the time.

Ever so slowly, inch by incremental inch, Louisiana was painstakingly brought back into the fold. Federal intercession and supervision was maintained until Louisiana could truly be accepted and trusted again as a full member of the Union. Just what that would take remained vague and undefined until 1868, when Louisiana was formally readmitted to the Union.

From Theory to Law

The techniques used by the military government during the occupation of Louisiana were an embodiment of Lincoln's philosophies, tempered by political necessities and expediency. Although negotiation was employed to effect change whenever possible, those compromises stayed within the framework of Lincoln's beliefs and values.

The goal was to win over a core group of influential people, either those who had Union sympathies to begin with or those susceptible to influence. Although they were being wooed, a hardline was used to bring the populace into compliance with certain inviolable rules of conduct.

After compliance was achieved, softer techniques were used whenever feasible. Some forms of reward for "good behavior" were given, and the needs of the population were addressed. The sympathizers seen as possible candidates for initial limited self-rule were further tested and influenced. As a state demonstrated trustworthiness and loyalty in incremental steps, greater freedom and self-rule was incrementally granted.

Notes and Orations _____

"I would be glad for her to make a new Constitution recognizing the emancipation proclamation, and adopting emancipation in those parts of the state to which the proclamation does not apply. And while she is at it, I think it would not be objectionable for her to adopt some practical system by which the two races could gradually live themselves out of their old relation to each other, and both come out better prepared for the new. Education for young blacks should be included in the plan. After all, the power, or element, of "contract" may be sufficient for this probationary period; and, by it's simplicity, and flexibility, may be the better."

—Abraham Lincoln, writing to Nathaniel Banks concerning Louisiana, August 5, 1863

Slowly, blacks were given equal rights and freedoms, while great effort was made to convince the white majority that their position of dominance would not be compromised. Great equalizers such as free public education were made available to black children as well as white. Other exclusive services and privileges long taken for granted by whites, such as access to the court system, were also slowly made available to blacks.

The lessons learned in Lincoln's Louisiana Experiment were applied throughout Reconstruction. Flexibility would be employed to deal with changing situations and events that didn't unfold as experience would suggest, but the principles tried and proven in Louisiana would serve the Union—and ultimately the South—well through the long, slow, and painful process of reconstruction.

The Least You Need to Know

- ◆ Union occupation of New Orleans started quite early in the Civil War, in March 1862.

- ◆ Military governance of Louisiana was in effect until proven Union loyalists could be placed throughout the state's political offices.

- ◆ Military governance of occupied states allowed Lincoln to manage reconstruction with minimal congressional interference.

- ◆ Emancipation was done in small, incremental steps to minimize instability and not unduly alarm the whites in dominant economic and political power.

Chapter 21

International Policy

In This Chapter

- Why Lincoln and the Union faced threats from overseas during America's Civil War

- How an international maritime incident almost started a war between the Union and Great Britain in 1861

- How Lincoln transformed public opinion in Europe to the Union's benefit

- How modern-day leaders emulate Lincoln's diplomatic style

Given all the domestic demands of the Civil War, we don't think of Abraham Lincoln as a foreign statesman. But in addition to the war effort at home, international policy and diplomacy were important issues in the Lincoln administration.

Considering that Lincoln had never traveled the world, he had to be a quick study when it came to foreign relations. With the help of his secretary of state, Lincoln and his administration averted possible war with England and France. And in the end, Lincoln earned international respect as a savvy world politician.

Southern Drawl or British Accent?

When Abraham Lincoln entered office in 1861, seven states had already seceded and four more were about to. Confederate forces had surrounded Fort Sumter in South Carolina. You'd think Lincoln's attention would have been totally focused on domestic matters.

However, it occurred to Lincoln and his administration that there was an outside threat as well. Because of the South's strong foreign trade ties and the North's support of exclusionary economic policies, other countries might come to the aid of the Confederacy. The United States had enjoyed generally cordial relationships with most European governments, but American tariffs on foreign goods had strained some of those relations. Northern legislators had pressed for the tariffs, which restricted import trade.

Economic Ties

Foreign alliances would give the Confederacy many advantages in a war. Overseas interests could provide an influx of cash, food supplies, and military manpower. Raw materials, manufactured goods, and weapons could be shipped to southern states, too. Moral support and military expertise could also be added to the mix, making it difficult for the Union to quell the rebellion. Of course, the other, greater threat was that foreign intervention might enlarge the domestic battle. What if other countries actually allied militarily with the Confederacy and attacked the Union?

In the first few days and weeks of the war, the gravity of the international situation wasn't immediately apparent to Lincoln or most of his Cabinet. But Lincoln's secretary of state, William H. Seward, recognized that the situation posed significant risks to the Union. Seward prepared and sent a letter to other nations, warning them to stay out of the conflict. His communiqué intimated that any nation recognizing the Confederacy as a sovereign nation would do so at its own peril.

After war began, the Union initiated blockades of Confederate ports to cut off incoming and outgoing supply shipments. The strategy was prudent from a military standpoint, but the Confederacy hoped that the action would be viewed as unduly interfering with international trade and damaging to foreign economies. The blockade of southern ports implied sovereignty, and that undermined Lincoln's theory about secession. This problem loomed large in the early days of the war.

Confederate leaders also figured the cutting off of cotton shipments to Europe would enrage Great Britain and other countries, causing European nations to recognize and side with the Confederate States of America. They hoped Great Britain would break the blockade of their "sovereign nation" and join the battle against the Union.

To the surprise of many in the South, England decided against direct involvement. Instead of breaking the blockade and risking war with the Union, England responded with a proclamation of neutrality in May of 1861. Other European countries followed Great Britain's lead.

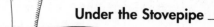

Under the Stovepipe

As the Union tightened its blockade of southern ports in 1861, the South's European customers turned to new sources of cotton even as economic realities forced the Confederacy to aggressively pursue recognition as an independent country. Recognition as a sovereign nation would allow the South to reopen trade and gain allies for its cause.

However, neutrality didn't exactly rule out all international involvement. A side effect of the declarations of neutrality by European nations was the unspoken acknowledgment of the Confederacy as a *belligerent power*. Among other rights, that status gave the Confederacy the power to obtain loans and purchase goods from neutral countries, and to exercise *belligerent rights* on the high seas.

Lincoln Lingo

An entity at war with an established nation, a **belligerent power** doesn't have the full status of a sovereign government but is recognized as an organized body. **Belligerent rights** are granted by international law and/or established nations and include key maritime rights: the right to stop, board, and inspect ships of neutral countries for war materiel intended for the belligerent's enemy; to capture vessels of the belligerent's enemy; and other rights reserved for a sovereign nation at war.

Delicate Diplomacy

Europe's tacit acknowledgment of the Confederacy's belligerent status angered many in the North. People figured it would only be a matter of time before this tentative recognition would evolve into full diplomatic recognition of the Confederacy. Great Britain was viewed as the greatest threat. Secretary of State Seward immediately instructed America's minister to England, Charles Adams, to warn Britain "not to fraternize with our domestic enemy" officially or otherwise, or they would risk war.

One of Lincoln's greatest, but largely unsung, achievements during the Civil War was avoiding war with England or France while convincingly threatening war to prevent recognition of the Confederacy. Many people in England closely watched the Civil War as it unfolded. A Union loss might have pleased some folks in Great Britain, which lost face in the War of 1812. However, people and parties in England held differing views. Even within the British government, there was fierce debate over the wisdom of any invention.

France and England's ruling classes sympathized with the Confederacy, since those countries considered the South to be an aristocracy, as they were. (The two countries appeared to overlook the fact that the South was, at its core, democratic in nature, not aristocratic.) To some, the idea that the American democratic "experiment" might fail was tantalizing.

Some individuals and groups in Britain and France felt a kinship with the Confederacy because all three (Britain, France, and the Confederacy) had been forced to operate under similar burdens of what they felt to be oppressive tariffs. But most people in France and England could not abide slavery. In fact, British and French newspapers blasted slavery as a relic of barbarism. Up until 1862, though, the federal government clearly conveyed the message that it was fighting to save the Union, not to abolish slavery per se, so before slavery became an issue in the war, the governments of the two European countries could reasonably side with the Confederacy without violating moral values.

However, the Confederacy's belief that Europe's economy was so dependent on southern cotton that it would give active support to the Confederacy turned out to be wrong.

The Trent Affair

There was some early involvement by the British, though, and one event brought the Union to the brink of yet another war. Although modern scholars believe the threat of war with England was overblown, the events of 1861 are nevertheless important historically.

Tensions between the Union and England and France grew as the Confederacy jockeyed for international recognition and favors. The matter eventually came to a head late in the fall of 1861.

To aid his cause, Confederate President Jefferson Davis took the bold step of officially naming ministers to England and France. James Mason of Virginia (grandson of George Mason, a framer of the Bill of Rights) and John Slidell of Louisiana were appointed as the Confederacy's diplomatic emissaries to Great Britain and France, respectively.

The two men left for Europe in October with the goal of obtaining recognition of the Confederacy as a sovereign nation and obtaining support for the South's cause. On October 12, Mason and Slidell boarded the *Gordon*, a small private steamer. The vessel left South Carolina's Charleston harbor at 1:00 in the morning. After dodging the Union blockade, the *Gordon* made its way to Cuba. There, the two newly minted statesmen boarded the British mail steamer *Trent*, bound for England's port at Southampton.

Under the Stovepipe

The Union warship commander who instigated the Trent Affair in 1861 also has an interesting biography. In 1838, then 40-year-old Lieutenant Charles Wilkes was in charge of a government expedition to South America and Antarctica. Wilkes led a squadron of six ships, more than 300 seamen, and a team of scientists and artists whose mission was to conduct research and create accurate naval charts of the region. The region Wilkes explored became known as Wilkes Land.

On November 8, 1861, the Union warship *USS San Jacinto*, under the command of Captain Charles Wilkes, intercepted the *Trent* 300 miles east of Cuba. The Union wasn't in the practice of stopping foreign vessels, but had received intelligence reports about the Confederacy's intentions and that the diplomats were likely onboard the *Trent*.

Wilkes halted the *Trent* on the high seas—international waters—by firing two shots across her bow. Armed Union marines from the *San Jacinto* boarded the *Trent* and forcibly removed the two Confederate diplomats and their secretaries. After the prisoners were onboard the *San Jacinto*, the *Trent* was allowed to proceed. The Union warship headed up the East Coast to Union territory.

When the *San Jacinto* pulled into Boston Harbor on November 23, the people of Boston greeted Wilkes and the ship's crew enthusiastically. The war had not been going well for the Union, and the seizure of the rebel diplomats boosted northern morale. Northern newspapers competed in honoring Wilkes, trying to out-do one another with articles of glowing praise. Congress recognized Wilkes's contributions to the

Union cause by issuing an official resolution. Meanwhile, the Confederate prisoners were incarcerated at nearby Fort Warren.

That might have been the end of the story—except the Union's actions on the high seas infuriated Great Britain. When news of the capture reached London on November 27, the British challenged the Union. Great Britain's government claimed that the captain of the *San Jacinto* had violated international maritime law.

The English prime minister, Lord Palmerston, called an emergency Cabinet meeting. While Palmerston was actually quite restrained in the conduct of the crisis, he dramatically opened the meeting by throwing his hat down on the table and exclaiming, "I don't know whether you are going to stand for this, but I'll be damned if I do!"

> **Under the Stovepipe**
>
> As news spread of the Union's capture of Confederate diplomats, Virginia rebels at Norfolk and Fort Monroe reportedly rejoiced. Confederates believed retaliation by England against the Union was imminent.

British officials crafted a strongly worded letter, demanding an immediate apology from the Union and return of the Confederate diplomats. Queen Victoria's consort, Prince Albert, urged restraint. A considerably softened letter was forwarded to Britain's Washington, D.C.-based minister Lord Lyons for delivery. Lyons presented Britain's demands to Seward on December 19, 1861.

The British maintained that the Union violated international law by stopping the *Trent*, boarding the vessel, and removing passengers. According to England, if the Union believed that a covert operation was underway, the ship and its entire crew should have been seized. The proper next step would have been to escort the vessel to a Union harbor where a *prize court* could be convened. The court would then decide whether the taking of prisoners from the ship was proper or not.

> **Lincoln Lingo**
>
> A **prize court** adjudicates disputes regarding the capture of goods and vessels at sea. During war, privately owned Confederate ships and also vessels from neutral countries that carry contraband—people or materials supporting enemy action—are subject to seizure. But title does not automatically pass to the captor. A prize court convened by the capturing nation must decide the fate of the ship and property using international law or other applicable statutes.

While this tenuous diplomacy was taking place, France suggested a tentative willingness to join with Britain in war against the United States. Aside from legal issues, Britain viewed the Union's action as insulting.

Lincoln faced a conundrum. Although he could ill afford war with England, complying with British demands seemed politically impossible—Captain Wilkes's action was just too popular in the North. Lincoln met with his Cabinet, and many heated arguments ensued. From these meetings arose Lincoln's philosophy of "one war at a time." He didn't deem it prudent to fight Great Britain and the Confederacy simultaneously. What had previously appeared to be "politically impossible" domestically became the best course of action from an international perspective.

Secretary Seward presented a carefully crafted letter to Lord Lyons announcing that the Union planned to release the Confederate prisoners. However, the Union challenged Britain's assertion that the entire ship should have been seized. Lincoln and his administration argued that out of the War of 1812, Britain had adopted the American ideal of neutral rights. Basically, the Union asserted that the *San Jacinto* had no right to seize the *Trent* because of its affiliation with a neutral country. What's more, Lincoln continually referred to the Confederate prisoners as "citizens of the United States," which further reduced the perception that the actions of the *San Jacinto* were warlike.

On January 1, 1862, Mason and Slidell were released and allowed to resume their trip to Europe. Britain backed off because releasing the prisoners constituted an implicit apology. The Union achieved its objectives of averting war and saving face, but the release of Mason and Slidell actually constituted a total surrender.

After all the uproar, the Confederacy's diplomatic mission ultimately failed. They were unable to convince any European nations to intervene on the Confederacy's behalf in the Civil War.

Notes and Orations

"In the month of June last there were some grounds to expect that the maritime powers which, at the beginning of our domestic difficulties, so unwisely and unnecessarily, as we think, recognized the insurgents as a belligerent, would soon recede from that position, which has proved only less injurious to themselves, than to our own country. But the temporary reverses which afterwards befell the national arms, and which were exaggerated by our own disloyal citizens abroad have hitherto delayed that act of simple justice."

—Abraham Lincoln, annual message to Congress, December 1, 1862

Lincoln and Seward's calm, sure handling of the Trent Affair earned the respect of the British government. Prior to the incident, Seward was viewed as a warmonger. But the Union's diplomacy showed British officials that they could work with Lincoln and that peace between the two countries was possible.

The outcome of the Trent Affair marked a major shift in British attitude toward the Union—and Lincoln personally. What's more, the peace accord remained in place even when future events strained the relationship.

Statesman Lincoln

Secretary William Seward deserves a lot of credit for what he accomplished for the Union during the Civil War. But the diplomatic strides made were the result of the Seward–Lincoln team. The combination of each man's unique individual strengths and shortcomings made the collaboration especially powerful.

Lincoln's folksy manner caused many people to underestimate him. Lord Lyons, British ambassador to the United States, is said to have once described Lincoln as a "rough westerner of the lowest origins." On the other hand, Seward was far more worldly, having traveled internationally and met with many foreign leaders. Seward's big-city sophistication made him a fine counterpart for Lincoln's homespun nature. But unlike Seward, Lincoln had a deep understanding of people—a key attribute of successful diplomats.

More than anything else, the tools of a statesman are his words. Whether written or uttered, properly chosen words delivered at the right time to the right person can defuse tensions, elicit cooperation, or break down barriers. Lincoln's simple, evocative eloquence in his speeches and correspondence demonstrated time and again the finest traditions of diplomacy.

Many people consider Seward to have been the consummate diplomat of the Lincoln presidency. When Lincoln initially wanted to issue the Emancipation Proclamation, Seward urged him to wait until the North enjoyed a significant military success. Lincoln took Seward's advice and waited until after the battle at Antietam before issuing this groundbreaking proclamation.

Arguably, Lincoln's biggest ongoing international challenge may have been to keep other nations from recognizing the Confederacy. Lincoln absolutely believed that secession was treasonous, and states that had seceded were still part of the nation—they just needed to be brought back into the fold. For the Confederacy to receive any sort of international recognition would be to legitimize their cause by establishing their independence from the United States.

Notes and Orations

"I have received the new year's address which you have sent me with a sincere appreciation of the exalted and humane sentiments by which it was inspired.

As those sentiments are manifestly the enduring support of the free institutions of England, so I am sure also that they constitute the only reliable basis for free institutions throughout the world.

The resources, advantages, and powers of the American people are very great, and they have, consequently, succeeded to equally great responsibilities. It seems to have devolved upon them to test whether a government, established on the principles of human freedom, can be maintained against an effort to build one upon the exclusive foundation of human bondage.

They will rejoice with me in the new evidences which your proceedings furnish, that the magnanimity they are exhibiting is justly estimated by the true friends of freedom and humanity in foreign countries.

Accept my best wishes for your individual welfare, and for the welfare and happiness of the whole British people."

—Abraham Lincoln, letter addressed "to the workingmen of London," February 2, 1863

Mediation and the Impact of Antietam

By 1862, it began to look like the Confederacy might win the war. The North had failed in its attempt to capture Richmond and been pushed out of Virginia. The Confederate army was on the offensive. The British government was beginning to listen to Confederate emissaries. The American minister in London, Charles Francis Adams, warned Seward that the British government might soon decide to mediate the differences between the North and South. If that decision was made and the North refused to mediate, Great Britain would acknowledge the Confederacy as a sovereign nation.

The situation grew even more serious when Confederates soundly defeated the Union army at Manassas (Bull Run) for a second time. As Robert E. Lee moved to invade the North, several British officials, including Prime Minister Palmerston, warned that if Lee was successful, the mediation idea would be brought to the British cabinet for its consideration. The British government had no hostile motive. Officials there simply believed the quarrel had gone on long enough. If the Confederacy was going to win, they reasoned, it was time to stop the bickering and end the war.

On September 17, 1862, 18 days after the Union's stunning defeat at the Second Battle of Manassas (Bull Run), Lee's invasion of the North culminated with the Battle of Antietam, in Maryland. Not only was this the first major Civil War engagement on Northern soil, it was the bloodiest single-day battle in American history. According to National Archives data, nine times as many Americans were killed or wounded that day than on June 6, 1944, D-day, the so-called "longest day" of World War II. (Losses at Antietam numbered about 23,000 while American casualties at Omaha and Utah beaches on D-day totaled 2,510.)

The battle was a turning point that changed the entire course of the Civil War, but also halted the Confederacy's efforts to have Great Britain intervene and mediate peace. The Union's victory at Antietam gave Lincoln the victory he needed to an-nounce the abolition of slavery in the South, and may have prevented England and France from lending support to a country that engaged in slavery.

Another Bid for Mediation

Another near miss occurred in 1863, when the influential Horace Greeley of the *New York Tribune* promoted the idea that the conflict between the North and South should be mediated by England, France, or Switzerland. Greeley's suggestion gained some momentum. The French government recommended a meeting between the Union and the Confederacy to discuss the possibilities of either a reunion or permanent sep-aration of the United States.

Seward rejected France's proposal out of hand—with Lincoln's full knowledge and support. Newspapers—presumably excluding the *New York Tribune*—almost univer-sally praised the Lincoln administration for this course of action, and commended both Seward and Lincoln for their wisdom and steadfastness. Not only did Lincoln think mediation was a bad idea on its own merits, he was certain it would also serve to offer at least tacit recognition of the Confederacy as a separate entity.

The whole issue of mediation and the international attention it drew made Lincoln realize that in addition to winning over popular opinion in the United States, he needed to do so overseas. His strategy worked so well that it is used by today's politicians.

Lincoln sent businessmen and clergymen to Europe as his personal emissaries—to carry his messages to key audiences. In England, for instance, Lincoln's communica-tions teams targeted unemployed workmen who'd lost their jobs because of the cotton shortage. The emissaries expressed sympathy but they blamed the Confederacy for the situation. Instead of siding with the Confederacy, the laborers came to view the

South as the instigator of their troubles. Lincoln's successful techniques for shifting public opinion are still in use today—by corporations, cause-related organizations, and, of course, politicians.

With Seward's able assistance, Lincoln's handling of foreign affairs during the Civil War had considerable influence on the war's outcome. His skillful parlay of the British in the Trent Affair began a sea change in how the British viewed their American cousins and the Union government in particular. The newfound international respect earned by the Union would strengthen over the years.

Lincoln's mixture of down-hominess and resolute firmness undoubtedly had a major impact on how the United States was regarded by other nations. This sometimes contradictory and sometimes complementary juxtaposition of strength and gentleness, firmness and conciliatoriness, continues to be used by American presidents and statesmen to this day, and continues to serve us well. You might think of it as playing "good cop, bad cop."

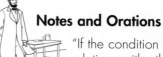

Notes and Orations

"If the condition of our relations with other nations is less gratifying than it has usually been at former periods, it is certainly more satisfactory than a nation so unhappily distracted as we are, might reasonably have apprehended."

—Abraham Lincoln, annual message to Congress, December 1, 1862

We Remember Abe

Lincoln's approach to diplomacy seemed rooted in an innate ability to read others, to use his common sense, and to come at a problem with certain conviction. Lincoln almost always knew where he stood on issues, and this certainty made it much easier for him to take and stick to a position. In turn, he could stand for that position and urge, threaten, cajole, entreat, or even use humor to win others over. At the very least he let his position be unmistakably understood. Although well served by advisors, Lincoln nonetheless always seemed able to synthesize the information he received and put it to its best use.

His considerable communication skills—written and oratory—that served him well in the courtroom also added to his expertise as a statesman.

> **Under the Stovepipe**
>
> Lincoln's secretary of state, William Seward, was an outspoken opponent of slavery. Because of his views and close alliance with Lincoln, Seward was also a target of John Wilkes Booth's assassination conspiracy. On April 14, 1865, while at home recovering from a serious injury caused by a carriage accident, Seward was stabbed in the throat by Booth associate Lewis Powell. Seward recovered from his wounds and served as secretary of state under Lincoln's successor, President Andrew Johnson. Unfortunately, Seward also adopted Johnson's conservative views.
>
> Seward might be best remembered for his involvement in the United States' 1867 purchase of Alaska from Russia. The government paid just more than $7 million for the territory, and the transaction was widely known as "Seward's Folly."

His ungainly, somewhat uncouth appearance often led others to underestimate him. He was quite aware of this perception, and he exploited it. Lincoln allowed others to see him as an unsophisticated hayseed, while using his uncommon wisdom and insight to best them. Those who thought Lincoln an unintelligent, common man were often surprised when getting their comeuppance. A similar down-home, unassuming manner has served other presidents well, including modern-day presidents Carter, Clinton, and George W. Bush.

Influencing public opinion was also important to Lincoln, and critical to his many successes. Given the immense costs of the Civil War both in terms of dollars and lives, maintaining a tenuous hold on public support was absolutely critical. Lincoln was able to do so with a great measure of success.

Recognizing the need to engender widespread public support was not new for politicians, but Lincoln recognized the need to win over the common man in other countries as well. Lincoln matured as a statesman through his presidency and gained a rather astute understanding of how the common man in Europe thought. Politicians would typically ignore this audience; if someone can't vote for a politician or directly influence someone who can, then that person is generally of little interest to the politician. Yet Lincoln recognized the influence that could be brought to bear by British workingmen, for instance, and sought to win them over. By all indications, he succeeded well.

In today's age of instant communication through television, radio, telephone, and the Internet, reaching an audience of regular folks in another country doesn't seem that exotic or difficult. But in Lincoln's time, reaching the common man in England was a pretty remarkable feat.

Yes, Lincoln used overseas intermediaries, agents, and emissaries. But undertaking that effort and being successful was a remarkable achievement in the nineteenth century. Instantaneous communication wasn't even a dream.

Lincoln was also a master of that political trait that is seemingly required of even the small-town mayor today—spin doctoring. Taking a situation—any situation—and portraying it in a manner most favorable to the politician is an art form.

The Least You Need to Know

- Lincoln and Secretary of State William Seward made a formidable team.

- Lincoln was much more involved in international policy and foreign relations than many people realize.

- One of Lincoln's major goals throughout the Civil War was preventing other nations from recognizing the Confederacy as a separate entity.

- The Trent Affair triggered a crisis between the Union and Great Britain.

- Lincoln understood the political expediency of winning widespread public support of his positions and actions.

- In addition to being a great leader and wartime president, Lincoln was also a highly effective diplomat and statesman.

Glossary

abolitionist   A person who believes in the abolishment, or elimination, of slavery.

affiant   A legal term used to describe a person who swears under oath as to the truth of certain facts, usually in the form of a written legal document known as an affidavit.

agrarian   Relating to or promoting the interests of agriculture, land, or farmers. The term is also used to define ownership of rural property or the division of land.

agriculture   A term derived from ancient Greek and Latin words meaning "related to the land." Agriculture is the practice—and some say the science, art, and business—of farming, generally for purposes of producing food. Farming is not limited to growing and harvesting crops like grain and corn. Agriculture is a huge industry that includes diverse pursuits with a common goal: sustaining society.

Amtrak   (National Railroad Passenger Corporation) A quasi-governmental agency that operates passenger rail service throughout the United States and parts of Canada. All Amtrak's stock is owned by the federal government, through the U.S. Department of Transportation.

Antietam, Battle of   A major battle between the Union and the Confederacy fought near Sharpsburg, Maryland, on September 17, 1862. The battle, which was won by the Union, ended General Robert E. Lee's first invasion of the North. Fought just 18 days after the Confederate victory at

Second Manassas (just 40 miles to the southeast in Virginia), the Battle of Antietam claimed more than 23,000 men killed, wounded, and missing—the bloodiest single-day battle in American history. The Union's victory at Antietam led to Lincoln's issuance of the Emancipation Proclamation. (The South called this major confrontation the Battle of Sharpsburg.)

Armstrong, Jack   Leader of a group of men in New Salem, Illinois, who challenged Lincoln to a wrestling match. The actual outcome of the match has been lost to obscurity, but Lincoln's conduct won the admiration and respect of Armstrong and his followers.

belligerent power   An entity at war with an established nation. A belligerent power doesn't have the full status of a sovereign government but is recognized as an organized body.

belligerent rights   Rights granted by international law and/or established nations to a party to a war, including key maritime rights: the right to stop, board, and inspect ships of neutral countries for war materiel intended for the belligerent's enemy; to capture vessels of the belligerent's enemy; and other rights reserved for a sovereign nation at war.

blab school   Once common, students at a blab school recited their lessons out loud—all at once! The teacher would listen closely as students repeated their lessons over and over, trying to catch and correct errors made by individual students.

Black Codes   After the Civil War ended, southern legislatures enacted laws, collectively known as black codes, designed to limit the rights of former slaves and to undermine the intent of the Thirteenth Amendment to the U.S. Constitution. Congress moved to defeat black codes by passing the Fourteenth Amendment to the U.S. Constitution.

Black Hawk War   A short-lived Indian war in 1832; the Sauk and Fox Indians left Iowa and returned to Illinois to reclaim land from a disputed treaty. Young Abraham Lincoln enlisted in the Illinois militia to protect his homeland in this brief but fierce conflict. He was quickly promoted to captain in the militia.

Booth, John Wilkes   An actor and southern sympathizer, Booth went to Ford's Theatre in Washington, D.C., on the night of April 14, 1865, with the hopes of undoing the still-fragile peace between the North and South. He placed a derringer to President Lincoln's head and pulled the trigger, mortally wounding the president. Finally tracked down in a tobacco barn in Virginia, Booth refused to come out, and was shot and killed by federal troops.

Buchanan, James Born into a prominent Pennsylvania family in 1791, Buchanan was the fifteenth president of the United States, and predecessor of President Abraham Lincoln. As president-elect in office, Democrat Buchanan relied on constitutional doctrine to settle the increasingly fierce debate over slavery in America's western territories. He believed that the issue would cease to be a problem after the Supreme Court ruled in the Dred Scott case, and stated as much in his inaugural speech. When the ruling was delivered two days after Buchanan's inauguration, northerners were outraged. His inaction on the issue led to a split of the Democratic Party in 1860, when northern and southern Democrats each nominated two presidential candidates. Buchanan has the distinction of being the only U.S. president never to marry.

Bull Run, First and Second Battles of (*See* Manassas, First and Second)

caisson Originating in the 1800s, a caisson is a flat-decked, wheeled cart that was first used to transport military artillery and was often pressed into service to carry dead soldiers from the battlefield. As it was in Lincoln's day, the use of a caisson and riderless horse are traditional elements of a funeral procession for a military leader. U.S. presidents are accorded this honor in recognition of their former role as commander in chief. The caisson that was used in President Reagan's funeral procession was built in 1918, and was attended by the Caisson Platoon of the 3rd U.S. Infantry Regiment, known as The Old Guard. The roots of this military regiment date back to 1784.

catafalque A catafalque (pronounced *cat-a-folk*) is a decorated platform used to hold a coffin while in state or repose during a funeral and for public exhibition of the body. Decorative additions might include an overhead canopy, extensive corner draping, and other such things. Fabric used to drape the structure's framework is almost always black. Sometimes the catafalque is used to transport the body to its final resting place.

circuit lawyer In Lincoln's time, court proceedings were held in one town after another, with lawyers and judges traveling along this circuit, representing local defendants and plaintiffs living near those towns. These traveling jurists would visit some 15 courthouses in about 10 weeks, and "Court Days," as they were known, became major social events in local communities.

Civil War Also known as the War Between the States (and more disparaging titles), the Civil War pitted northern states, the Union, and southern states, the Confederacy, against one another. The conflict commenced after southern states began seceding, or withdrawing, from the Union. When Confederate troops surrounded Union forces at Fort Sumter, in Charleston Harbor, South Carolina, and ultimately attacked, civil war began. Lasting from 1861 to 1865, the Civil War was the costliest in American history, with more than 618,000 dead, more than in all the wars from the Revolution through Vietnam combined.

Compromise of 1850   Settled the slavery issue for lands acquired in the Mexican War. California was admitted as a free state, and the territories of Utah and New Mexico (which included land later to become Arizona and Nevada) were given the right to decide the slavery issue for themselves.

Confiscation Act of 1862   Congress approved the Confiscation Act of 1862, also known as the Second Confiscation Act, on July 16, 1862. It was the first measure to specifically call for emancipation of slaves in rebel states. The act declared that slaves residing in Washington, D.C., as well as slaves in the Confederacy who sought refuge behind Union lines, were to be set free. However, emancipation under the act was at the convenience of the federal government—the Act outlined a judicial process that would free slaves on a cumbersome case-by-case basis, and the measure offered blacks no civil rights guarantees.

Davis, Jefferson   President of the Confederate States of America from 1861 to 1865, Jefferson Davis was a former United States representative and senator, as well as U.S. secretary of war. Like Lincoln, Davis was born in Kentucky. His father, Samuel Emory Davis, and his uncles were all Revolutionary War soldiers in 1776. Davis was captured by Union soldiers on May 10, 1865, and indicted for treason in 1866. Davis was imprisoned from 1865 until 1867, when influential northerners posted bail to gain his release. In 1868, the Union dropped all charges.

demand notes   Printed in $5, $10, and $20 denominations, demand notes, called "greenbacks" because of their green color, were the first paper money issued since the Continentals. Only about $10 million worth were issued, and most that remain today are in the hands of collectors. Unlike Confederacy currency, any Union currency issued from 1861 forward is still considered valid and can be redeemed for cash at face value. (*See also* greenbacks.)

Douglas, Stephen   Douglas was a longtime rival of Lincoln's—in love and in politics. He vied against Lincoln for the affections of Mary Todd and later competed against Lincoln in Illinois politics, and ultimately for the presidency in 1860. The Lincoln–Douglas debates of 1858, when the two opposed each other for a U.S. Senate seat, are likely the most famous in United States history. As a senator, Douglas sponsored the Kansas–Nebraska Act, which would allow these newly admitted states to decide the slavery question on their own, in violation of the Missouri Compromise of 1820.

emigration   Moving *from* one's country or region to settle elsewhere. (From the Latin word *emigrare*, which means "to move.")

enfranchisement   The act of bestowing citizenship rights upon an individual or group. The term originates from the old French *enfranchir*, "to set free." Suffrage is the right to vote. In a democracy, a citizen's right to vote is a crucial element of enfranchisement. Accordingly, voting rights and enfranchisement are commonly used interchangeably.

Father Abraham   A nickname given to Abraham Lincoln in a poem titled "We Are Coming, Father Abraham," published in the *New York Post* on August 16, 1862. The poem was written by James Sloan Gibbons, a northern abolitionist Quaker, as a call to arms directed at northerners.

filibuster   An activity designed to prevent a legislative body from taking action on proposed legislation. The activity usually involves prolonged speechmaking and refusal to yield the floor to a fellow member of Congress.

Force Bill of 1833   A law that authorized President Jackson to use military force to enforce federal law, including tariffs.

Ford's Theatre   A theatre located in downtown Washington, D.C. On April 14, 1865, President Lincoln, his wife, Mary, and another couple were seated watching the play *Our American Cousin* when actor John Wilkes Booth entered the box, placed a derringer to Lincoln's head, and fired, wounding him mortally. Today, the theatre is a part of the Ford's Theatre National Historic Site, maintained by the U.S. National Park Service.

Fort Stevens   A Union fort in Washington, near the Maryland border. Lincoln traveled to Fort Stevens in July 1864 to get a firsthand look at the enemy, and to determine the strength of the Confederate forces. While engaged in a conversation, Lincoln's party came under fire. Ignoring the gunfire, Lincoln continued talking until someone yelled, "Get down, you fool!" Lincoln remains one of only two United States presidents to have been fired upon on the field of battle while in office. The other was James Madison during the War of 1812.

Fort Sumter   A small Union fort on a tiny island in Charleston Harbor, South Carolina, this facility played a pivotal role in the beginnings of the Civil War. Confederate troops surrounded the fort, not allowing Union soldiers out or supplies in. Lincoln had dispatched a small expeditionary force to take provisions to the troops at Fort Sumter, with strict orders not to fire at the rebels unless first fired upon. What Lincoln didn't know at the time was that the Confederacy had already decided to take the first shot. On April 12, 1861, rebels attacked Fort Sumter, which fell three days later.

freedman   A slave made free.

Freedmen's Bureau   Established by the War Department in 1865 at Lincoln's initiation but after his death, the Freedmen's Bureau was officially known as the Bureau of Refugees, Freedmen, and Abandoned Lands. The bureau managed the process of providing rations, clothing, and medicine for freed slaves and dealing with confiscated property in the former slave and border states. Created with the support of Abraham Lincoln, the Freedmen's Bureau was the first federal government welfare agency in U.S. history.

Free-Soilers   A political party whose members were against slavery but were not abolitionists. They believed that white men should receive property in the western territories free of charge. Some Free-Soilers sought to ban all blacks from these newly acquired lands.

Gettysburg   Located 50 miles northwest of Baltimore, the small town of Gettysburg, Pennsylvania, was the site of the largest battle ever waged during the American Civil War. Fought in the first three days of July 1863, the battle resulted in victory for the Union and ended Lee's second invasion of the North. Historians have referred to the battle as the "High Water Mark of the Confederacy." It was also the bloodiest single battle of the war (the bloodiest single day was Antietam), resulting in more than 51,000 soldiers killed, wounded, captured, or missing.

Grant, General Ulysses S.   General-in-Chief of the Union army starting in 1864 after victories at Shiloh and Vicksburg, Grant successfully ran for president in 1868, succeeding Andrew Johnson.

greenbacks   One of many slang terms used for paper money, the expression originated in the 1860s after passage of the Legal Tender Act, a measure pushed by Lincoln. United States currency notes printed under the authority of the act were to be considered "legal tender" for virtually any use. Printed in green ink on one side, the notes became known as "greenbacks." (*See also* demand notes.)

habeas corpus   The Medieval Latin translation of the term habeas corpus is "you shall have the body." Also known as the Great Writ, the writ of habeas corpus is an order that may be issued to release a person from unlawful restraint; the protection against imprisonment without cause, one of the personal liberties guaranteed by the United States Constitution. When Lincoln suspended the writ of habeas corpus in selected areas in the spring of 1861, some citizens no longer had this constitutional right. Congress later formally approved Lincoln's initiatives.

Hell on Wheels   The term "Hell on Wheels" grew out of the rowdy behavior of some of the workers on the railroad construction project. As these men usually arrived riding in a wheeled car on the railroad tracks, these hellions were often described as "Hell on Wheels."

Herndon, William   Lawyer with whom Abraham shared a law practice, beginning in 1844. Herndon later wrote a biography of Lincoln in an attempt to show him as a mortal and let people know of Lincoln the man.

homestead   A dwelling with adjoining buildings and land occupied as a principle residence.

Homestead Act   A law signed by Abraham Lincoln in 1862 that offered prospective settlers free land. The deal was relatively simple: One only had to stake a claim, submit an application at a land office, and pay a $10 filing fee and $2 commission fee to the land agent. In return, the homesteader received a grant of 160 acres of virtually untouched, publicly owned land in the West. After the equivalent of a title search was completed, the homesteader was given a temporary claim to the land—and was required to reside on the property continuously for a period of five years. During that span, the homesteader was required to "improve" the land. At a minimum, that meant constructing a 12-by-14 residential dwelling, soil cultivation, and crop production. Upon filing proof that the requirements were met, the homesteader received clear title to the property.

illegitimacy   Being born to unmarried parents. In Lincoln's day, illegitimate children were not entitled to financial support by their father nor were they entitled to inherit money or property.

immigration   Moving *to* a place.

industrial   Relates to companies involved in the manufacture and/or distribution of products.

Jim Crow Laws   Restricted access of blacks to public areas, accommodations, water fountains, waiting rooms, courthouse exits and entrances, and theatres. Some jurisdictions set curfews and employment restrictions for blacks.

John Brown's Raid   Abolitionist John Brown and a group of followers raided the federal armory and arsenal at Harper's Ferry, West Virginia, at the confluence of the Potomac and Shenandoah Rivers on October 16, 1859, with the intent of bringing attention to the plight of slavery. Brown's raid was stopped; several people on both sides of the conflict died. Brown was captured and tried for treason, found guilty, and hanged. The raid was arguably a partial success as it did raise the visibility of the slavery issue.

Johnson, Andrew Lincoln's vice-president, southern Democrat Johnson ascended to the presidency upon Lincoln's assassination. Radical Republicans embattled him almost immediately. After dismissing Secretary of War Edwin Stanton, Johnson was impeached for violating presidential restrictions enacted by the Radical Republicans. He was acquitted by a single vote in 1867. Born in North Carolina in 1808, Johnson grew up in poverty and championed the cause of the common man, while condemning plantation aristocracy. While representing Tennessee as U.S. senator, Johnson refused to give up his congressional seat, making him a hated man in the South.

Kansas–Nebraska Act Stephen Douglas proposed the Kansas–Nebraska Act that would divide a large tract of land in the plains into Nebraska and Kansas. Under this act, these two territories were allowed to decide the slavery question on their own. Part of the act's language repealed the Missouri Compromise of 1820, which allowed Missouri to enter the Union as a slave state, but at the same time prohibited slavery in western territories north of Missouri's southern border. Passage of the Kansas–Nebraska Act appalled Lincoln and compelled him to return to public life and run for national office.

Knob Creek The Lincoln family moved from Sinking Spring Farm to Knob Creek, about 10 miles away, after the land at Sinking Spring was found to be infertile. Both farms were located in Kentucky.

Know-Nothings A political party that opposed foreign immigration and were widely believed to be anti-Catholic.

land grant colleges Land grant colleges are designated either by Congress or the state to reap the benefits of the Morrill Act of 1862, a measure supported by President Lincoln. The act was expanded in 1890 and later years. The original mission of these schools was to teach agriculture, military tactics, mechanical arts, and the classics to the working class so they could get a practical and affordable liberal education—and the Union army could get badly needed officers to help win the Civil War. The Morrill Act of 1890 expanded on the first by prohibiting the sending of funds to institutions that made distinctions as to race, unless other land grant institutions in that state were available to blacks. The United States Department of Agriculture plays a large role in the administration of land grant funds.

Land of Lincoln A phrase coined after Lincoln's death that refers to the entire state of Illinois. It is now the state motto.

Lee, General Robert E. A Virginia native and graduate of the United States Military Academy at West Point, then-Major General Lee was asked by President

Lincoln to command the Union army. Two days later, Virginia seceded, and General Lee felt compelled to refuse the appointment, unwilling to take arms against his home state. Lee was appointed a brigadier general in the Confederate army. His various commands included the Department of Northwestern Virginia (July–October 1861), the Department of South Carolina, Georgia, and Florida (November 1861–March 1862, commanded from a desk in Richmond), the Army of Northern Virginia (June 1, 1862–April 9, 1865). In February 1865, Lee was appointed General-in-Chief, leading the entire Confederate army. Lee's family home in Arlington, Virginia, was quickly seized by the Union, and the grounds made into a cemetery (now Arlington National Cemetery) to forever deny its return to the Lee family.

Legal Tender Act   Signed into law by Lincoln in 1862 during the Civil War, the Legal Tender Act authorized the printing of $150,000,000 in United States notes (and later increased to $450,000,000) to be treated as legal tender for virtually all purposes, to help finance the war. This act was quite controversial at the time, and was challenged in court in several states.

lie in state, to   In the United States, the term used exclusively to describe the formal honor of placing a person's remains in the Rotunda of the United States Capitol. When placed anywhere else for public or private viewing, the body is said to be lying *in repose*.

Lincoln, Edward Baker   Abraham's second son, born March 10, 1846. Died February 1, 1850, probably of pulmonary tuberculosis.

Lincoln, Mary Todd   A Kentucky belle, Mary Todd married Abraham in 1842 after several false starts. Several members of the Todd family were not fond of Lincoln, thinking him too uncultured for Mary. She bore Lincoln four sons, and was by his side when he was shot at Ford's Theatre in 1865.

Lincoln, Nancy Hanks   Abraham's mother, born February 5, 1784, Hampshire County, Virginia (now West Virginia). Died October 5, 1818, age 34, of "milk sickness."

Lincoln, Robert Todd   Abraham Lincoln's firstborn son, born August 1, 1843, at the Globe Tavern. He became a successful businessman, secretary of war, and later a diplomat. Robert Todd Lincoln died in his sleep at Hildene, his summer home in Vermont, on July 26, 1926. He was the only Lincoln child to survive to adulthood. The Lincoln bloodline ended with the death of Robert's great-grandson, Robert Lincoln Beckwith, who was born in 1904 and died in 1984.

Lincoln, Sarah Bush Johnston   Abraham's stepmother, born December 13, 1788, in Hardin County, Kentucky. Married Daniel Johnston in 1806, who died in 1816. Wed widower Thomas Lincoln in 1819. Died April 12, 1869, age 80.

Lincoln, Thomas   Abraham's father, born January 6, 1778, to Bathsheba and Abraham Lincoln in Rockingham County, Virginia. Thomas lived until January 17, 1851, age 73.

Lincoln, Thomas "Tad"   Born April 4, 1853, Abraham's fourth son had a large head and small body, earning him the nickname "Tadpole" or Tad for short. Tad died on July 15, 1871, in Chicago, probably of tuberculosis.

Lincoln, William "Willie" Wallace   Abraham's third son, born December 21, 1850. Willie died at the age of 11 on February 20, 1862, probably of typhoid fever, while Lincoln was president.

Lincoln–Douglas Debates   This series of seven debates, one in each of the Illinois congressional districts in which Lincoln and Douglas had not already spoken, pitted Stephen Douglas against Abraham Lincoln in a race for a U.S. Senate seat. Douglas advocated popular sovereignty, which would allow states to individually decide the slavery issue, while Lincoln argued that the nation could not survive with half-slavery, half-free states.

Lincolniana   A term to describe virtually anything having to do with Abraham Lincoln, including primary and secondary research materials. A few examples are letters, speeches, and other writings; fiction and nonfiction works that feature Lincoln as a key character; and biographies about Lincoln, his family members, and key associates.

literacy tests   Some states previously required voter registration applicants to prove they could read and write. These tests typically evaluated far more than simple reading and writing, and were used to prevent blacks from voting. This was especially true in the southern states of Alabama, Georgia, Louisiana, Mississippi, Texas, and Virginia.

Logan, Stephen T.   A lawyer with whom Abraham shared a law practice in Springfield, Illinois, from 1841 to 1844.

Louisiana Purchase   In 1803, the United States purchased from France a great tract of land, covering 828,000 acres that would later become 13 states. The transaction cost the United States about $15 million, or about 6 cents an acre.

Manassas, First and Second   Two major Civil War battles (also known as the First and Second Battles of Bull Run) fought near Manassas, a town in northern Virginia. First Manassas, fought on July 21, 1861, was the first major battle of the Civil War. Second Manassas was fought from August 28 to 30, 1862. The South won both battles. Today, the site of these two clashes between the Union and the Confederacy is known as Manassas National Battlefield Park and is maintained by the National Park Service.

Manifest Destiny   A nineteenth-century doctrine that viewed U.S. territorial expansion as its obvious fate. Many Americans in the 1840s believed the destiny of the United States of America was to expand across the entire continent, holding all land from the Atlantic to the Pacific oceans. What's more, they believed it was God's will that this expansion take place. Interestingly, no U.S. president or secretary of state ever outlined this doctrine. The term was coined by a journalist, and the concept provoked a great deal of controversy at the time.

McClellan, General George   McClellan was General-in-Chief of the Union army and Commander of the Army of the Potomac, and led the army during the decisive battle at Antietam, Maryland, which saw the costliest single day of the Civil War. He and Lincoln were at odds about many aspects of running the war, and McClellan was relieved of his post as General-in-Chief, replaced by General Henry W. Halleck. He was relieved as Commander of the Army of the Potomac in 1862, replaced by General Ambrose Burnside. McClellan then ran against Lincoln in the 1864 presidential race—and lost.

Mexican–American War   The Republic of Texas applied for statehood in 1845 after being annexed by the United States. The Mexican government refused to give up the land, and the United States went to war to bring Texas into the Union. Then-president James K. Polk not only wanted Texas but the Mexican territories of California, New Mexico, and Utah.

migration   The movement of a large group *to* a place.

milk sick   A disease characterized by nausea, vomiting, trembling, dizziness, and severe intestinal pain, eventually found to be caused by drinking the milk of cows who had eaten white snakeroot plants. Without medicine, symptoms worsened and ultimately led to coma and death.

Missouri Compromise   An 1820 federal legislative measure to settle slavery issues related to lands acquired from France in the Louisiana Purchase. The Missouri Compromise allowed Missouri to enter as a slave state, while prohibiting slavery in western territories north of Missouri's southern border.

New Salem, Illinois   Now gone, this was the "big city" on the Sangamon River where Abraham went to seek his fortune after first leaving home. About 100 folks called New Salem home at the time. Here he worked as a surveyor, railsplitter, shopkeeper's assistant, shopkeeper, and postmaster.

New Salem Debating Society   This debate club consisted of a group of men in New Salem, Illinois, who gathered for the purposes of scholarly debate. Lincoln joined the society, furthering his reputation with fellow villagers who admired his knowledge, reasoned arguments, and presentation.

Oak Ridge Cemetery   Abraham Lincoln's final resting place in Springfield, Illinois, though it took a while for him to really rest in peace. After a lengthy procession by train to help a grieving nation mourn for the loss of its larger-than-life president, Lincoln's body was moved no fewer than 17 times after arriving at Oak Ridge. Members of a counterfeiting ring acted on a plot to steal Lincoln's body and hold it for ransom for the release of one of their colleagues. Fortunately, a Secret Service agent had infiltrated the ring, and he summoned waiting detectives to arrest the gang before they could make off with the body of the former president. Also interred in the Lincoln tomb are his wife, Mary, and three of his four sons—Willie, Eddie, and Thomas "Tad."

oratory   The art and science of delivering an eloquently crafted speech designed to sway an audience. Oratory's origins arise from ancient Greece and Rome, when such skills were highly valued and taught as part of a classical curriculum. The word oratory is derived from the Latin term *orare*, "to pray." Political oratory emerged as a major force in the American colonies and in Europe in the eighteenth century. Today, the term oratory is erroneously used for all public speaking and is sometimes defined as a "pompous" speech. Oratory techniques and skills are most commonly employed in law, politics, and religion.

Owens, Mary   An early fiancée of Lincoln's, he proposed to and then spurned Owens. He had a change of heart and proposed marriage to her again seven months later, but this time was rejected by Mary.

Pacific Railway Act   Passed by Congress in 1862, the Pacific Railway Act was a measure supported by Lincoln. The act identified the thirty-second parallel as the initial transcontinental railroad route, and provided huge land grants for the purpose of establishing that railway. The Union Pacific and Central Pacific Railroads were authorized to construct the railway. The Union Pacific began building west from Omaha, and the Central Pacific began building east from Sacramento, coming together near Promontory, Utah, in 1869.

pardon   An official pardon is when an executive forgives an offense and reduces or eliminates the convicted person's punishment.

parole   A conditional release of a prisoner who has not yet served his full term. In Civil War times, the term *parole of honor* was synonymous with "word of honor." A Civil War prisoner could be granted freedom simply by promising not to engage in combat until formally exchanged.

Petersen House   Sometimes described inaccurately as a private home or residence, the Petersen House was a boarding house located across the street from Ford's Theatre to which Lincoln was carried after being shot on April 14, 1865. After lingering through the night, Lincoln died there the following morning. The modest room only held a small number of people, but artists over the years have depicted as many as 47 people in the room at once, including many who were not even in Washington at the time!

Pinkerton, Allan   A Scottish immigrant, Pinkerton formed the first detective agency in the United States. Performing unrelated work for the Philadelphia, Wilmington, & Baltimore Railroad, Pinkerton uncovered a plot to kill Lincoln. To ensure Lincoln's safe passage from Baltimore to Washington for his inaugural, Pinkerton and his operatives served as Lincoln's bodyguards. Lincoln named Pinkerton head of the United States Secret Service, though at the time the Secret Service investigated counterfeit crime and did not protect the president. Pinkerton was nicknamed "The Eye" and the sign above the door of his detective agency office included a painted human eye as a logo—the origin of "private eye," a slang term for a private detective.

primogeniture   The state of being firstborn. The *rule of primogeniture* comes from ancient English law, holding that the right of inheritance of a man's estate belongs solely to his eldest male child. That meant younger male siblings and females, including daughters and wives, inherited nothing. Primogeniture was not uniformly followed in the American colonies, but when Thomas Jefferson, as a state legislator, abolished Virginia's statutes in the late 1700s, other colonies later followed suit

prize court   Adjudicates disputes regarding the capture of goods and vessels at sea. During war, privately owned ships and also vessels from neutral countries that carry contraband—people or materials supporting enemy action—are subject to seizure. But title does not automatically pass to the captor. A prize court convened by the capturing nation must decide the fate of the ship and property using international law or other applicable statutes.

pulmonary tuberculosis   A contagious bacterial infection caused by Mycobacterium tuberculosis, known as TB. The infection primarily involves the lungs but can spread to other organs. In Lincoln's time, there was no known cure for the infection and it was usually fatal.

Reconstruction   The period in U.S. history that spanned from 1863, as the Union openly dealt with the challenges of managing conquered southern territory, to the final withdrawal of federal troops from the South in 1877. The term is also used to describe the attempt made during this time period to solve social, economic, and political problems that rose from the readmission of the 11 states that had seceded from the Union.

relic   A memento kept because of its association with the past; often used to denote an object of religious veneration, including personal belongings of a saint or a piece of the saint's body. Many people collected relics of Lincoln's—even the surgeon general appears to have helped himself to a lock of Lincoln's hair.

rifle volleys   Full military honors at the interment (or burial) of a president of the United States typically include the firing of three rifle volleys over the fallen leader's grave. This long-standing tradition arose from the practice of halting battlefield fighting to allow for the removal of dead soldiers on both sides of a conflict. After the field had been cleared, three volleys were fired to signal that the battle could be resumed. In modern times, seven service members usually fire the three volleys. But don't confuse this high honor with the 21-gun salute. That's something completely different.

Scott, Dred   Scott was a slave who sued for his freedom upon the demise of his master, and is the namesake of one of the most memorable and outrageous legal decisions in American history. Scott claimed that because he lived with his master for several years in free states, his time in those lands made him a free man. The case took 10 long years to wind its way through the legal system. Ultimately, the United States Supreme Court ruled, in a 7-2 decision, that Scott was not legally a citizen and therefore had no right to sue his master. The justices further declared that blacks were inferior to whites and were owned property, on par with cattle and mules. Furthermore, the justices decided that Congress had no constitutional right to bar slavery, nullifying the Missouri Compromise and all other laws limiting or controlling slavery.

section   A section of land is a unit of measurement in real estate parlance equal to 640 square acres.

Sharpsburg, Battle of (*See* Antietam, Battle of)

Shields, James   A prominent local politician of Springfield, Illinois. He was offended when he read three separate 1842 editorials critical of him in the Springfield newspaper. Incorrectly assuming that Lincoln had written them all—Lincoln's former fiancée, Mary Todd, and her friend Julia Jayne had written two of them, Lincoln only one—Shields challenged Lincoln to a duel. Friends of both Lincoln and Shields talked them out of it. The situation brought Lincoln and Mary Todd together again, ultimately to become engaged again and marry later that year.

Sinking Spring, Kentucky   Site of the Lincoln family farm where Abraham was born in 1809, near Hodgenville.

Special Field Order 15   As Union General William T. Sherman marched to the sea in Savannah, tens of thousands of freed blacks left inland plantations and followed Sherman's forces. Afterward, Sherman met with a group of black men to determine how to deal with all those people. Reverend Garrison Frazier told Sherman the best way they could take care of themselves was to have land. On January 16, 1865, Sherman responded by issuing Special Field Order 15, which set the expectation among slaves that each freed slave would receive "forty acres and a mule." Sherman's order distributed abandoned plantations on Charleston's southern coast and the barrier islands of South Carolina and Georgia—40,000 freed blacks settled these lands. Lincoln's successor, Andrew Johnson, would undo Sherman's good deed when he ordered that confiscated lands be returned to their former owners.

Springfield, Illinois   Now the state capital, Lincoln's home for much of his adult life, and the home base for his law practice.

state funeral   A tradition- and protocol-steeped funeral of high honor, afforded to all United States presidents, whether in office at the time of their death or not. The secretary of state, as representative of the sitting president, is responsible for planning the state funeral.

Stephens, Alexander H.   Vice-president of the Confederate States of America under Jefferson Davis, Stephens was an old friend of Lincoln's and someone Abe thought would support him and the Union.

Stuart, Major John Todd   A fellow Illinois legislator, Lincoln and Stuart met during the Black Hawk War. Stuart encouraged Lincoln to become a lawyer, and loaned him law books to study. He was also Lincoln's first law partner.

subscriber   To offset construction costs, railroads in the 1850s often solicited financial pledges, or "subscriptions," from investors, who were typically folks who stood to benefit from the railroad's route—individuals, businesses, and even entire towns. People who purchased these subscriptions were commonly known as subscribers.

suffrage   The right to vote. In a democracy, a citizen's right to vote is a crucial element of enfranchisement. Accordingly, voting rights and enfranchisement are commonly used interchangeably.

Taney, Chief Justice Roger B.   Chief architect and author of the 1857 Dred Scott decision, stripping African Americans of all rights and eliminating all laws limiting slavery, Taney was a Maryland slaveholder himself. One can only imagine how chagrined Taney was four years later, when he had the duty of swearing in our sixteenth president, Abraham Lincoln, whose policies Taney detested.

"Taps"   The military call signaling soldiers to "extinguish lights." Written in 1862 by Brigadier General Daniel Butterfield of the Army of the Potomac, the bugle call was later adopted in 1863 throughout the Union military. Lincoln's funeral was the first presidential funeral at which "Taps" was played.

tariff   A form of government tax levied on raw or manufactured goods as they move in or out of a country. The term tariff is synonymously used with customs tax or duty. Tariffs are commonly collected by the government of the country importing goods but can also be applied to exported as well as local goods.

Trent Affair   The Trent Affair nearly brought the United States and Great Britain to war in 1861. Confederate President Jefferson Davis sent James Mason to be Confederate minister to Great Britain and John Slidell to be Confederate minister to France. The two eluded the Union blockade and made their way to Cuba, where they boarded the British steamer *Trent* for passage across the Atlantic. The *USS San Jacinto* of the Union navy intercepted the *Trent*, seized the two Confederate diplomats, and allowed the *Trent* to continue on her way. The British were offended by this event and demanded an apology and the return of the Confederate diplomats; France expressed willingness to side with the British against the United States. Ultimately, the two Confederate diplomats were released and made their way to Europe, where they failed to enlist any assistance to the Confederacy.

United States Department of Agriculture (USDA)   Founded by President Lincoln in 1862 as "the people's department," the USDA made quality seeds and education available to the then 58 percent of the population who were farmers.

Vandalia, Illinois   Vandalia was the second state capital of Illinois, where Abraham served as a state legislator.

Whig   A now defunct political party, the Whig Party existed from about 1834 to 1856. Abraham Lincoln was a Whig for most of his political career, until he joined the Republican Party, which came into existence in 1854. Whig platforms included strong interest in "internal improvements," a term similar to what's known today as infrastructure—roads, waterways, and so forth.

word of honor   A promise based on one's personal honor and integrity.

Appendix B

For Further Reading

Baker, Jean Harvey. *Civil War and Reconstruction*. New York: W.W. Norton, 2001.

———. *Mary Todd Lincoln: A Biography*. New York: W.W. Norton, 1987.

Borritt, Gabor (Ed.) *Of the People, By the People, For the People*. New York: Columbia University Press, 1996.

Bryan, George S. *The Great American Myth*. New York: Carrick and Evans, 1940.

Burkhimer, Michael. *100 Essential Lincoln Books*. Nashville: Cumberland House Publishing, Inc., 2003. (Probably your best place to start.)

Cuomo, Mario M. *Why Lincoln Matters: Today More Than Ever*. New York: Harcourt, 2004.

Donald, David Herbert. *Lincoln*. New York: Simon and Schuster, 1995.

———. *We Are Lincoln Men: Abraham Lincoln and His Friends*. New York: Simon and Schuster, 2003.

Fehrenbacher, Don E. *Prelude to Greatness: Lincoln in the 1850s*. Stanford: Stanford University Press, 1962.

Guelzo, Allen. *Lincoln's Emancipation Proclamation: The End of Slavery in America*. New York: Simon and Schuster, 2004.

Harris, William C. *Lincoln's Last Months*. Boston: Harvard University Press, 2004.

Helm, Katherine Mary. *Wife of Lincoln*. New York: Harper & Brothers, 1928. (The author is Mary Todd Lincoln's niece.)

Herndon, William H. *Herndon's Life of Lincoln: The History and Personal Recollections of Abraham Lincoln*. Greenwich, Connecticut: Fawcett, 1961.

Holzer, Harold. *The Lincoln Mailbag: America Writes to the President, 1861–1865*. Carbondale, Illinois: Southern Illinois University Press, 1998.

———. *Lincoln at Cooper Union: The Speech That Made Abraham Lincoln President*. New York: Simon and Schuster, 2004.

———. *The Lincoln-Douglas Debates: The First Complete, Unexpurgated Text*. New York: Fordham University Press, 2004.

———. *Lincoln Seen and Heard*. Lawrence, Kansas: University Press of Kansas, 2001.

———. *Dear Mr. Lincoln: Letters to the President*. New York: Perseus Books, 1995.

———. *Lincoln as I Knew Him: Gossip, Tributes and Revelations from His Best Friends and Worst Enemies*. Chapel Hill, North Carolina: Algonquin Books of Chapel Hill, 1999.

Holzer, Harold, William D. Pederson, and John Y. Simon. *The Lincoln Forum: Abraham Lincoln, Gettysburg and the Civil War*. Mason City, Iowa: Savas Publishing Company, 1999.

Miller, William Lee. *Lincoln's Virtues*. New York: Vintage, 2003.

Neely, Mark E., Jr. *The Abraham Lincoln Encyclopedia*. New York: McGraw–Hill Book Company, 1982.

———. *The Fate of Liberty: Abraham Lincoln and Civil Liberties*. New York: Oxford University Press, 1991.

———. *The Last Best Hope of Earth: Abraham Lincoln and the Promise of America*. Boston: Harvard University Press, 1993.

Nicolay, John G., and John Hay. *Abraham Lincoln: A History*. New York: The Century Company, 1890 (10 volumes).

Paludan, Philip. *The Presidency of Abraham Lincoln*, Lawrence: University of Kansas Press, 1994

Perret, Geoffrey. *Lincoln's War: The Untold Story of America's Greatest President as Commander in Chief*. New York: Random House, 2004.

Pinsker, Matthew. *Lincoln's Sanctuary: Abraham Lincoln and the Soldiers' Home.* New York: Oxford University Press, 2003.

Sandburg, Carl. *Abraham Lincoln: The Prairie Years.* New York: Harcourt, Brace, 1926 (2 volumes).

———. *Abraham Lincoln: The War Years.* New York: Harcourt, Brace, 1939 (4 volumes).

———. *Abraham Lincoln: The Prairie Years and the War Years.* New York: Harvest/HBJ, 2002 (new version of previously published work, 800 pages).

Steers, Edward Jr. *Blood on the Moon: The Assassination of Abraham Lincoln.* Lexington, Kentucky: University Press of Kentucky, 2001.

Wills, Garry. *Lincoln at Gettysburg: The Words That Remade America.* New York: Touchstone, 1992.

Wilson, Douglas L. *Honor's Voice: The Transformation of Abraham Lincoln.* New York: Vintage, 1999.

Reference Works

Basler, Roy P., ed. *Abraham Lincoln: His Speeches and Writings.* New York: DaCapo Press, Inc., reprinted 1990.

———. *The Collected Works of Abraham Lincoln.* New Brunswick: Rutgers University Press, 1953 (9 volumes).

Fehrenbacher, Don E., and Fehrenbacher, Virginia, (Eds.). *Recollected Works of Abraham Lincoln.* Stanford: Stanford University Press, 1996.

Lincoln Societies

The Abraham Lincoln Association
Old State Capitol
Springfield, Illinois 62701
www.alincolnassoc.com

The Abraham Lincoln Institute of the Mid-Atlantic
721 Dartmouth Avenue
Silver Spring, Maryland 20910
www.lincoln-institute.org

International Lincoln Association
24775 Fern Valley Road
PO Drawer L
Idyllwild, California 92549-1108

Lincoln Association of Indiana
1010 E. 86th Street, Suite 61–J
Indianapolis, Indiana 46240
317-848-9361

Lincoln Association of Jersey City
Mr. Paul Pantozzi
830 Bergen Avenue
Jersey City, New Jersey 07306
201-333-1000

Lincoln Fellowship of Pennsylvania
PO Box 3372
Gettysburg, Pennsylvania 17325
www.gettysburg.edu

Lincoln Fellowship of Wisconsin
Steven K. Rogstad, Secretary and Editor
5419 Idlewood Drive
Racine, Wisconsin 53402
414-681-4972

The Lincoln Forum
www.thelincolnforum.org

Lincoln Group of Florida
901 Palmer Avenue
Winter Park, Florida 32789

Lincoln Group of Illinois
Illinois Benedictine University
5700 College Road
Lisle, Illinois 60532-0900

The Lincoln Group of New York
PO Box 220
Newton, New Jersey 07860
www.lincolngroupny.org

The Lincoln Group of the District of Columbia, Inc.
PO Box 5676
Washington, D.C. 20016
www.lincolngroup.org

The Lincoln Society
PO Box 1–31
Hwakang, Taipei 11114
Taiwan, Republic of China

Louisiana Lincoln Group
One University Place, 148 BH
Shreveport, Louisiana 71115-2301

Tokyo Lincoln Center
Meisei University
Box 5001
Hino–Shi Tokyo, Japan 191

Online Resources

Abraham Lincoln Historical Digitization Project
lincoln.lib.niu.edu/

A project sponsored by the Illinois State Library to digitize historical documents about Lincoln; many items are available online.

Abraham Lincoln Online
showcase.netins.net/web/creative/lincoln.html

A vast resource with organized and indexed links to internal and external pages about Lincoln.

Abraham Lincoln Presidential Library
www.state.il.us/hpa/lib

An online resource from the Illinois Historic Preservation Agency about the history of Illinois and President Lincoln.

Abraham Lincoln Presidential Library and Museum
www.alincolnmuseum.com/home.html

This is the virtual presence of the 200,000-square-foot facility located in the heart of Springfield, Illinois.

Abraham Lincoln Research Site
members.aol.com/RVSNorton/Lincoln2.html

A user-friendly site with lots of fascinating information about Lincoln—operated by a former history teacher.

Abraham Lincoln: Savior of the Union
www.jeannepasero.com/lincoln.html

A friendly, informal site that includes resources for teachers and activities for kids.

Lanesville City Schools, Lincoln Resources List
www.lanesville.k12.in.us/LCSYellowpages/Lincoln/lincoln.htm

Nice, comprehensive set of links to various Lincoln resources.

Mr. Lincoln's White House
http://www.mrlincolnswhitehouse.org/

A description of the White House during Lincoln's time in office, produced by the Lehrman Institute and the Lincoln Institute.

Mr. Lincoln's Virtual Library at the Library of Congress
memory.loc.gov/ammem/alhtml/alhome.html

Online resources from two large Lincolniana collections at the Library of Congress. You can see images of scanned documents in Lincoln's own handwriting online.

Presidents of the United States
www.presidentsusa.net/lincoln.html

Nicely organized and categorized links to numerous Abraham Lincoln resources.

The A. Lincoln Bibliophile
webpages.charter.net/lincolnbooks/

A rather remarkable site that catalogs an immense number of books about Lincoln, primarily more contemporary volumes. Contains a number of interesting and useful reviews of Lincoln books, and information on a large number of soon-to-be-published titles.

The Abraham Lincoln Bicentennial Commission
www.lincolnbicentennial.gov/

Appointed by the president and members of Congress, the 15 members of the Commission are focused on informing the public about the impact Abraham Lincoln had on the development of our nation and finding the best possible ways to honor his accomplishments. The Commission website contains educational material, plans for the bicentennial celebration of Lincoln's birth in 2009, and a schedule of events.

The Collected Works of Abraham Lincoln
www.hti.umich.edu/l/lincoln/

An online version of The Collected Works of Abraham Lincoln, a multivolume collection of Lincoln's speeches, correspondence, and other writings—compiled and annotated by a team of researchers over a five-year period.

The Huntington Library
www.huntington.org

A renowned research library in San Marino, California, The Huntington Library has numerous resources and papers pertaining to Abraham Lincoln.

The Lincoln Herald
web.mountain.net/~niddk/

An online, quarterly publication of the Lincoln Memorial University in Harrogate, Tennessee.

The Lincoln Institute
http://www.abrahamlincoln.org

Dedicated to supporting Lincoln scholars, the Institute produces printed matter, Internet content, and seminars to further the awareness and study of Lincoln. Many resources for teachers and students are available online.

The Lincoln Museum: Fort Wayne, Indiana
www.thelincolnmuseum.org/

Information about the museum and online resources about Abraham Lincoln.

The Papers of Abraham Lincoln
www.papersofabrahamlincoln.org/

A project of the Illinois Historic Preservation Agency, the Abraham Lincoln Library and Museum, and the University of Illinois at Springfield, this site contains online versions of Lincoln's personal papers, with a goal of digitizing all documents written by or to Lincoln in his lifetime.

The Presidential Papers of Abraham Lincoln Online
www.presidentialpapersofabrahamlincolnonline.org/

This site is the result of a collaborative project to make all of Lincoln's presidential papers available online by 2009, the bicentennial of President Lincoln's birth.

The White House Presidential Biographies
www.whitehouse.gov/history/presidents/al16.html

Lincoln's official presidential biography at the White House website.

Lincoln Destinations and Events

Historic Sites and Memorials

The following list is a sampling of the many historic sites, memorials, and libraries dedicated to Lincoln and his legacy that are located throughout the United States.

California

The Lincoln Memorial Shrine
125 West Vine Street
Redlands, California
www.lincolnshrine.org

This extravagant shrine was built by Robert and Alma Watchorn in 1932 as a tribute to both Lincoln and their son, Emory Ewart, who died of wounds received in World War I. The shrine houses the Carrara marble bust of Lincoln sculpted by George Gray Barnard along with thousands of volumes of books, original manuscripts, and other relics.

District of Columbia

Ford's Theatre National Historic Site
511 10th Street NW
Washington, D.C.
www.nps.gov/foth/index2.htm

Ford's Theatre is the site of Lincoln's assassination and also houses the Lincoln Museum, which includes a large exhibit containing many Lincoln and assassination relics. Across the street from the theatre is Petersen's Boarding House, to which Lincoln was taken after he was shot and where he died on April 15, 1865.

Lincoln Cottage
President Lincoln and Soldiers' Home National Monument
Washington, D.C.
www.nationaltrust.org

This cottage, on the grounds of the Soldiers' Home in Washington, D.C., served as a retreat for Lincoln between 1862 and 1864.

Lincoln Memorial
The Mall
Washington, D.C.
www.nps.gov/linc/

Perhaps the best-known tribute to Abraham Lincoln, this monument sits at one end of the Washington Mall, faced at the opposite end by the Washington Monument, with several other memorials and monuments in between. The reflecting pond lies at the foot of the Lincoln Memorial, and the plaza in between has been the site of many historic protests, demonstrations, and rallies.

Illinois

Abraham Lincoln Monument
Lincoln Park at Dearborn Street
Chicago, Illinois
www.ci.chi.il.us/Landmarks/L/LincolnMonument.html

Dating back to 1887, with Stanford White as the architect and Augustus Saint-Gaudens the sculptor, this tribute is considered one of Chicago's most important public sculptures. It was designated a Chicago landmark in December 2001.

Abraham Lincoln Presidential Library
112 North Street
Springfield, Illinois
www.illinoishistory.gov/lib

A research facility, this library is operated by the Illinois Historic Preservation Agency and contains material about Illinois history as well as an extensive Lincoln collection that includes manuscripts, audiovisuals, relics, and other artifacts. In 2004, the library received a donation that included Lincoln's presidential satchel and a dress worn by Mary Todd Lincoln, among other items.

Lincoln–Herndon Law Offices State Historic Site
Sixth and Adams Streets
Springfield, Illinois

This restored building is where Lincoln's first law office was in 1843 and is one of the locations where the Lincoln–Herndon law offices was located.

Lincoln Home National Historic Site
Springfield, Illinois
www.nps.gov/liho/

Lincoln's home until 1861, this house has been restored to its 1860s appearance.

Lincoln Memorial Garden and Nature Center
2301 East Lake Shore Drive
Springfield, Illinois
www.lmgnc.com

Founded in 1936 by Mrs. Harriet Knudson, these grounds, now more than 100 acres, were intended as a living tribute to President Lincoln.

Lincoln's New Salem Historic Site
Petersburg, Illinois
www.lincolnsnewsalem.com

The town where Lincoln's future began might have ceased operation in 1847, but its buildings and roads have been reconstructed for all to see. A nine-foot bronze sculpture by Avard Fairbanks—located next to the visitor center—portrays a young Lincoln picking up law books and discarding his axe.

Lincoln Statue
State Capitol Building
Springfield, Illinois

By Andrew O'Connor, this impressive statue stands outside the State Capitol.

Lincoln's Tomb
Oak Ridge Cemetery
Springfield, Illinois
www.state.il.us/HPA/hs/Tomb.htm

This monument to Lincoln contains the remains not only of Abraham, but also of his wife Mary Todd Lincoln, and three of Lincoln's four children—Eddie, Willie, and Tad. (Eldest son Robert was buried in Arlington National Cemetery in Arlington, Virginia.)

Vandalia State House
315 West Gallatin
Vandalia, Illinois

Vandalia became the second capital of Illinois in 1820, and it is here that Abraham Lincoln served his first statewide office, beginning on December 1, 1834. In 1836, Lincoln began his second term in this building, which replaced an earlier one. The last Illinois state legislative session to meet here, before Springfield was named the state's new capital, took place in 1839.

Indiana

Lincoln Boyhood National Memorial
Lincoln City, Indiana
www.nps.gov/libo/

The Lincoln Boyhood National Memorial preserves the site of the farm where Abraham Lincoln spent 14 formative years of his life, from the age of 7 to 21. The farm is a re-created pioneer homestead with a cabin, outbuildings, split-rail fences, farm animals, vegetable and herb gardens, and field crops. Rangers in period clothing perform a variety of activities typical of the 1820s era.

Lincoln Memorial Bridge and Statue
Vincennes, Indiana
www.vincennes.org/attractions.htm

This bridge, crossing the Wabash River, was dedicated in 1933, and marks the spot where the Lincoln family crossed the Wabash in 1830. A statue of Lincoln adorns the Illinois side of this bridge.

The Lincoln Museum
Fort Wayne, Indiana
http://www.thelincolnmuseum.org/

The world's largest museum dedicated to Abraham Lincoln. The museum's mission is to interpret and preserve Lincoln's history and legacy through education, research, preservation, and exhibits.

Iowa

Lincoln Monument
Council Bluffs, Iowa
www.councilbluffsiowa.com/tourism/attractions.asp

Commemorates the spot where Lincoln stood in 1859 to choose the eastern terminus of the transcontinental railroad.

Lincoln and Tad Monument

Lafayette Avenue near Fairview Cemetery
State Capitol Grounds
Des Moines, Iowa
www.state.ia.us/vrtour/grounds/lincoln.html

By renowned Lincoln sculptor Fred Torrey, this monument is said to be the only one depicting Lincoln as a father. Fred Torrey's wife Mabel, a child sculpture specialist, created Tad. The monument was financed by a penny drive from school children throughout Iowa, and was commissioned in 1959 to mark the one hundred fiftieth anniversary of Lincoln's birth.

Kentucky

Abraham Lincoln Birthplace National Historic Site
Near Elizabethtown, Kentucky
www.nps.gov/abli/

A monument and a cabin representative of those that might have been found here in 1809 at the site of Lincoln's birthplace near Sinking Spring in what was then the Commonwealth of Virginia.

Mary Todd Lincoln House
578 West Main Street
Lexington, Kentucky
www.mtlhouse.org/

This is the house in which Mary Todd was born in 1818.

Louisiana

International Lincoln Center Library
Louisiana State University
One University Place
Shreveport, Louisiana
www.lsus.ed/lincoln/library.asp

This library houses a unique collection of documents and artifacts that focus on Lincoln's legacy in the United States and abroad. Included are an international stamp collection, books, journals, a map of Lincoln Island near Vietnam, and the Argentina chapter of the International Lincoln Association.

Maryland

Antietam National Battlefield
Antietam, Maryland
www.nps.gov/anti/

On September 17, 1862, 23,000 men were killed, wounded, or missing after the Battle of Antietam. This immense tragedy produced the Union victory Lincoln needed to issue the Emancipation Proclamation.

Nebraska

Lincoln Statues
Capitol Building
Lincoln, Nebraska
www.lincoln.org/visiting/attractions/museums/statue.htm

A replica of the Daniel Chester French statue of Lincoln at Gettysburg is at the west entrance of the Capitol building. Another statue of Lincoln is at the east entrance of the Justice and Law Enforcement building at Tenth Street and Lincoln Mall.

New York

The Cooper Union for the Advancement of Science and Art
Cooper Square
New York, New York
www.cooper.edu

Established in 1859, this college is one of the nation's oldest and is the only private, full-scholarship college in the United States that prepares students for careers in art, architecture, and engineering. Lincoln spoke at the Great Hall at Cooper Union, which opened a year before the college. Its podium continues to draw great Americans and thought-provoking lecturers. Check its website for public events.

Pennsylvania

Gettysburg National Military Park
Gettysburg, Pennsylvania
www.nps.gov/gett/

The battle that turned the tide of the Civil War was fought here; also the site of one of Lincoln's most memorable speeches. In the town of Gettysburg, the Wills House is also a must-see.

Wills House
Six Lincoln Square
Gettysburg, Pennsylvania

The former home of attorney David Wills and the place where Lincoln spent the night before delivering his renowned Gettysburg Address. Lincoln finished the speech in Wills's upstairs guest room.

South Dakota

Mount Rushmore National Memorial
Near Rapid City, South Dakota
www.nps.gov/moru/

Arguably one of America's most famous memorials, Lincoln's head, along with those of Thomas Jefferson, George Washington, and Teddy Roosevelt, is carved into the side of a mountain in rural South Dakota.

Tennessee

Abraham Lincoln Library and Museum at Lincoln Memorial College
Harrogate, Tennessee
www.lmunet.edu/Museum/index.htm

Located on the campus of Lincoln Memorial College, the library and museum contain tens of thousands of books and other documents as well as other relics, including "life masks" of both Abraham and Mary Todd and the cane Abe carried to Ford's Theatre on the night of his death.

Off the Beaten Path

Although hundreds of statues and monuments to Lincoln have been constructed all over the world, here are a few that are a bit out of the way—or a little quirky.

Illinois

Lincoln Watermelon Statue
Lincoln, Illinois

This full-size statue of a watermelon slice commemorates the day that Lincoln reportedly christened the town with watermelon juice. The town of Lincoln, Illinois, claims to be the only one named after Lincoln with his consent.

Pennsylvania

Lincoln Statue
Fairmount Park
Philadelphia, Pennsylvania
www.andropogon.com/news/lincoln.htm

This statue of Lincoln rests on a large pedestal in a heavily trafficked area and is seen by many motorists and pedestrians each day.

Wisconsin

The Lincolns in Granite
East Park
Racine, Wisconsin
Statue of Abraham and Mary Todd Lincoln

Miss Lena Rosewall left her entire $20,000 estate for the creation and home of this statue, which depicts Abraham and Mary Todd Lincoln in the early days of their marriage, before the trials of the presidency. Dedicated in 1943, the statue is the first of Abraham and Mary together.

Wyoming

Lincoln Monument
Near Laramie, Wyoming
www.roadsideamerica.com/attract/WYLARlincoln.html

Commissioned by the state of Wyoming in 1959 to commemorate the one hundred fiftieth anniversary of Lincoln's birth, this 12-foot-high bronze sculpture of Lincoln's head sits atop a 30-foot-high pedestal of rocks.

Nationwide

The Lincoln Highway
The Lincoln Highway Association
www.lincolnhighwayassoc.org

Named for Abraham Lincoln and conceived in 1913, this historic road stretches from New York to San Francisco, and is the first transcontinental highway specifically designed for automotive travel. The highway and the association helped pave the way for America's nationwide highway network.

United Kingdom

Lincoln Monument
Old Calton Cemetery
Edingburgh, Scotland
www.rampantscotland.com/know/blknow_lincoln.htm

Built in memory of Scottish soldiers who fought in the Civil War, this was reportedly the first memorial to Lincoln outside the United States.

Lincoln Statue
Parliament Square
London, England

An Augustus Saint-Gaudens statue, this is a full-sized replica of the original in Chicago's Lincoln Park.

Annual Events

Here are a few of the most prominent events held throughout the country each year to remember Lincoln and his contributions to America. (And don't forget to celebrate Lincoln's birthday on February 12!)

January Through March

Annual Symposium (February)
Abraham Lincoln Institute
College Park, Maryland
www.lincoln-institute.org/

Free symposium for Lincoln scholars and the general public alike; co-sponsored by the National Archive.

Lincoln Home Birthday Events (February)
Lincoln Home National Historic Site
Lincoln City, Indiana
www.nps.gov/liho/pphtml/eventdetail15359.html

Various events each year, including lectures and other activities.

Wreath Laying on Lincoln's Birthday (February)
Lincoln Monument
Washington, D.C.
www.nps.gov/linc/

Each year on February 12th, a wreath is laid and the Gettysburg Address is read to commemorate Lincoln's birthday.

April Through May

Scouting Pilgrimage (April)
Springfield, Illinois
www.alincolnbsa.org/pilgrimage/

Each year since the 1950s, thousands of scouts and other young people gather at Lincoln's Tomb at the Oak Ridge Cemetery in Springfield, Illinois, to pay homage to America's sixteenth president.

Scouting Pilgrimage (April)
Redlands, California
http://www.lincolnshrine.org/

Scouts on the West Coast also engage in a pilgrimage to the Lincoln Shrine located in Redlands, California.

June Through September

Young Abe Lincoln, A Musical (June Through August)
Lincoln Amphitheater at the Lincoln State Park
Lincoln City, Indiana
www.usi.edu/lincoln/

This musical, by Billy Edd Wheeler, is performed annually at the Lincoln Amphitheater and tells the true story of young Abe's boyhood years in Indiana. The amphitheater's sides are open to the environment, but a roof provides protection from the sun and elements.

Abraham Lincoln National Railsplitting Contest and Craft Fair (September)
Lincoln, Illinois
www.geocities.com/findinglincolnillinois/specialevents1.htm

Contests for railsplitting, cross-cut sawing, rail tossing, watermelon eating, corn shelling, and log rolling, along with a Girl Scout Jamboree and craft fair, are held each year in Lincoln.

October Through December

Lincoln Forum Symposium (November)
Gettysburg, Pennsylvania
www.thelincolnforum.org/

This is the annual gathering and symposium of The Lincoln Forum, an organization dedicated to furthering knowledge about Lincoln through symposia, tours, student essays, a newsletter, and an annual award that recognizes special contributions to Lincoln studies.

Annual Remembrance Day (November)
Gettysburg, Pennsylvania
www.gettysburg.com

A parade is held followed by a wreath laying and reading of the Gettysburg Address at the Albert Woodson memorial.

Annual Lincoln Observance (November)
Gettysburg, Pennsylvania
www.gettysburg.com
www.nps.gov/gett/events.htm

Commemorates the anniversary of Lincoln's Gettysburg Address and the dedication of the Cemetery at Gettysburg. Events include memorial services, a reading of Lincoln's address, Civil War encampments, and more. At Soldiers' National Cemetery during the annual observance, luminary candles are placed on each Civil War grave as a testament to the sacrifices made there in 1863.

Events Related to Lincoln's Bicentennial

Abraham Lincoln Bicentennial Commission
Washington, D.C.
www.lincolnbicentennial.gov

The Commission's website includes events leading up to and including Lincoln's bicentennial celebration in 2009.

A Lincoln Timeline

1809   February 12, Lincoln is born at Sinking Spring in Hardin County, Kentucky, joining sister, Sarah, who was born in 1807.

1809   Abraham's father, Thomas Lincoln, moves his family to Knob Creek, a 230-acre farm 10 miles from Sinking Spring.

1812   Abraham's brother, Thomas, is born then dies in infancy.

1816   The Lincoln family moves from Kentucky to Indiana.

1818   Abraham's mother, Nancy Hanks Lincoln, dies from milk sickness.

1819   Lincoln's father, Thomas Lincoln, weds widow Sarah Bush Johnston.

1826   Abraham's sister, Sarah, marries Aaron Grigsby.

1828   Abraham works on a flatboat to move cargo to New Orleans.

1828   Abraham's sister, Sarah, dies in childbirth.

1830   The Lincoln family moves from Indiana to Illinois by wagon train, settling on the Sangamon River.

1831   Abraham Lincoln leaves home permanently and moves to New Salem, Illinois, and later works as a surveyor, storekeeper's assistant, and postmaster.

1832   Lincoln runs for the Illinois state legislature.

1832   Just as his campaign for elective office begins, the Black Hawk War breaks out and Abe enlists in state militia.

1832   Lincoln's first run at political office for Illinois state legislature ends in defeat.

1833   Lincoln and William Berry buy a general store in New Salem.

1834   Lincoln runs for state office for the second time and is elected, beginning his term as an Illinois legislator at the capital city of Vandalia, Illinois.

1836   Lincoln obtains a law license without ever setting foot in law school.

1836   Lincoln sends a love letter to Mary Owens in New Salem.

1837   Lincoln moves to Springfield (when that city is named the new capital of Illinois) and establishes a law practice there with John T. Stuart.

1837   Lincoln protests an antiabolitionist resolution passed in the Illinois State House—his first public attack against slavery.

1838   Lincoln breaks off his engagement with Mary Owens.

1839   Lincoln becomes a traveling "circuit lawyer," practicing law in the Eighth Judicial Circuit of Illinois.

1839   December, Lincoln meets Mary Todd at a cotillion ball.

1841   Stuart and Lincoln dissolve their law practice and Abraham and Stephen T. Logan form a new law office.

1841   Lincoln and Mary Todd break up, and Abraham suffers from extreme depression as a result.

1842   Lincoln is challenged to a duel, but others intervene and the event is called off; Abraham and Mary reconcile.

1842   November 4, Lincoln marries Mary Todd.

1843   August 1, son Robert Todd Lincoln is born.

1844   Abraham Lincoln buys his first home, located in Springfield.

1844   Lincoln enters a law partnership with William Herndon.

1846   March 10, son Edward Baker Lincoln is born.

1846   Lincoln is elected to the United States Congress, taking his seat in December 1847, and within less than a month of his arrival in Washington, publicly challenges Democratic President James K. Polk's actions in the Mexican War.

1847   In Congress, Lincoln reads his amendment to abolish slavery in the District of Columbia, but his backers abandon him and he never formally introduces his proposal.

1849	Lincoln is admitted to practice before the United States Supreme Court.
1850	February 1, son Edward Baker Lincoln dies.
1850	December 21, son William "Willie" Wallace Lincoln is born.
1853	April 4, son Thomas "Tad" Lincoln is born.
1854	May 30, passage of the Kansas–Nebraska Act compels Lincoln to reenter politics.
1856	May 29, Lincoln aligns himself with the newly formed Republican Party.
1859	January 6, Lincoln loses U.S. Senate race to Democrat Stephen A. Douglas.
1860	May 18, Lincoln receives presidential nomination from the Republican Party.
1860	November 6, Lincoln wins the presidential election.
1860	December 20, South Carolina secedes from the Union, the first state to do so.
1861	February 18, the Confederate States of America inaugurate former U.S. Senator Jefferson Davis as its president.
1861	March 4, Abraham Lincoln is inaugurated as the President of the United States at the age of 52.
1861	April 12, the American Civil War begins when Fort Sumter in Charleston, South Carolina, is fired upon by Confederate troops.
1861	June 3, Stephen Douglas dies.
1862	February 20, Lincoln's cherished son Willie dies.
1863	January 1, Lincoln issues the Emancipation Proclamation.
1863	July 1–3, the Battle of Gettysburg turns tide of the war.
1863	November 19, Lincoln delivers his address at the dedication of the cemetery at Gettysburg, Pennsylvania.
1864	November 8, President Lincoln is elected to a second term.
1865	March 4, Lincoln's second inauguration.
1865	April 9, the surrender of Confederate General Robert E. Lee at Appomattox Court House, Virginia, ends the Civil War.
1865	April 11, Lincoln delivers his last public address.
1865	April 14, Lincoln is shot by John Wilkes Booth at Ford's Theatre in Washington, D.C.

1865 April 15, across the street from Ford's Theatre at Petersen's Boarding House, Abraham Lincoln dies at 7:22 A.M.

1865 May 4, Lincoln is interred in a public receiving vault in Oak Ridge Cemetery in Springfield, Illinois.

1901 September 26, Lincoln is permanently interred in the Lincoln Tomb at Oak Ridge Cemetery in Springfield, Illinois.

Lincoln's Great Speeches

The Gettysburg Address

Address Delivered at the Dedication of the Cemetery at Gettysburg,
Gettysburg, Pennsylvania
November 19, 1863

Four score and seven years ago our fathers brought forth on this continent, a new nation, conceived in Liberty, and dedicated to the proposition that all men are created equal.

Now we are engaged in a great civil war, testing whether that nation, or any nation so conceived and so dedicated, can long endure. We are met on a great battle-field of that war. We have come to dedicate a portion of that field, as a final resting place for those who here gave their lives that that nation might live. It is altogether fitting and proper that we should do this.

But, in a larger sense, we can not dedicate—we can not consecrate—we can not hallow—this ground. The brave men, living and dead, who struggled here, have consecrated it, far above our poor power to add or detract. The world will little note, nor long remember what we say here, but it can never forget what they did here. It is for us the living, rather, to be dedicated here to the unfinished work which they who fought here have thus far so nobly advanced. It is rather for us to be here dedicated to the great task remaining before us—that from these honored dead we take increased devotion to that cause for which they gave the last full measure of devotion—that we here highly resolve that these dead shall not have died in vain—that this nation, under God, shall have a new birth of freedom—and that government of the people, by the people, for the people, shall not perish from the earth.

Abraham Lincoln

Source: The Collected Works of Abraham Lincoln, *edited by Roy P. Basler; used courtesy of The Abraham Lincoln Association.*

The Emancipation Proclamation

January 1, 1863
By the President of the United States of America:
A Proclamation.

Whereas, on the twenty-second day of September, in the year of our Lord one thousand eight hundred and sixty-two, a proclamation was issued by the President of the United States, containing, among other things, the following, to wit:

"That on the first day of January, in the year of our Lord one thousand eight hundred and sixty-three, all persons held as slaves within any State or designated part of a State, the people whereof shall then be in rebellion against the United States, shall be then, thenceforward, and forever free; and the Executive Government of the United States, including the military and naval authority thereof, will recognize and maintain the freedom of such persons, and will do no act or acts to repress such persons, or any of them, in any efforts they may make for their actual freedom.

"That the Executive will, on the first day of January aforesaid, by proclamation, designate the States and parts of States, if any, in which the people thereof, respectively, shall then be in rebellion against the United States; and the fact that any State, or the people thereof, shall on that day be, in good faith, represented in the Congress of the United States by members chosen thereto at elections wherein a majority of the qualified voters of such State shall have participated, shall, in the absence of strong countervailing testimony, be deemed conclusive evidence that such State, and the people thereof, are not then in rebellion against the United States."

Now, therefore I, Abraham Lincoln, President of the United States, by virtue of the power in me vested as Commander-in-Chief, of the Army and Navy of the United States in time of actual armed rebellion against the authority and government of the United States, and as a fit and necessary war measure for suppressing said rebellion, do, on this first day of January, in the year of our Lord one thousand eight hundred and sixty-three, and in accordance with my purpose so to do publicly proclaimed for the full period of one hundred days, from the day first above mentioned, order and designate as the States and parts of States wherein the people thereof respectively, are this day in rebellion against the United States, the following, to wit:

Arkansas, Texas, Louisiana, (except the Parishes of St. Bernard, Plaquemines, Jefferson, St. John, St. Charles, St. James Ascension, Assumption, Terrebonne, Lafourche, St. Mary, St. Martin, and Orleans, including the City of New Orleans) Mississippi, Alabama, Florida, Georgia, South Carolina, North Carolina, and Virginia, (except the forty-eight counties designated as West Virginia, and also the counties of Berkley, Accomac, Northampton, Elizabeth City, York, Princess Ann, and Norfolk, including the cities of Norfolk and Portsmouth[)], and which excepted parts, are for the present, left precisely as if this proclamation were not issued.

And by virtue of the power, and for the purpose aforesaid, I do order and declare that all persons held as slaves within said designated States, and parts of States, are, and henceforward shall be free; and that the Executive government of the United States, including the military and naval authorities thereof, will recognize and maintain the freedom of said persons.

And I hereby enjoin upon the people so declared to be free to abstain from all violence, unless in necessary self-defence; and I recommend to them that, in all cases when allowed, they labor faithfully for reasonable wages.

And I further declare and make known, that such persons of suitable condition, will be received into the armed service of the United States to garrison forts, positions, stations, and other places, and to man vessels of all sorts in said service.

And upon this act, sincerely believed to be an act of justice, warranted by the Constitution, upon military necessity, I invoke the considerate judgment of mankind, and the gracious favor of Almighty God.

In witness whereof, I have hereunto set my hand and caused the seal of the United States to be affixed.

Done at the City of Washington, this first day of January, in the year of our Lord one thousand eight hundred and sixty-three, and of the Independence of the United States of America the eighty-seventh.

By the President: ABRAHAM LINCOLN
WILLIAM H. SEWARD, Secretary of State.

Source: The Collected Works of Abraham Lincoln, *edited by Roy P. Basler; used courtesy of The Abraham Lincoln Association.*

Last Public Address

Washington, D.C.
April 11, 1865

We meet this evening, not in sorrow, but in gladness of heart. The evacuation of Petersburg and Richmond, and the surrender of the principal insurgent army, give hope of a righteous and speedy peace whose joyous expression can not be restrained. In the midst of this, however, He from whom all blessings flow, must not be forgotten. A call for a national thanksgiving is being prepared, and will be duly promulgated. Nor must those whose harder part gives us the cause of rejoicing, be overlooked. Their honors must not be parcelled out with others. I myself was near the front, and had the high pleasure of transmitting much of the good news to you; but no part of the honor, for plan or execution, is mine. To Gen. Grant, his skillful officers, and brave men, all belongs. The gallant Navy stood ready, but was not in reach to take active part.

By these recent successes the re-inauguration of the national authority—reconstruction—which has had a large share of thought from the first, is pressed much more closely upon our attention. It is fraught with great difficulty. Unlike a case of a war between independent nations, there is no authorized organ for us to treat with. No one man has authority to give up the rebellion for any other man. We simply must begin with, and mould from, disorganized and discordant elements. Nor is it a small additional embarrassment that we, the loyal people, differ among ourselves as to the mode, manner, and means of reconstruction.

As a general rule, I abstain from reading the reports of attacks upon myself, wishing not to be provoked by that to which I can not properly offer an answer. In spite of this precaution, however, it comes to my knowledge that I am much censured for some supposed agency in setting up, and seeking to sustain, the new State government of Louisiana. In this I have done just so much as, and no more than, the public knows. In the Annual Message of Dec. 1863 and accompanying Proclamation, I presented *a* plan of re-construction (as the phrase goes) which, I promised, if adopted by any State, should be acceptable to, and sustained by, the Executive government of the nation. I distinctly stated that this was not the only plan which might possibly be acceptable; and I also distinctly protested that the Executive claimed no right to say when, or whether members should be admitted to seats in Congress from such States. This plan was, in advance, submitted to the then Cabinet, and distinctly approved by every member of it. One of them suggested that I should then, and in that connection, apply the Emancipation Proclamation to the theretofore excepted parts of Virginia and Louisiana; that I should drop the suggestion about apprenticeship for freed-people, and that I should omit the protest against my own power, in regard to the admission of members to Congress; but even he approved every part and parcel of the plan which has since been employed or touched by the action of Louisiana. The new constitution of Louisiana, declaring emancipation for the whole State, practically applies the Proclamation to the part previously excepted. It does not adopt apprenticeship for freed-people; and it is silent, as it could not well be otherwise, about the admission of members to Congress. So that, as it applies to Louisiana, every member of the Cabinet fully approved the plan. The message went to Congress, and I received many commendations of the plan, written and verbal; and not a single objection to it, from any professed emancipationist, came to my knowledge, until after the news reached Washington that the people of Louisiana had begun to move in accordance with it. From about July 1862, I had corresponded with different persons, supposed to be interested, seeking a reconstruction of a State government for Louisiana. When the message of 1863, with the plan before mentioned, reached New-Orleans, Gen. Banks wrote me that he was confident the people, with his military co-operation, would reconstruct, substantially on that plan. I wrote him, and some of them to try it; they tried it, and the result is known. Such only has been my agency in getting up the Louisiana government. As to sustaining it, my promise is out, as before stated. But, as bad promises are better broken than kept, I shall treat this as a bad promise, and break it, whenever I shall be convinced that keeping it is adverse to the public interest. But I have not yet been so convinced.

I have been shown a letter on this subject, supposed to be an able one, in which the writer expresses regret that my mind has not seemed to be definitely fixed on the question whether the seceding States, so called, are in the Union or out of it. It would perhaps, add astonishment to his regret, were he to learn that since I have found professed Union men endeavoring to make that question, I have *purposely* forborne any public expression upon it. As appears to me that question has not been, nor yet is, a practically material one, and that any discussion of it, while it thus remains practically immaterial, could have no effect other than the mischievous one of dividing our friends. As yet, whatever it may hereafter become, that question is bad, as the basis of a controversy, and good for nothing at all—a merely pernicious abstraction.

We all agree that the seceded States, so called, are out of their proper relation with the Union; and that the sole object of the government, civil and military, in regard to those States is to again get them into that proper practical relation. I believe it is not only possible, but in fact, easier to do this, without deciding, or even considering, whether these States have ever been out of the Union, than with it. Finding themselves safely at home, it would be utterly immaterial whether they had ever been abroad. Let us all join in doing the acts necessary to restoring the proper practical relations between these States and the Union; and each forever after, innocently indulge his own opinion whether, in doing the acts, he brought the States from without, into the Union, or only gave them proper assistance, they never having been out of it.

The amount of constituency, so to speak, on which the new Louisiana government rests, would be more satisfactory to all, if it contained fifty, thirty, or even twenty thousand, instead of only about twelve thousand, as it does. It is also unsatisfactory to some that the elective franchise is not given to the colored man. I would myself prefer that it were now conferred on the very intelligent, and on those who serve our cause as soldiers. Still the question is not whether the Louisiana government, as it stands, is quite all that is desirable. The question is, "Will it be wiser to take it as it is, and help to improve it; or to reject, and disperse it?" "Can Louisiana be brought into proper practical relation with the Union *sooner* by *sustaining*, or by *discarding* her new State government?"

Some twelve thousand voters in the heretofore slave-state of Louisiana have sworn allegiance to the Union, assumed to be the rightful political power of the State, held elections, organized a State government, adopted a free-state constitution, giving the benefit of public schools equally to black and white, and empowering the Legislature to confer the elective franchise upon the colored man. Their Legislature has already voted to ratify the constitutional amendment recently passed by Congress, abolishing slavery throughout the nation. These twelve thousand persons are thus fully committed to the Union, and to perpetual freedom in the state—committed to the very things, and nearly all the things the nation wants—and they ask the nations recognition and it's assistance to make good their committal. Now, if we reject, and spurn them, we do our utmost to disorganize and disperse them. We in effect say to the white men "You are worthless, or worse—we will neither help you, nor be helped by you." To the blacks we say "This cup of liberty which these, your old masters, hold to your lips, we will dash from you, and leave you to the chances of gathering the spilled and scattered contents in some vague and undefined when, where, and how." If this course, discouraging and paralyzing both white and black, has any tendency to bring Louisiana into proper practical relations with the Union, I have, so far, been unable to perceive it. If, on the contrary, we recognize, and sustain the new government of Louisiana the converse of all this is made true. We encourage the hearts, and nerve the arms of the twelve thousand to adhere to their work, and argue for it, and proselyte for it, and fight for it, and feed it, and grow it, and ripen it to a complete success. The colored man too, in seeing all united for him, is inspired with vigilance, and energy, and daring, to the same end. Grant that he desires the elective franchise, will he not attain it sooner by saving the already advanced steps toward it, than by running backward over them? Concede that the new government of Louisiana is only to what it should be as the egg is to the fowl, we shall sooner have the fowl by hatching the egg than by smashing it? Again, if we reject Louisiana, we also reject one vote in favor of the proposed amendment to the national Constitution. To meet this proposition, it has been argued that no more than three-fourths of those States which have not attempted secession are necessary to validly ratify the amendment. I do not commit myself against this, further than to say that such a ratification would be questionable, and sure to be persistently questioned; while a ratification by three-fourths of all the States would be unquestioned and unquestionable.

I repeat the question, "Can Louisiana be brought into proper practical relation with the Union *sooner* by *sustaining* or by *discarding* her new State Government?

What has been said of Louisiana will apply generally to other States. And yet so great peculiarities pertain to each state, and such important and sudden changes occur in the same state; and withal, so new and unprecedented is the whole case, that no exclusive, and inflexible plan can be safely prescribed as to details and colatterals [*sic*]. Such exclusive, and inflexible plan, would surely become a new entanglement. Important principles may, and must, be inflexible.

In the present "*situation*" as the phrase goes, it may be my duty to make some new announcement to the people of the South. I am considering, and shall not fail to act, when satisfied that action will be proper.

Source: The Collected Works of Abraham Lincoln, *edited by Roy P. Basler; used courtesy of The Abraham Lincoln Association.*

Cooper Union Address

New York, New York
February 27, 1860

Mr. President and fellow citizens of New York:

The facts with which I shall deal this evening are mainly old and familiar; nor is there anything new in the general use I shall make of them. If there shall be any novelty, it will be in the mode of presenting the facts, and the inferences and observations following that presentation.

In his speech last autumn, at Columbus, Ohio, as reported in "The New-York Times," Senator Douglas said:

"Our fathers, when they framed the Government under which we live, understood this question just as well, and even better, than we do now."

I fully indorse this, and I adopt it as a text for this discourse. I so adopt it because it furnishes a precise and an agreed starting point for a discussion between Republicans and that wing of the Democracy headed by Senator Douglas. It simply leaves the inquiry: "What was the understanding those fathers had of the question mentioned?"

What is the frame of government under which we live?

The answer must be: "The Constitution of the United States." That Constitution consists of the original, framed in 1787, (and under which the present government first went into operation,) and twelve subsequently framed amendments, the first ten of which were framed in 1789.

Who were our fathers that framed the Constitution? I suppose the "thirty-nine" who signed the original instrument may be fairly called our fathers who framed that part of the present Government. It is almost exactly true to say they framed it, and it is altogether true to say they fairly represented the opinion and sentiment of the whole nation at that time. Their names, being familiar to nearly all, and accessible to quite all, need not now be repeated.

I take these "thirty-nine," for the present, as being "our fathers who framed the Government under which we live."

What is the question which, according to the text, those fathers understood "just as well, and even better than we do now?"

It is this: Does the proper division of local from federal authority, or anything in the Constitution, forbid our *Federal Government* to control as to slavery in *our Federal Territories?*

Upon this, Senator Douglas holds the affirmative, and Republicans the negative. This affirmation and denial form an issue; and this issue—this question—is precisely what the text declares our fathers understood "better than we."

Let us now inquire whether the "thirty-nine," or any of them, ever acted upon this question; and if they did, how they acted upon it—how they expressed that better understanding?

In 1784, three years before the Constitution—the United States then owning the Northwestern Territory, and no other, the Congress of the Confederation had before them the question of prohibiting slavery in that Territory; and four of the "thirty-nine" who afterward framed the Constitution, were in that Congress, and voted on that question. Of these, Roger Sherman, Thomas Mifflin, and Hugh Williamson voted for the prohibition, thus showing that, in their understanding, no line dividing local from federal authority, nor anything else, properly forbade the Federal Government to control as to slavery in federal territory. The other of the four—James M'Henry—voted against the prohibition, showing that, for some cause, he thought it improper to vote for it.

In 1787, still before the Constitution, but while the Convention was in session framing it, and while the Northwestern Territory still was the only territory owned by the United States, the same question of prohibiting slavery in the territory again came before the Congress of the Confederation; and two more of the "thirty-nine" who afterward signed the Constitution, were in that Congress, and voted on the question. They were William Blount and William Few; and they both voted for the prohibition—thus showing that, in their understanding, no line dividing local from federal authority, nor anything else, properly forbids the Federal Government to control as to slavery in Federal territory. This time the prohibition became a law, being part of what is now well known as the Ordinance of '87.

The question of federal control of slavery in the territories, seems not to have been directly before the Convention which framed the original Constitution; and hence it is not recorded that the "thirty-nine," or any of them, while engaged on that instrument, expressed any opinion on that precise question.

In 1789, by the first Congress which sat under the Constitution, an act was passed to enforce the Ordinance of '87, including the prohibition of slavery in the Northwestern Territory. The bill for this act was reported by one of the "thirty-nine," Thomas Fitzsimmons, then a member of the House of Representatives from Pennsylvania. It went through all its stages without a word of opposition, and finally passed both branches without yeas and nays, which is equivalent to a unanimous passage. In this Congress there were sixteen of the thirty-nine fathers who framed the original Constitution. They were John Langdon, Nicholas Gilman, Wm. S. Johnson, Roger Sherman, Robert Morris, Thos. Fitzsimmons, William Few, Abraham Baldwin, Rufus King, William Paterson, George Clymer, Richard Bassett, George Read, Pierce Butler, Daniel Carroll, James Madison.

This shows that, in their understanding, no line dividing local from federal authority, nor anything in the Constitution, properly forbade Congress to prohibit slavery in the federal territory; else both their fidelity to correct principle, and their oath to support the Constitution, would have constrained them to oppose the prohibition.

Again, George Washington, another of the "thirty-nine," was then President of the United States, and, as such approved and signed the bill; thus completing its validity as a law, and thus showing that, in his understanding, no line dividing local from federal authority, nor anything in the Constitution, forbade the Federal Government, to control as to slavery in federal territory.

No great while after the adoption of the original Constitution, North Carolina ceded to the Federal Government the country now constituting the State of Tennessee; and a few years later Georgia ceded that which now constitutes the States of Mississippi and Alabama. In both deeds of cession it was made a condition by the ceding States that the Federal Government should not prohibit slavery in the ceded territory. Besides this, slavery was then actually in the ceded country. Under these circumstances, Congress, on taking charge of these countries, did not absolutely prohibit slavery within them. But they did interfere with it—take control of it—even there, to a certain extent. In 1798, Congress organized the Territory of Mississippi. In the act of organization, they prohibited the bringing of slaves into the Territory, from any place without the United States, by fine, and giving freedom to slaves so bought. This act passed both branches of Congress without yeas and nays. In that Congress were three of the "thirty-nine" who framed the original Constitution. They were John Langdon, George Read and Abraham Baldwin. They all, probably, voted for it. Certainly they would have placed their opposition to it upon record, if, in their understanding, any line dividing local from federal authority, or anything in the Constitution, properly forbade the Federal Government to control as to slavery in federal territory.

In 1803, the Federal Government purchased the Louisiana country. Our former territorial acquisitions came from certain of our own States; but this Louisiana country was acquired from a foreign nation. In 1804, Congress gave a territorial organization to that part of it which now constitutes the State of Louisiana. New Orleans, lying within that part, was an old and comparatively large city. There were other considerable towns and settlements, and slavery was extensively and thoroughly intermingled with the people. Congress did not, in the Territorial Act, prohibit slavery; but they did interfere with it—take control of it—in a more marked and extensive way than they did in the case of Mississippi. The substance of the provision therein made, in relation to slaves, was:

First. That no slave should be imported into the territory from foreign parts.

Second. That no slave should be carried into it who had been imported into the United States since the first day of May, 1798.

Third. That no slave should be carried into it, except by the owner, and for his own use as a settler; the penalty in all the cases being a fine upon the violator of the law, and freedom to the slave.

This act also was passed without yeas and nays. In the Congress which passed it, there were two of the "thirty-nine." They were Abraham Baldwin and Jonathan Dayton. As stated in the case of Mississippi, it is probable they both voted for it. They would not have allowed it to pass without recording their opposition to it, if, in their understanding, it violated either the line properly dividing local from federal authority, or any provision of the Constitution.

In 1819–20, came and passed the Missouri question. Many votes were taken, by yeas and nays, in both branches of Congress, upon the various phases of the general question. Two of the "thirty-nine"—Rufus King and Charles Pinckney—were members of that Congress. Mr. King steadily voted for slavery prohibition and against all compromises, while Mr. Pinckney as steadily voted against slavery prohibition and against all compromises. By this, Mr. King showed that, in his understanding, no line dividing local from federal authority, nor anything in the Constitution, was violated by Congress prohibiting slavery in federal territory; while Mr. Pinckney, by his votes, showed that, in his understanding, there was some sufficient reason for opposing such prohibition in that case.

The cases I have mentioned are the only acts of the "thirty-nine," or of any of them, upon the direct issue, which I have been able to discover.

To enumerate the persons who thus acted, as being four in 1784, two in 1787, seventeen in 1789, three in 1798, two in 1804, and two in 1819–20—there would be thirty of them. But this would be counting John Langdon, Roger Sherman, William Few, Rufus King, and George Read each twice, and Abraham Baldwin, three times. The true number of those of the "thirty-nine" whom I have shown to have acted upon the question, which, by the text, they understood better than we, is twenty-three, leaving sixteen not shown to have acted upon it in any way.

Here, then, we have twenty-three out of our thirty-nine fathers "who framed the government under which we live," who have, upon their official responsibility and their corporal oaths, acted upon the very question which the text affirms they "understood just as well, and even better than we do now;" and twenty-one of them—a clear majority of the whole "thirty-nine"—so acting upon it as to make them guilty of gross political impropriety and willful perjury, if, in their understanding, any proper division between local and federal authority, or anything in the Constitution they had made themselves, and sworn to support, forbade the Federal Government to control as to slavery in the federal territories. Thus the twenty-one acted; and, as actions speak louder than words, so actions, under such responsibility, speak still louder.

Two of the twenty-three voted against Congressional prohibition of slavery in the federal territories, in the instances in which they acted upon the question. But for what reasons they so voted is not known. They may have done so because they thought a proper division of local from federal authority, or some provision or principle of the Constitution, stood in the way; or they may, without any such question, have voted against the prohibition, on what appeared to them to be sufficient grounds of expediency. No one who has sworn to support the Constitution can conscientiously vote for what he understands to be an unconstitutional measure, however expedient he may think it; but one may and ought to vote against a measure which he deems constitutional, if, at the same time, he deems it inexpedient. It, therefore, would be unsafe to set down even the two who voted against the prohibition, as having done so because, in their understanding, any proper division of local from federal authority, or anything in the Constitution, forbade the Federal Government to control as to slavery in federal territory.

The remaining sixteen of the "thirty-nine," so far as I have discovered, have left no record of their understanding upon the direct question of federal control of slavery in the federal territories. But there is much reason to believe that their understanding upon that question would not have appeared different from that of their twenty-three compeers, had it been manifested at all.

For the purpose of adhering rigidly to the text, I have purposely omitted whatever understanding may have been manifested by any person, however distinguished, other than the thirty-nine fathers who framed the original Constitution; and, for the same reason, I have also omitted whatever understanding may have been manifested by any of the "thirty-nine" even, on any other phase of the general question of slavery. If we should look into their acts and declarations on those other phases, as the foreign slave trade, and the morality and policy of slavery generally, it would appear to us that on the direct question of federal control of slavery in federal territories, the sixteen, if they had acted at all, would probably have acted just as the twenty-three did. Among that sixteen were several of the most noted anti-slavery men of those times—as Dr. Franklin, Alexander Hamilton and Gouverneur Morris—while there was not one now known to have been otherwise, unless it may be John Rutledge, of South Carolina.

The sum of the whole is, that of our thirty-nine fathers who framed the original Constitution, twenty-one—a clear majority of the whole—certainly understood that no proper division of local from federal authority, nor any part of the Constitution, forbade the Federal Government to control slavery in the federal territories; while all the rest probably had the same understanding. Such, unquestionably, was the understanding of our fathers who framed the original Constitution; and the text affirms that they understood the question "better than we."

But, so far, I have been considering the understanding of the question manifested by the framers of the original Constitution. In and by the original instrument, a mode was provided for amending it; and, as I have already stated, the present frame of "the Government under which we live" consists of that original, and twelve amendatory articles framed and adopted since. Those who now insist that federal control of slavery in federal territories violates the Constitution, point us to the provisions which they suppose it thus violates; and, as I understand, that all fix upon provisions in these amendatory articles, and not in the original instrument. The Supreme Court, in the Dred Scott case, plant themselves upon the fifth amendment, which provides that no person shall be deprived of "life, liberty or property without due process of law;" while Senator Douglas and his peculiar adherents plant themselves upon the tenth amendment, providing that "the powers not delegated to the United States by the Constitution" "are reserved to the States respectively, or to the people."

Now, it so happens that these amendments were framed by the first Congress which sat under the Constitution—the identical Congress which passed the act already mentioned, enforcing the prohibition of slavery in the Northwestern Territory. Not only was it the same Congress, but they were the identical, same individual men who, at the same session, and at the same time within the session, had under consideration, and in progress toward maturity, these Constitutional amendments, and this act prohibiting slavery in all the territory the nation then owned. The Constitutional amendments were introduced before, and passed after the act enforcing the Ordinance of '87; so that, during the whole pendency of the act to enforce the Ordinance, the Constitutional amendments were also pending.

The seventy-six members of that Congress, including sixteen of the framers of the original Constitution, as before stated, were pre- eminently our fathers who framed that part of "the Government under which we live," which is now claimed as forbidding the Federal Government to control slavery in the federal territories.

Is it not a little presumptuous in any one at this day to affirm that the two things which that Congress deliberately framed, and carried to maturity at the same time, are absolutely inconsistent with each other? And does not such affirmation become impudently absurd when coupled with the other affirmation from the same mouth, that those who did the two things, alleged to be inconsistent, understood whether they really were inconsistent better than we—better than he who affirms that they are inconsistent?

It is surely safe to assume that the thirty-nine framers of the original Constitution, and the seventy-six members of the Congress which framed the amendments thereto, taken together, do certainly include those who may be fairly called "our fathers who framed the Government under which we live." And so assuming, I defy any man to show that any one of them ever, in his whole life, declared that, in his understanding, any proper division of local from federal authority, or any part of the Constitution, forbade the Federal Government to control as to slavery in the federal territories. I go a step further. I defy any one to show that any living man in the whole world ever did, prior to the beginning of the present century, (and I might almost say prior to the beginning of the last half of the present century,) declare that, in his understanding, any proper division of local from federal authority, or any part of the Constitution, forbade the Federal Government to control as to slavery in the federal territories. To those who now so declare, I give, not only "our fathers who framed the Government under which we live," but with them all other living men within the century in which it was framed, among whom to search, and they shall not be able to find the evidence of a single man agreeing with them.

Now, and here, let me guard a little against being misunderstood. I do not mean to say we are bound to follow implicitly in whatever our fathers did. To do so, would be to discard all the lights of current experience—to reject all progress—all improvement. What I do say is, that if we would supplant the opinions and policy of our fathers in any case, we should do so upon evidence so conclusive, and argument so clear, that even their great authority, fairly considered and weighed, cannot stand; and most surely not in a case whereof we ourselves declare they understood the question better than we.

If any man at this day sincerely believes that a proper division of local from federal authority, or any part of the Constitution, forbids the Federal Government to control as to slavery in the federal territories, he is right to say so, and to enforce his position by all truthful evidence and fair argument which he can. But he has no right to mislead others, who have less access to history, and less leisure to study it, into the false belief that "our fathers who framed the Government under which we live" were of the same opinion—thus substituting falsehood and deception for truthful evidence and fair argument. If any man at this day sincerely believes "our fathers who framed the Government under which we live," used and applied principles, in other cases, which ought to have led them to understand that a proper division of local from federal authority or some part of the Constitution, forbids the Federal Government to control as to slavery in the federal territories, he is right to say so. But he should, at the same time, brave the responsibility of declaring that, in his opinion, he understands their principles better than they did themselves; and especially should he not shirk that responsibility by asserting that they "understood the question just as well, and even better, than we do now."

But enough! *Let all who believe that "our fathers, who framed the Government under which we live, understood this question just as well, and even better, than we do now," speak as they spoke, and act as they acted upon it. This is all Republicans ask—all Republicans desire—in relation to slavery. As those fathers marked it, so let it be again marked, as an evil not to be extended, but to be tolerated and protected only because of and so far as its actual presence among us makes that toleration and protection a necessity. Let all the guarantees those fathers gave it, be, not grudgingly, but fully and fairly, maintained.* For this Republicans contend, and with this, so far as I know or believe, they will be content.

And now, if they would listen—as I suppose they will not—I would address a few words to the Southern people.

I would say to them: You consider yourselves a reasonable and a just people; and I consider that in the general qualities of reason and justice you are not inferior to any other people. Still, when you speak of us Republicans, you do so only to denounce us as reptiles, or, at the best, as no better than outlaws. You will grant a hearing to pirates or murderers, but nothing like it to "Black Republicans." In all your contentions with one another, each of you deems an unconditional condemnation of "Black Republicanism" as the first thing to be attended to. Indeed, such condemnation of us seems to be an indispensable prerequisite—license, so to speak—among you to be admitted or permitted to speak at all. Now, can you, or not, be prevailed upon to pause and to consider whether this is quite just to us, or even to yourselves? Bring forward your charges and specifications, and then be patient long enough to hear us deny or justify.

You say we are sectional. We deny it. That makes an issue; and the burden of proof is upon you. You produce your proof; and what is it? Why, that our party has no existence in your section—gets no votes in your section. The fact is substantially true; but does it prove the issue? If it does, then in case we should, without change of principle, begin to get votes in your section, we should thereby cease to be sectional. You cannot escape this conclusion; and yet, are you willing to abide by it? If you are, you will probably soon find that we have ceased to be sectional, for we shall get votes in your section this very year. You will then begin to discover, as the truth plainly is, that your proof does not touch the issue. The fact that we get no votes in your section, is a fact of your making, and not of ours. And if there be fault in that fact, that fault is primarily yours, and remains until you show that we repel you by some wrong principle or practice. If we do repel you by any wrong principle or practice, the fault is ours; but this brings you to where you ought to have started—to a discussion of the right or wrong of our principle. If our principle, put in practice, would wrong your section for the benefit of ours, or for any other object, then our principle, and we with it, are sectional, and are justly opposed and denounced as such. Meet us, then, on the question of whether our principle, put in practice, would wrong your section; and so meet it as if it were possible that something may be said on our side. Do you accept the challenge? No! Then you really believe that the principle which "our fathers who framed the Government under which we live" thought so clearly right as to adopt it, and indorse it again and again, upon their official oaths, is in fact so clearly wrong as to demand your condemnation without a moment's consideration.

Some of you delight to flaunt in our faces the warning against sectional parties given by Washington in his Farewell Address. Less than eight years before Washington gave that warning, he had, as President of the United States, approved and signed an act of Congress, enforcing the prohibition of slavery in the Northwestern Territory, which act embodied the policy of the Government upon that subject up to and at the very moment he penned that warning; and about one year after he penned it, he wrote LaFayette that he considered that prohibition a wise measure, expressing in the same connection his hope that we should at some time have a confederacy of free States.

Bearing this in mind, and seeing that sectionalism has since arisen upon this same subject, is that warning a weapon in your hands against us, or in our hands against you? Could Washington himself speak, would he cast the blame of that sectionalism upon us, who sustain his policy, or upon you who repudiate it? We respect that warning of Washington, and we commend it to you, together with his example pointing to the right application of it.

But you say you are conservative—eminently conservative—while we are revolutionary, destructive, or something of the sort. What is conservatism? Is it not adherence to the old and tried, against the new and untried? We stick to, contend for, the identical old policy on the point in controversy which was adopted by "our fathers who framed the Government under which we live;" while you with one accord reject, and scout, and spit upon that old policy, and insist upon substituting something new. True, you disagree among yourselves as to what that substitute shall be. You are divided on new propositions and plans, but you are unanimous in rejecting and denouncing the old policy of the fathers. Some of you are for reviving the foreign slave trade; some for a Congressional Slave-Code for the Territories; some for Congress forbidding the Territories to prohibit Slavery within their limits; some for maintaining Slavery in the

Territories through the judiciary; some for the "gur-reat pur-rinciple" that "if one man would enslave another, no third man should object," fantastically called "Popular Sovereignty;" but never a man among you is in favor of federal prohibition of slavery in federal territories, according to the practice of "our fathers who framed the Government under which we live." Not one of all your various plans can show a precedent or an advocate in the century within which our Government originated. Consider, then, whether your claim of conservatism for yourselves, and your charge or destructiveness against us, are based on the most clear and stable foundations.

Again, you say we have made the slavery question more prominent than it formerly was. We deny it. We admit that it is more prominent, but we deny that we made it so. It was not we, but you, who discarded the old policy of the fathers. We resisted, and still resist, your innovation; and thence comes the greater prominence of the question. Would you have that question reduced to its former proportions? Go back to that old policy. What has been will be again, under the same conditions. If you would have the peace of the old times, readopt the precepts and policy of the old times.

You charge that we stir up insurrections among your slaves. We deny it; and what is your proof? Harper's Ferry! John Brown!! John Brown was no Republican; and you have failed to implicate a single Republican in his Harper's Ferry enterprise. If any member of our party is guilty in that matter, you know it or you do not know it. If you do know it, you are inexcusable for not designating the man and proving the fact. If you do not know it, you are inexcusable for asserting it, and especially for persisting in the assertion after you have tried and failed to make the proof. You need to be told that persisting in a charge which one does not know to be true, is simply malicious slander.

Some of you admit that no Republican designedly aided or encouraged the Harper's Ferry affair, but still insist that our doctrines and declarations necessarily lead to such results. We do not believe it. We know we hold to no doctrine, and make no declaration, which were not held to and made by "our fathers who framed the Government under which we live." You never dealt fairly by us in relation to this affair. When it occurred, some important State elections were near at hand, and you were in evident glee with the belief that, by charging the blame upon us, you could get an advantage of us in those elections. The elections came, and your expectations were not quite fulfilled. Every Republican man knew that, as to himself at least, your charge was a slander, and he was not much inclined by it to cast his vote in your favor. Republican doctrines and declarations are accompanied with a continual protest against any interference whatever with your slaves, or with you about your slaves. Surely, this does not encourage them to revolt. True, we do, in common with "our fathers, who framed the Government under which we live," declare our belief that slavery is wrong; but the slaves do not hear us declare even this. For anything we say or do, the slaves would scarcely know there is a Republican party. I believe they would not, in fact, generally know it but for your misrepresentations of us, in their hearing. In your political contests among yourselves, each faction charges the other with sympathy with Black Republicanism; and then, to give point to the charge, defines Black Republicanism to simply be insurrection, blood and thunder among the slaves.

Slave insurrections are no more common now than they were before the Republican party was organized. What induced the Southampton insurrection, twenty-eight years ago, in which, at least three times as many lives were lost as at Harper's Ferry? You can scarcely stretch your very elastic fancy to the conclusion that Southampton was "got up by Black Republicanism." In the present state of things in the United States, I do not think a general, or even a very extensive slave insurrection is possible. The indispensable concert of action cannot be attained. The slaves have no means of rapid communication; nor can incendiary freemen, black or white, supply it. The explosive materials are everywhere in parcels; but there neither are, nor can be supplied, the indispensable connecting trains.

Much is said by Southern people about the affection of slaves for their masters and mistresses; and a part of it, at least, is true. A plot for an uprising could scarcely be devised and communicated to twenty individuals before some one of them, to save the life of a favorite master or mistress, would divulge it. This is the rule; and the slave revolution in Hayti was not an exception to it, but a case occurring under peculiar circumstances. The gunpowder plot of British history, though not connected with slaves, was more in point. In that case, only about twenty were admitted to the secret; and yet one of them, in his anxiety to save a friend, betrayed the plot to that friend, and, by consequence, averted the calamity. Occasional poisonings from the kitchen, and open or stealthy assassinations in the field, and local revolts extending to a score or so, will continue to occur as the natural results of slavery; but no general insurrection of slaves, as I think, can happen in this country for a long time. Whoever much fears, or much hopes for such an event, will be alike disappointed.

In the language of Mr. Jefferson, uttered many years ago, "It is still in our power to direct the process of emancipation, and deportation, peaceably, and in such slow degrees, as that the evil will wear off insensibly; and their places be, *pari passu*, filled up by free white laborers. If, on the contrary, it is left to force itself on, human nature must shudder at the prospect held up."

Mr. Jefferson did not mean to say, nor do I, that the power of emancipation is in the Federal Government. He spoke of Virginia; and, as to the power of emancipation, I speak of the slaveholding States only. The Federal Government, however, as we insist, has the power of restraining the extension of the institution—the power to insure that a slave insurrection shall never occur on any American soil which is now free from slavery.

John Brown's effort was peculiar. It was not a slave insurrection. It was an attempt by white men to get up a revolt among slaves, in which the slaves refused to participate. In fact, it was so absurd that the slaves, with all their ignorance, saw plainly enough it could not succeed. That affair, in its philosophy, corresponds with the many attempts, related in history, at the assassination of kings and emperors. An enthusiast broods over the oppression of a people till he fancies himself commissioned by Heaven to liberate them. He ventures the attempt, which ends in little else than his own execution. Orsini's attempt on Louis Napoleon, and John Brown's attempt at Harper's Ferry were, in their philosophy, precisely the same. The eagerness to cast blame on old England in the one case, and on New England in the other, does not disprove the sameness of the two things.

And how much would it avail you, if you could, by the use of John Brown, Helper's Book, and the like, break up the Republican organization? Human action can be modified to some extent, but human nature cannot be changed. There is a judgment and a feeling against slavery in this nation, which cast at least a million and a half of votes. You cannot destroy that judgment and feeling—that sentiment—by breaking up the political organization which rallies around it. You can scarcely scatter and disperse an army which has been formed into order in the face of your heaviest fire; but if you could, how much would you gain by forcing the sentiment which created it out of the peaceful channel of the ballot-box, into some other channel? What would that other channel probably be? Would the number of John Browns be lessened or enlarged by the operation?

But you will break up the Union rather than submit to a denial of your Constitutional rights.

That has a somewhat reckless sound; but it would be palliated, if not fully justified, were we proposing, by the mere force of numbers, to deprive you of some right, plainly written down in the Constitution. But we are proposing no such thing.

When you make these declarations, you have a specific and well-understood allusion to an assumed Constitutional right of yours, to take slaves into the federal territories, and to hold them there as property. But no such right is specifically written in the Constitution. That instrument is literally silent about any such right. We, on the contrary, deny that such a right has any existence in the Constitution, even by implication.

Your purpose, then, plainly stated, is that you will destroy the Government, unless you be allowed to construe and enforce the Constitution as you please, on all points in dispute between you and us. You will rule or ruin in all events.

This, plainly stated, is your language. Perhaps you will say the Supreme Court has decided the disputed Constitutional question in your favor. Not quite so. But waiving the lawyer's distinction between dictum and decision, the Court have decided the question for you in a sort of way. The Court have substantially said, it is your Constitutional right to take slaves into the federal territories, and to hold them there as property. When I say the decision was made in a sort of way, I mean it was made in a divided Court, by a bare majority of the Judges, and they not quite agreeing with one another in the reasons for making it; that it is so made as that its avowed supporters disagree with one another about its meaning, and that it was mainly based upon a mistaken statement of fact—the statement in the opinion that "the right of property in a slave is distinctly and expressly affirmed in the Constitution."

An inspection of the Constitution will show that the right of property in a slave is not "*distinctly* and *expressly* affirmed" in it. Bear in mind, the Judges do not pledge their judicial opinion that such right is *impliedly* affirmed in the Constitution; but they pledge their veracity that it is "*distinctly* and *expressly*" affirmed there—"distinctly," that is, not mingled with anything else—"expressly," that is, in words meaning just that, without the aid of any inference, and susceptible of no other meaning.

If they had only pledged their judicial opinion that such right is affirmed in the instrument by implication, it would be open to others to show that neither the word "slave" nor "slavery" is to be found in the Constitution, nor the word "property" even, in any connection with language alluding to the things slave, or slavery; and that wherever in that instrument the slave is alluded to, he is called a "person;"—and wherever his master's legal right in relation to him is alluded to, it is spoken of as "service or labor which may be due,"—as a debt payable in service or labor. Also, it would be open to show, by contemporaneous history, that this mode of alluding to slaves and slavery, instead of speaking of them, was employed on purpose to exclude from the Constitution the idea that there could be property in man.

To show all this, is easy and certain.

When this obvious mistake of the Judges shall be brought to their notice, is it not reasonable to expect that they will withdraw the mistaken statement, and reconsider the conclusion based upon it?

And then it is to be remembered that "our fathers, who framed the Government under which we live"—the men who made the Constitution—decided this same

Constitutional question in our favor, long ago—decided it without division among themselves, when making the decision; without division among themselves about the meaning of it after it was made, and, so far as any evidence is left, without basing it upon any mistaken statement of facts.

Under all these circumstances, do you really feel yourselves justified to break up this Government unless such a court decision as yours is, shall be at once submitted to as a conclusive and final rule of political action? But you will not abide the election of a Republican president! In that supposed event, you say, you will destroy the Union; and then, you say, the great crime of having destroyed it will be upon us! That is cool. A highwayman holds a pistol to my ear, and mutters through his teeth, "Stand and deliver, or I shall kill you, and then you will be a murderer!"

To be sure, what the robber demanded of me—my money—was my own; and I had a clear right to keep it; but it was no more my own than my vote is my own; and the threat of death to me, to extort my money, and the threat of destruction to the Union, to extort my vote, can scarcely be distinguished in principle.

A few words now to Republicans. *It is exceedingly desirable that all parts of this great Confederacy shall be at peace, and in harmony, one with another. Let us Republicans do our part to have it so. Even though much provoked, let us do nothing through passion and ill temper. Even though the southern people will not so much as listen to us, let us calmly consider their demands, and yield to them if, in our deliberate view of our duty, we possibly can. Judging by all they say and do, and by the subject and nature of their controversy with us, let us determine, if we can, what will satisfy them.*

Will they be satisfied if the Territories be unconditionally surrendered to them? We know they will not. In all their present complaints against us, the Territories are scarcely mentioned. Invasions and insurrections are the rage now. Will it satisfy them, if, in the future, we have nothing to do with invasions and insurrections? We know it will not. We so know, because we know we never had anything to do with invasions and insurrections; and yet this total abstaining does not exempt us from the charge and the denunciation.

The question recurs, what will satisfy them? Simply this: We must not only let them alone, but we must somehow, convince them that we do let them alone. This, we know by experience, is no easy task. We have been so trying to convince them from the very beginning of our organization, but with no success. In all our platforms and speeches we have constantly protested our purpose to let them alone; but this has had no tendency to convince them. Alike unavailing to convince them, is the fact that they have never detected a man of us in any attempt to disturb them.

These natural, and apparently adequate means all failing, what will convince them? This, and this only: cease to call slavery *wrong*, and join them in calling it *right*. And this must be done thoroughly—done in *acts* as well as in *words*. Silence will not be tolerated—we must place ourselves avowedly with them. Senator Douglas' new sedition law must be enacted and enforced, suppressing all declarations that slavery is wrong, whether made in politics, in presses, in pulpits, or in private. We must arrest and return their fugitive slaves with greedy pleasure. We must pull down our Free State constitutions. The whole atmosphere must be disinfected from all taint of opposition to slavery, before they will cease to believe that all their troubles proceed from us.

I am quite aware they do not state their case precisely in this way. Most of them would probably say to us, "Let us alone, do nothing to us, and say what you please about slavery." But we do let them alone—have never disturbed them—so that, after all, it is what we say, which dissatisfies them. They will continue to accuse us of doing, until we cease saying.

I am also aware they have not, as yet, in terms, demanded the overthrow of our Free-State Constitutions. Yet those Constitutions declare the wrong of slavery, with more solemn emphasis, than do all other sayings against it; and when all these other sayings shall have been silenced, the overthrow of these Constitutions will be demanded, and nothing be left to resist the demand. It is nothing to the contrary, that they do not demand the whole of this just now. Demanding what they do, and for the reason they do, they can voluntarily stop nowhere short of this consummation. Holding, as they do, that slavery is morally right, and socially elevating, they cannot cease to demand a full national recognition of it, as a legal right, and a social blessing.

Nor can we justifiably withhold this, on any ground save our conviction that slavery is wrong. If slavery is right, all words, acts, laws, and constitutions against it, are themselves wrong, and should be silenced, and swept away. If it is right, we cannot justly object to its nationality—its universality; if it is wrong, they cannot justly insist upon its extension—its enlargement. All they ask, we could readily grant, if we thought slavery right; all we ask, they could as readily grant, if they thought it wrong. Their thinking it right, and our thinking it wrong, is the precise fact upon which depends the whole controversy. Thinking it right, as they do, they are not to blame for desiring its full recognition, as being right; but, thinking it wrong, as we do, can we yield to them? Can we cast our votes with their view, and against our own? In view of our moral, social, and political responsibilities, can we do this?

Wrong as we think slavery is, we can yet afford to let it alone where it is, because that much is due to the necessity arising from its actual presence in the nation; but can we, while our votes will prevent it, allow it to spread into the National Territories, and to overrun us here in these Free States? If our sense of duty forbids this, then let us stand by our duty, fearlessly and effectively. Let us be diverted by none of those sophistical contrivances wherewith we are so industriously plied and belabored—contrivances such as groping for some middle ground between the right and the wrong, vain as the search for a man who should be neither a living man nor a dead man—such as a policy of "don't care" on a question about which all true men do care—such as Union appeals beseeching true Union men to yield to Disunionists, reversing the divine rule, and calling, not the sinners, but the righteous to repentance—such as invocations to Washington, imploring men to unsay what Washington said, and undo what Washington did.

Neither let us be slandered from our duty by false accusations against us, nor frightened from it by menaces of destruction to the Government nor of dungeons to ourselves. LET US HAVE FAITH THAT RIGHT MAKES MIGHT, AND IN THAT FAITH, LET US, TO THE END, DARE TO DO OUR DUTY AS WE UNDERSTAND IT.

Abraham Lincoln

Source: The Collected Works of Abraham Lincoln, *edited by Roy P. Basler; used courtesy of The Abraham Lincoln Association.*

Second Inaugural Address

Washington, D.C.
March 4, 1865

At this second appearing to take the oath of the presidential office, there is less occasion for an extended address than there was at the first. Then a statement, somewhat in detail, of a course to be pursued, seemed fitting and proper. Now, at the expiration of four years, during which public declarations have been constantly called forth on every point and phase of the great contest which still absorbs the attention, and engrosses the energies of the nation, little that is new could be presented. The progress of our arms, upon which all else chiefly depends, is as well known to the public as to myself; and it is, I trust, reasonably satisfactory and encouraging to all. With high hope for the future, no prediction in regard to it is ventured.

On the occasion corresponding to this four years ago, all thoughts were anxiously directed to an impending civil war. All dreaded it—all sought to avert it. While the inaugeral [sic] address was being delivered from this place, devoted altogether to *saving* the Union without war, insurgent agents were in the city seeking to *destroy* it without war—seeking to dissole [sic] the Union, and divide effects, by negotiation. Both parties deprecated war; but one of them would *make* war rather than let the nation survive; and the other would *accept* war rather than let it perish. And the war came.

One eighth of the whole population were colored slaves, not distributed generally over the Union, but localized in the Southern part of it. These slaves constituted a peculiar and powerful interest. All knew that this interest was, somehow, the cause of the war. To strengthen, perpetuate, and extend this interest was the object for which the insurgents would rend the Union, even by war; while the government claimed no right to do more than to restrict the territorial enlargement of it. Neither party expected for the war, the magnitude, or the duration, which it has already attained. Neither anticipated that the *cause* of the conflict might cease with, or even before, the conflict itself should cease. Each looked for an easier triumph, and a result less fundamental and astounding. Both read the same Bible, and pray to the same God; and each invokes His aid against the other. It may seem strange that any men should dare to ask a just God's assistance in wringing their bread from the sweat of other men's faces; but let us judge not that we be not judged. The prayers of both could not be answered; that of neither has been answered fully. The Almighty has his own purposes. "Woe unto the world because of offences! for it must needs be that offences come; but woe to that man by whom the offence cometh!" If we shall suppose that American Slavery is one of those offences which, in the providence of God, must needs come, but which, having continued through His appointed time, He now wills to remove, and that He gives to both North and South, this terrible war, as the woe due to those by whom the offence came, shall we discern therein any departure from those divine attributes which the believers in a Living God always ascribe to Him? Fondly do we hope—fervently do we pray—that this mighty scourge of war may speedily pass away. Yet, if God wills that it continue, until all the wealth piled by the bond-man's two hundred and fifty years of unrequited toil shall be sunk, and until every drop of blood drawn with the lash, shall be paid by another drawn with the sword, as was said three thousand years ago, so still it must be said "the judgments of the Lord, are true and righteous altogether."

With malice toward none; with charity for all; with firmness in the right, as God gives us to see the right, let us strive on to finish the work we are in; to bind up the nation's wounds; to care for him who shall have borne the battle, and for his widow, and his orphan—to do all which may achieve and cherish a just and lasting peace, among ourselves, and with all nations.

Source: The Collected Works of Abraham Lincoln, *edited by Roy B. Basler; used courtesy of The Abraham Lincoln Association.*

Index

U

V

W–X–Y–Z

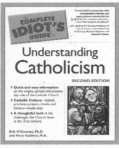

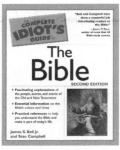

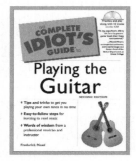

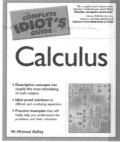